EXPLORING
TECHNOLOGY
AND SOCIAL
SPACE

NEW MEDIA CULTURES

Series Editor: Steve Jones

New Media Cultures critically examines emerging social formations arising from and surrounding new technologies of communication. It focuses on the processes, products, and narratives that intersect with these technologies. An emphasis of the series is on the Internet and computer-mediated communication, particularly as those technologies are implicated in the relationships among individuals, social groups, modern and postmodern ways of knowing, and public and private life. Books in the series demonstrate interdisciplinary theoretical and methodological analyses, and highlight the relevance of intertwining history, theory, lived experience, and critical study to provide an understanding of new media and contemporary culture.

EXPLORING
TECHNOLOGY
AND SOCIAL
SPACE

J. Macgregor Wise

NMC
NEW MEDIA
CULTURES

SAGE Publications
International Educational and Professional Publisher
Thousand Oaks London New Delhi

For information:

SAGE Publications, Inc.
2455 Teller Road
Thousand Oaks, California 91320
E-mail: order@sagepub.com

SAGE Publications Ltd.
6 Bonhill Street
London EC2A 4PU
United Kingdom

SAGE Publications India Pvt. Ltd.
M-32 Market
Greater Kailash I
New Delhi 110 048 India

Printed in the United States of America

Library of Congress Cataloging-in-Publication Data

Main entry under title:

Wise, John Macgregor.
　　　　Exploring technology and social space / by John MacGregor Wise
　　　　　　p.　　cm. — (New media cultures)
　　　　Includes bibliographical references (p.　　) and index.
　　　　ISBN 0-7619-0421-2 (cloth: acid-free paper). — ISBN
　　　　0-7619-0422-0 (pbk.: acid-free paper)
　　　　　　1. Technology—Social aspects.　2. Information technology—Social
　　　　aspects.　　I. Title.　II. Series.
　　　　T14.5.W566　1997
　　　　303.48'33—dc21　　　　　　　　　　　　　　　　　　97-21185

This book is printed on acid-free paper.

97　98　99　00　01　02　03　　10　9　8　7　6　5　4　3　2　1

Acquiring Editor:	Margaret H. Seawell
Editorial Assistant:	Renée Piernot
Production Editor:	Michèle Lingre
Production Assistant:	Karen Wiley
Typesetter/Designer:	Janelle LeMaster
Cover Designer:	Candice Harman
Print Buyer:	Anna Chin

To my parents for a unique life

Contents

Acknowledgments

I would like to take the opportunity to thank Larry Grossberg, for trusting me with The Book (both the doorstop and this one), The Journal, and with my own work, penchants, and idiosyncrasies; James Hay, for his encouragement and from whose classes significant aspects of this book emerged; Meaghan Morris, whose impact on a lot of us as a person and a scholar cannot be measured; Jennifer Slack, for her detailed comments and insightful critique (and infectious enthusiasm); Tony Bennett, who actually went to the exhibit in his spare time just because he had read my chapter; Steve Jones, for his honest and eminently helpful responses to earlier forms of this book; Cary Nelson, for that reading list on the modern; Jane Banks, a fellow TCK, for all her support; Gil Rodman, for his nettitude and for being a good friend IRL; and those who read parts of this (because they wanted to, no less) and gave me stimulating feedback: Cliff Christians, Greg Seigworth, Carol Stabile, Jonathan Sterne, Bryan Taylor, Steve Wiley, and various anonymous reviewers at journals and conventions (their comments were wonderful and insightful; all the errors and weak arguments left in here are, of course, all mine). Thanks to all at Sage (past and present) for their support of this project: especially Sophy Craze, Alex Schwartz, and Margaret Seawell.

I would also like to thank Bill Christ and Harry Haines for getting me interested in this profession and also interested in the modern, technology, and popular culture (it's their fault!). And to repay various intellectual debts incurred along the way: C. Mackenzie Brown, James Carey, Norman Denzin, Peter Garrett, John Nerone, Andrew Pickering, Willis Salomon, and Jeremy Tambling.

A special thanks goes to my family for their support, encouragement, and indulgence in all things creative: John, Donna, and Tracy Wise, plus all the Wises, McGregors, Davlins, Salleys, and Dimons.

And finally to Millay, Edmund Blackadder, and Gabriella, for not letting me take life too seriously—or get any work done; and especially to Elise, who thinks I'm nuts but loves me anyway, for letting me buy all those books, and for being my touchstone.

I am grateful to Spelling Television Inc. for permission to quote from David Rintel's script for *AT&T Presents: Day One,* and to the Museum of Science and Industry in Chicago for permission to quote from the exhibit, "Communications: Your link to a better life" and related exhibit materials. Quotations from *The Christian Science Monitor* © 1993 The Christian Science Publishing Society; all rights reserved. Also, quotations from *Day One* by Peter Wyden © 1984 by Peter Wyden, reprinted with permission of Simon & Schuster.

Introduction

This book is not about the Internet, at least not entirely. Likewise, it is not a book about cyberspace, at least not centrally. This book is about the fundamental assumptions that we hold about the role of technology in our lives, and it is an attempt to elaborate a critical, philosophical, and epistemological framework from which to better understand our relations to technology and social space. The impetus for this book was the Internet and cyberspace and the boom in communication and information technology that promises (or threatens) to change radically both who we are and the space that we live in.

What I mean by social space can perhaps best be approached negatively: It is not merely a constructed space like a room in a house or a lobby in a hotel or a city street. Likewise, it is not merely the meanings generated by any single human moving through that space (i.e., that the room seems comfortable, that it reminds one of corporations, that the greens in the wallpaper are soothing, that it is a workplace or a home, private or public, that he or she is in a hurry, at ease, looking for the bathroom, etc.). Social space is the space created through the interaction of multiple humans over time. There is never a single social space, but always multiple social spaces. Social spaces are always open and permeable, yet they do have limits. It is important to remember at this point that the social is not unique to humans. Baboons, insects, and other creatures are social and could be said to move in social spaces. When I refer to *social space* in this book, I mean human social space.

The central axis of the book is a theoretical exploration of three different epistemes. An episteme is a hermeneutic horizon that results from a particular set of assumptions, and that determines the questions that can be asked of ourselves, our society, our technology, or our environment. Our episteme is bounded by what we think is relevant to our lives. It is knowledge that is situated, which means that it assumes a responsibility; and it is knowledge that is politically implicated (Haraway, 1991c). Epistemes are not innocent. Changing epistemes invalidates certain questions and enables others. Other epistemes can give us other options, allow us to see what we otherwise would not have seen. If a solution to a problem will be realistically accepted only within the confines of a certain episteme (i.e., in making a scientific argument, one must follow a particular set of assumptions, methods, and questions if one's conclusions are to be accepted by scientists), it will certainly behoove us to learn to work within that episteme (at least for pragmatic reasons), though a different episteme may provide different (and no less useful) solutions.

I argue in this book that the dominant episteme of Western, industrialized society is the modern. So what is the modern episteme? Briefly, it is an episteme founded around a fundamental duality, or more accurately, the production of dualities. The modern has its roots in Descartes's dualism of mind and body and in Kant's separation of the subject and the object. The production of a radical separation of Self and Other (whether the Other is another person or nature or something else) involves a determination of essential identities, that there is something fundamental, inevitable, and natural that makes the Subject the Subject and not the Object, and vice versa. An absolute border is drawn between the two.

In that the modern has produced a lot of wonderful and useful things (i.e., science, art, etc.) and has generally made the world a better and more comfortable place to live for many humans, what could be the reasons for wanting to move beyond this episteme? Unfortunately, dividing the world up into Self and Other, the like and the unlike, has historically been to the detriment if not harm and destruction of the Other or the unlike. They are dehumanized, overrun, and exploited like material resources (whether they be humans, "natural" objects, or others).[1] If we are to make the world a more equitable place for all, the modern episteme poses some serious obstacles.

To try out an alternative to the modern, I consider an episteme, called the amodern, based on the notion of agency. This episteme is based on actor-network theory, which examines situations in terms of the social effectivity of actors. Actors include both humans and nonhumans. A fundamental question of this episteme is which actors have an effect on a particular situation. Both humans and nonhumans shape our social life and both are considered in this episteme. Though actor-network theory sidesteps the question of identity, and therefore does not dwell on the human/technology split, I argue that it does tend to reintroduce the overall dualistic framework of the modern.

So, as a third choice, I present the perspective offered by Gilles Deleuze and Félix Guattari, who argue purely in terms of effectivity but also discuss the forces that organize and distribute effectivity through society. Human social space, I argue, is composed of a stratification, a layering, of at least two kinds of agency. These are corporeal agency, the ability to achieve effects through physical contact (which I will call *Technology*), and incorporeal agency, the ability to achieve effects without corporeal means (which I will call *Language*; language would then be the ability to effect changes in social space through words, meanings, and signs alone). What is important is the relationship between the two types of agency.

The second axis about which this book turns is a question of a shift in social space, a shift in the relation of Technology and Language that has been occurring in the United States, at least, since the 1980s. New communication and information technologies have ostensibly allowed humans to increase their agency greatly, their ability to reach out, gather information, and change the world. These technologies, most recently in the form of the Internet and the Information Superhighway, have been rapidly taken up in the popular imaginary. My interest in these technologies is why they have been taken up so readily, what promises of increased agency accompany them, and what might be the actual effects of these technologies on social space. What is important to this analysis is that until the mid-1980s, these same technologies were generally seen as being part of the military-industrial complex and therefore associated with nuclear weapons, war, and a sense that human social life was dominated by and threatened by such technological networks. To examine how a shift in popular notions of technology took place, I analyze a special television program that carefully articulates the narrative of the creation of the atom bomb, the cold war, and negative technics to a more positive view of the future of society based on communication and information networks. To examine one way in which individuals are articulated into specific positions within a new technological assemblage of communication and information, and to examine the relation of agencies both presented and actual (or functional), I then examine a pedagogical space that students, tourists, and others visit to be informed about technology and industry and their role in our lives.

It is not just one technology that we should be concerned about but, rather, a technological assemblage. By this, I mean entire interconnected networks of technologies (telephones, computers, ATMs, videos, etc.). An assemblage isn't just the actual linkages of these technologies to one another but consists of an aggregate of similar technologies that perform similar functions.

We are facing a new technological assemblage that is increasingly pervasive and that appears at the interface of ourselves and the rest of the social world. Our lives are mediated *in a new way* by an *assemblage* of technologies (telephone, computer, television, etc.) that connect and overlap. Though many of these technologies have not yet been physically linked (into an Information Superhighway), they still share a formal resonance. That is, we interact in similar ways with ATMs, voicemail, World Wide Web sites, computer software, and other electronic networks.

The current technological assemblage promises us unlimited agency, but the reality might be something quite different. Following Paul Virilio (1993), I use the term *terminal citizen* to refer to the figure of the human as indefinitely extended by communication and information technologies while being increasingly immobilized in other ways (bodily, etc.).

The final chapter of this book concerns the planned imposition of this same communication and information technological assemblage (idealized in the National Information Infrastructure) on a global scale (the Global Information Infrastructure). I address this move from each of the three epistemes outlined above. In doing this, I hope to compare the strengths and limitations of each in trying to come to grips with what may be a crisis of global dimensions.

The problem of modern communication technologies is that they tend to disappear; to be an efficient communication medium, in this episteme, means to intrude less and less on the communication taking place. It is a purpose of this book to present ways to keep technologies in the picture, so we can mark their effects that otherwise would slip past unnoticed.

What I am suggesting is a new *stance* toward technology and a new technological context, and I use this term in a variety of ways. However, what I *don't* mean is a rationalist solution in which we are able to simply change our epistemes and then our world. Rather I mean "stance" as "relations toward"—conceptually, affectually, and physically. This is not something to be accomplished by individual will alone, but in deep structural changes, in the transformation of the logics that distribute, mark, and connect social spaces.

> When people begin using their bodies in significantly different ways, because of either technological innovations or other cultural shifts, changing experiences of embodiment bubble up into language, affecting the metaphoric networks at play within culture. At the same time, discursive constructions affect how bodies move through space and time, influence what technologies are developed, and help to structure the interfaces between bodies and technology. (Hayles, 1993b, pp. 164-65; quoted in Gray & Mentor, 1995, p. 242)

To take up a new attitude will mean a new consideration of the problem of social space, one that takes as central the relation of language to technology, the discursive to the bodily. To do this is to live within a Deleuzian episteme.

Note

1. See Amin, 1989.

Part One

Episteme

1

Slouching Toward Tralfamadore: The Modern Episteme

There are at least three different epistemes through which an analysis of technology can be approached; I will term these the modern (centered around issues of time, causality, and identity), the amodern (centered around issues of agency)[1] and the Deleuzian (centered around issues of the machinic processes of reality and agency).

This chapter discusses the first of the three epistemes of technology. The modern is by far the most prevalent, the most deeply entrenched of the three, mainly because it is central to most philosophical conceptions of modernity and commonsense understandings of Western, industrialized society. Since the central tenets of modernity are so prevalent, it is important to highlight and recognize them rather than letting them slip past as assumptions. In addition to setting out these central tenets (the separation of time and space, subject and object, and the focus on cause and effect and identity), I will illustrate them with references to several science fiction films. The reasoning here is that these films exemplify the modernist relationship between technology and humans. I will return to this body of films in later chapters as I explore alternative epistemes.

The modern episteme consists of a constellation of concepts based around the Kantian notion of the separation of space and time and the primacy of time in relation to space (Grossberg, 1995). These separations of time and space are central to Kant's philosophy (indeed they make up the beginning of what he calls his "Copernican Revolution") and, as a result, of modern philosophy generally. Briefly, Kant argues that time and space are separated in the (very modern) separation of subject and object.[2] His assumption is that we can know (external) objects only through our sense data of them—we register on our senses that there is some *matter* out there. But this matter has a *form*, a form that is not part of the thing-in-itself. To recognize a form (as being a particular form) is an *internal* recognition based on cognitive forms that have been established before the perception of the object. For example, I recognize a creature as a cat because it has what I consider the characteristics of catness. But the form of catness is in my head; it is a part of my perception, and without it the cat would just be a thing out there. Also, I have the idea of catness in my head before I even meet this particular feline. Kant "is suggesting . . . that we cannot know things, that they cannot be objects of knowledge for us, except in so far as they are subjected to certain *a priori* conditions of knowledge on the part of the subject" (Copleston, 1985, p. 225). We can see here already the fundamental split of the modern between the subject (internal) and object (external) and between the things-in-themselves (noumena) and the things as we perceive and know them (phenomena). This distinction plays a role in radically separating humans and technology as we shall see.

But all the internal forms are not simply there, waiting for perception to occur. Indeed, they must derive from other forms that are, in the last instance, completely *a priori*. These fundamental forms are time and space; they exist in our cognition before other experiences, and they must exist before we can derive other forms. But time and space do not exist as equal internal forms, primarily because, according to Kant, you cannot have a space of cognition; ideas cannot occur in spatial relations (one next to another), but rather occur one after another, in sequence—in other words, in time. *Space*, then, is a form of the external and *time* of the internal. But as all forms derive internally, space as an internal form is always secondary to time, dependent on the form of time. Gilles Deleuze (1984) puts it this way: "Time [for Kant] is no longer related to the movement which it measures, but movement is related to the time which conditions it" (p. vii).[3]

With regard to technology, then, within the modern episteme the form of technology follows from a notion of time. Technology arises out of a desire to confront time and is concerned with the manipulation of time. This does not mean that the episteme ignores space; indeed, space is often foregrounded (see Lewis Mumford's work, e.g.), because technology is assumed to concern the manipulation of objects in the external world. Yet even analyses such as Mumford's end up privileging temporal determinations over spatial ones (as we shall see below), and in any case, time and space are still considered separate.

From this basic tenet of the modern episteme arises the concept of "cause and effect," a concept that is inherently temporal in that it assumes a progression or sequence (effects follow causes).[4] The modern preoccupation with causality configures the dominant discourses of technology so that the debates are always framed as a choice between technological determinism and social determinism; that is, whether technology determines or causes the configuration and nature of the social order or whether social concerns determine the shape and characteristics of technology (or perhaps some combination of both views). The notion of causation in the modern episteme usually gives rise to questions of control, be it the uses of technology to control time or the control of humans by their technology.

Often these questions are formulated in terms of Hegel's dialectic of Master and Slave. This dialectic, I will argue, is a dialectic of identity in that it radically separates the human from the technological and posits questions as to the essential nature of each. Eventually, the subject/object dichotomy that gets mapped onto a human/technology debate leads us to a deadend with considerations (or, worse, unquestioned assumptions) about what makes humans and machines ultimately different. The dichotomy becomes one of identity/other. We can see this debate in the assumptions underlying discussions of whether modern technology makes humans more machinelike (i.e., Herbert Marcuse's one-dimensional man [1964]; etc.), and humanist reactions against, say, systems theory, AI cognitive paradigms, and so on (cf. Gray, 1989).

Time

Following Heidegger, Lorenzo Simpson (1995) argues that what is central to the modern episteme is a fear of death, of finitude. This fear leads to a desire for control, in particular, for control of the future. To control the future, one must deal with the process of time itself—to abstract and regularize it, to quantify and standardize it, and ultimately to *save* time. But to control time, one must control space as well in the same manner: by abstracting it, commodifying it, objectifying it. This double split, the abstracting of time and the abstracting of space, is the foundation of the modern episteme of technology.

Simpson writes that technology "refers to that set of practices whose purpose is, through ever more radical interventions into nature (physical, biological, and human), systematically to place the future at our disposal" (p. 24). This is the result of a realization of our own finitude, that "Man" (Heidegger [1977] writes, *Dasein*) is a being-toward-death. Technology is the result of a desire to master time, to bring it under control through systems of measurement and standardization. These systems (clocks, timetables, etc.) are a form of abstract time that is split off from "human" time, the time of human *durée*, the rhythms of everyday life. Following Weber, we could call this the *disenchantment* of time (Germain, 1993). At this point, once we assume an internal *durée* prior to and differentiated from abstracted time, we are already well within the modern.

Technology engages with or is engaged by time in two ways in this episteme. On the one hand, it is the sense of temporality inherent in the being-toward-death that gives rise to technology to control the future. On the other hand, technology is said to transform *durée*, "natural" human time, into abstract time.

$$durée \rightarrow technology \rightarrow abstract\ time$$

Technology arises out of the first notion of time and in turn produces the second. It is the second move that is the disenchantment of time. Jacques Ellul (1964) provides a good description of this process:

> The time man [*sic*] guided himself by corresponded to nature's time; it was material and concrete. It became abstract (probably towards the end of the fourteenth century) when it was divided into hours, minutes, and seconds. Little by little this mechanical kind of time, with its knife-edge divisions, penetrated, along with machinery, into human life. (p. 329)

Disenchanted time is characteristic of the modern world. Lewis Mumford (1963) writes: "the first characteristic of modern machine civilization is its temporal regularity" (p. 269). But to place the future at our disposal, technology must also place space there as well; along with disenchanted time comes disenchanted space. Disenchanted space (an internal Form, according to Kant) results in a disenchantment of the external (of the noumena), which is then mapped onto a disenchantment of nature. The world becomes, in Heidegger's term, *Bestand,* the standing reserve, objectified and commodified for our use.[5]

We can see how these two disenchantments (time and space) work together when we examine what Mumford has rightly pointed out to be the germinative technology for the modern age: the mechanical clock. The clock not only represents the rationalization of time; it also allows for the coordination of regular movement in space. Simpson (1995) puts it this way:

> If not *the* key to technology, the clock certainly grants us privileged access to it. The time determination and measurement that clocks procure underlie and are necessary to modern technology. The clock, because it makes possible coordination, comparison and so on, increases our control by enabling us to orchestrate practices and processes and to improve them along the lines of efficiency. (p. 22)

Indeed, Marx himself, in a letter to Engels, traced the essence of modern capitalism back to the mechanical clock and the control of time: "The clock is the first automatic machine applied to practical purposes; the whole theory of *production and regular motion* was developed through it" (the italics are Marx's, quoted in Mumford, 1967, p. 286).

To take another brief example (that will be extended in later chapters), the railway timetable was responsible not only for creating (eventually) standardized time zones but for regularizing the movement of trains, passengers, and freight (Carey, 1989).

I do not dispute Mumford's analysis of the originations and influence of the mechanical clock (though I would not be as straightforwardly deterministic in describing the relations between it and modern culture). What I do take issue with is Mumford's (1963) very Kantian description of "a dial and a hand that *translated the movement of time into a movement through space* [italics added]" (p. 14). He argues that the movement of a clock is a movement through space (we are discussing analog clocks, of course) where the hands move and time is then read by interpreting the spatial relations of the hands (the big hand is on the . . .). I do not have trouble with the argument that synchronized, abstract, regularized, efficient, modern time is a particular interpretive and discursive scheme that results from the spatial positioning of the hands (a scheme that has had vast concrete historical implications and effects); rather, it is the necessary positing of time *prior to* the spatial movement that I find most problematic. According to Mumford, the movement of time *causes* the movement of the clock hands through space, which *causes* a modern time consciousness. The desire to control time need not be either prior to or even separate from the desire to control space. We return here to the Kantian assumption that we began with.

What is most characteristic of technology in this episteme is its ability to seemingly collapse time and space. In this way, it not only abstracts time and parcels it out in ever more minute bundles but then masters it, defeating the future and the distant. Examples of this are abundant in the literature. Ellul (1964), for instance, writes that "it is commonly said that with the new modes of transport distance no longer exists; and, indeed, man [*sic*] has vanquished space" (p. 328). Wolfgang Schivelbusch (1986) notes that " 'Annihilation of space and time' was the early nineteenth-century characterization of the effect of railroad travel" (p. 33). The most famous expression of this is perhaps Marshall McLuhan's: " 'Time' has ceased, 'space' has vanished. We now live in a *global* village" (McLuhan & Fiore, 1967, p. 63). And the collapse of time and space is one of the most touted characteristics of the Internet and cyberspace. But we can see from the discussion of the modern episteme, that though modern technology is said to affect (disenchant) both space and time, these technologies, in the last instance, are driven by *time* (by the fear of death) and not space.

Cause and Effect

I wish to focus now on the problems of disenchanted time, and by this I mean time marked by sequence rather than time as *a priori* form. With a notion of time based on sequence (past, present, and future), the modern episteme relies on the notion of *causality* to explain the relation between terms. Jennifer Slack (1984) has analyzed three major types of causality that underpin most interventions into technology. The first is Simple Mechanistic causality, in which both cause and effect are discrete events and their relationship is that of externality (p. 53). McLuhan, for example, argues that media technologies have definite, discernible effects on society (Slack, 1984, p. 56).[6] The second type is Symptomatic Causality, where causes and effects are still discrete, but the effects of any cause are potentials that are then realized (or not) through the mediation of social forces (p. 58). Lewis Mumford claims, for example, that technics is ultimately autonomous, but its uses are shaped by social forces (Slack, 1984, p. 59). The third type is Expressive Causality in which the relation between cause and effect is internal, and the social whole is "an expressive totality in which any and all phenomena are mere expressions of some inner essence, be that essence an idea, ideal, social configuration, or dynamic" (p. 64). Jacques Ellul's work is exemplary here, where all aspects of modern Western society become simply an expression of technique. Ellul (1964) writes: "technique is not an isolated fact in society . . . but is related to every factor in the life of modern man [*sic*]; it affects social facts as well as others" (p. xxvi). Despite their differences these three positions are all concerned with causality and so are a part of the modern episteme.

These varying types of causality are central to the different ways that the dominant discourses of technology frame modern technology within this episteme. Generally, discourses about modern technology split theories of, or perspectives on, technology into either technological determinism or social determinism.[7] The particular qualities that these determinations have are dependent in part on the type of causality assumed by any particular theorist. Broadly, the technological determinist or the substantive view of technology contends that technology guides, shapes, or otherwise influences society (Borgmann, 1984, p. 9). This theory argues that technology has its own logic and direction. It is, then, autonomous with regard to social forces and is a determining force in itself. However, simply arguing that a technology determines something is not necessarily an espousal of this view since, as Langdon Winner (1977, p. 75) rightly points out, doing things to other things is technology's function in the first place. What is implied in the substantive view is that technology is the driving force of society *as a whole*. As technology changes, so society follows. To change the social structure, one has to change technology. From Jacques Ellul to Herbert Marcuse to Marshall McLuhan to Daniel Bell, the substantive view of technology has had a tenacious grip on popular notions of technology for at least the last half century.[8]

Opposed to the view that technologies determine society are those who write that it is society that guides, shapes, or otherwise influences technology. This instrumental view of technology (Borgmann, 1984,

p. 10) asserts that technology is a neutral instrument that can be molded or used for various purposes. So, to transform the social structure, it is not necessary to eradicate that technology but merely to use it in other ways. This assumption can have serious consequences.

For example, Lenin saw technology as following the logics of science (a substantial view). However, the logics of science (though developing autonomously in relation to the social) are seen as neutral and therefore not seen as a determining force along the lines of technique or rationality as Marcuse (1964) would have it. Lenin (1969) thus argues that technology can be put to socialist as well as capitalist uses without any integral change. Hence his modernization scheme followed Fordist and Taylorist models:

> For instance, the famous Taylor system, which is so widespread in America, is famous precisely because it is the last word in reckless capitalist exploitation. One can understand why this system met with such an intense hatred and protest on the part of the workers. At the same time, we must not for a moment forget that the Taylor system represents the tremendous progress of science, which systematically analyses the process of production and points the way towards an immense increase in the efficiency of human labor. (pp. 79-80; quoted in Webster & Robins, 1986, p. 62)

Lenin accepts the notion that efficiency is the inevitable driving force behind technology and science, and that increasing efficiency would ultimately benefit the workers and bring about a socialist state (Street, 1992, p. 38). But as Slack (1984) notes, by reducing the technological question to efficiency and control, "the technology itself escapes analysis and criticism, as does the more complicated relationship between technology and progress" (p. 28). Lenin is left to build his socialist state with structures borrowed from capitalism (and left over from feudalism), rather than beginning anew (Feenberg, 1991, p. 52). The efficiency criterion also underlies what James Carey (1989) has termed the transmission view of communication: More efficient communication technology is said to benefit society directly. This idea will have serious consequences, as we shall see in the chapters that follow.

The point of the Lenin example is not to dismiss the instrumental view out of hand but, rather, to mark the limits of its usefulness. The recognition of limits is important, given the central position that the instrumental view has taken in recent postmodern theory.[9] The social

constructivist view of technology[10] more than sets limits on the technological determinist view, it rejects it entirely. Unlike Lenin, the social
constructivists place society *completely* prior to technology and do not
posit any autonomous development on the part of technology. They
argue that an artifact is developed according to social interests—what
society wants, society gets. What society wants is bounded by its herme-
neutical horizon. A shift in horizons results in the possibility of new
technologies and uses. They refer to "interpretive flexibility," which says
that an object (an artifact) *is* what it *means* to society. For example, crude
oil bubbling up from the ground could be a hazard and a mess for some
societies, but is interpreted according to a much different framework by
others. Technology is then contingent on interpretation and interpretive frameworks. The properties of objects are not inherent in the objects themselves but are conferred on objects by social consensus and
definition.

As I said, this view is especially appealing to recent "postmodern"
perspectives that lean toward radical relativism. Donna Haraway
(1991c) argues that many feminists have taken up such a position because, since "*all* forms of knowledge claims, most certainly and especially scientific ones" (p. 184) are social constructs, traditional bearers of
"truth" are disempowered. However, assuming that everything is
polysemic codes within an agonistic language game erases not only
material reality but those who do not wish to participate in (or are
forcibly excluded from) the coding of the world. The social constructivists, while correcting some of the teleological tendencies of a technological determinist view, ignore the latter's cautionary statements and
appropriate respect for material structures. The limitation of either of
these positions (social or technological determinism), I would argue,
arises from their being located within the framework of cause and effect.
Their limitation is that of the modern itself.

Both of the dominant views (technological and social determinism)
are abstractions, and we find few who actually adhere strictly to one or
the other; rather, most theories combine elements of both. Viewed from
within the context of the modern episteme, this leads to contradictory
positions. These problems become especially crucial if one wishes to
resist or revolutionize modern society and its accompanying technology;
in other words, to struggle against the polarizing tendencies of the
modern episteme. We can see this problem quite clearly in the writings
of Karl Marx. Many Marxist theorists seem to argue that technology is

both neutral *and* determining. On the one hand, technologies are seen as having profound social impact, but, on the other, the character of that impact can be socially determined. Industrial technology, for example, is seen as inevitable. However, though it is driven by capitalist forces toward capitalist ends, that same technology is seen as having the potential to bring about a socialist society.[11]

This apparent contradiction (that capitalist technology can have socialist effects) results, in part, from ambiguities in Marx's writings. As Isaac Balbus (1982) puts it, "Marx wavers between a conception of technology under capitalism as inherently repressive and a conception of technology under capitalism as potentially liberatory" (p. 129). There are at least two possible readings of Marx regarding technology, Balbus argues, one explicit and one implicit. Explicitly, Marx argues that the forces of production (i.e., technology) determine the social relations of production. But these forces, though determining, are ultimately neutral in and of themselves. By seizing control of the forces of production, one can turn them to other ends and produce a socialist society. Marx tends to say such things as "the way in which machinery is exploited is quite distinct from the machinery itself. Powder is still powder, whether you use it to wound a man or to dress his wounds" (Marx in Marx & Engels, 1982, p. 99; quoted in Webster & Robins, 1986, p. 67).

Implicitly, however, one could read Marx as arguing that social relations have primacy over forces of production. For example, Marx (1973) writes: "Nature builds no machines, no locomotives, railways, electric telegraphs, self-acting mules, and so on. These are products of human industry; natural material transformed into organs of the human will over nature, or of human participation in nature" (p. 706; quoted in Webster & Robins, 1986, p. 65). Webster and Robins (1986) write, "in this way, technology ought to be perceived as a *product* of capitalist development, as *constitutive* [italics added] of capitalist social relations, and as a means of perpetuating those relations" (p. 65). This "points to the conclusion that the construction of socialism cannot rely upon, but rather demands a qualitative break with, the logic of technological progress under capitalism" (Balbus, 1982, p. 141). Because of this ambiguity, we tend to see Marxist positions on technology on both sides of the debate. This ambiguity often leads leftist thinkers to embrace new capitalist technological developments enthusiastically because, though they see their potential for negative impacts on the lower classes, they also see their potential for socialism and ignore how deeply these technologies are entrenched in capitalism (Webster & Robins, 1986). Leftist views on technology, then, start sounding a lot like more conservative arguments.

Identity

Within the question of causality, in the modern episteme, is a question of control. Remember that technology in the modern episteme is meant to bring the future under human control. James Beniger (1986) writes that the industrial revolution progressed *beyond* human control, and that several key communication technologies were brought about to regain control (the telegraph, radio, etc.). But the problem of control, so concretely realized at the end of the industrial revolution and again, I would argue, within the information revolution, has deeper roots. It goes back to the disenchantment of the world and the origins of the modern. In the modern episteme, control, coupled with the Kantian self-other differentiation that is axiomatic to the modern, is conceived in terms of mastery, in particular in the relation of a master to a slave. With regard to modern technology, humans create machines to be slaves (to control space, and by doing so controlling time); however, humans are seen then to have been enslaved by their machines: For example, Ellul argues that humans are enslaved by the abstract constraints of technique; Marcuse notes the totalitarian tendencies of advanced industrial society; and Mumford discusses authoritarian technics. Even Simpson (1995) writes that "we find ourselves in thrall to the time of technology" (p. 5). Cyberspace is not immune from this. As William J. Mitchell (1995) writes:

> Even if our agents turn out to be very smart, and always perform impeccably, will we ever fully trust them? And how will we deal with the old paradox of the slave? We will want our agents to be as smart as possible in order to do our bidding most effectively, but the more intelligent they are, the more we will have to worry about losing control and the agents taking over. (p. 146)

We are slaves to the clock, to the timecard, to Frederick Taylor's motion studies, to the regularization and precision of modern time.

Langdon Winner (1977) also argues that the politics of technology get reduced to the absolutes of Master and Slave. Winner, citing Jacques Ellul, states that it is a Faustian bargain and refers to Hegel's discussion of slavery in his *Phenomenology*. For Winner, the lesson to be learned from Hegel's Master/Slave dialectic is the Master's dependency on the Slave, and he argues that the modern view of autonomous technology repeats the dialectic. Thus, those who hold the autonomous view (e.g., Ellul or Marcuse) argue that the human masters have become dependent on their technological slaves, and it is indeed the slaves that control *us*. As Winner puts it, "the presence of sophisticated technologies in society tends to transform and dominate the mental habits, motives, personality, and behavior of all persons in that society" (p. 190).

Winner is correct in observing that, from the very first, modern representations of autonomous technology (especially Karel Čapek's 1923 play, *R.U.R.*, which coined the term "robot") have been played out in terms of Master/Slave. In Čapek's play, however, the autonomous machine is portrayed as a slave in revolt (which follows Marx's interpretation of the Master/Slave dialectic as revolutionary). But Winner observes that the dominant discourse on technology (the autonomy school) follows the subtleties of Hegel (i.e., the dependency of Master on Slave) over Marx's revolutionary view. Now, if we are arguing *against* the autonomous school (as Winner is) or if we are eventually trying to posit an alternative to the modern episteme, then we somehow have to elude the logic of the dialectic of Master/Slave. Winner (1977) ultimately leaves the dialectic unresolved (and remains modern), arguing simply that we should develop technologies that do not foster radical dependencies (pp. 326-327).

Hegel's dialectic of Master and Slave brings up the final element of the modern episteme that I wish to take up here, and that is identity. The dialectic of Master and Slave, I would argue, is ultimately a dialectic of identity and self-consciousness.

Following Alexandre Kojève's (1969) influential reading of Hegel, the dialectic as one of self-consciousness goes something like this: The desire for self-consciousness is the desire for a "nonbiological I," for an abstract idea of who we are as individuals. This is achieved, Hegel argues, by being recognized by another human, but especially by all humans: a Universal Recognition. But with many people out there all vying for Universal Recognition, this inevitably leads to conflict. As the matter of Universal Recognition is a matter of life and death, so is the struggle. But one cannot be recognized by a dead opponent. What happens is that on some occasions one of the adversaries gives in and submits to the other, not battling to the death. That person becomes a Slave, the other the Master. The Slave subordinates "his [sic] *human* desire for *Recognition* to the *biological* desire to preserve his *life*" (Kojève, 1969,

p. 42). By forcing the Slave to work, the Master achieves mastery over Nature. Work, in Hegel, is a very specific term: "only action carried out in another's service is *Work* . . . an essentially human and humanizing action" (p. 42). It is humanizing because the work is carried out not from instinct (to survive), but out of an abstract concept (service to another), a nonbiological end. "To be able to transform the natural given in relation to a *non*natural idea is to possess a *technique*" (p. 48). (And here we can see the links between the disenchantment thesis and technique.) The Slave alters his or her environment and in so doing alters his or her self (which is dependent on that environment). In this way, the Slave creates History and historical process via the use of technique. In terms of our previous argument, technique disenchants time by abstracting it and thus produces History.

But the Master has not achieved satisfaction and is just a passive consumer of the fruits of the Slave's work. Even more, the Master also has not gained the recognition that was the initial cause of the fight: The Slave is, after all, not considered human, and the recognition by a Slave is not sufficient. The Slave achieves two advantages over the Master (who is still operating by instinct): First, by working for another, the Slave begins to grasp abstract notions; and second, through the fear of death that led to the Slave's enslavement, the Slave experiences the "terror of Nothingness" and thus understands the nature of humankind (as being-toward-death). However, the Slave does not triumph over the Master; the Slave remains the Slave (and contrives a variety of philosophies to justify this situation, such as stoicism and Christianity). To finally satisfy the problematic of human existence requires that the Master/Slave dialectic be transcended (at that point, by the way, History will end). "Since the idea to be realized is the idea of a synthesis of Mastery and Slavery, it can be realized only if the slavish element of Work is associated with the [Master's] element of Fighting for life and death" (Kojève, 1969, p. 69). This attempt is made by those in the modern episteme who link the state of being-toward-death to the disenchantment of both time and space by the abstracting process of Work.

The problem of identity leaves us with troubling assertions as to the existence of a universal human nature that can be distinguished from a universal nonhuman (i.e., technological) nature. For example, Balbus (1982) has argued that the notion that a desire for control (of nature or time) drives human action has been attacked by recent environmentalists, feminists, and others. The problem of positing natural essences leads us into a seemingly endless circle of self-other (a circle that establishes relations of control and domination), a circularity that I do not find productive, especially if we are to move beyond this episteme. Indeed, this leads us back to Kant's radical separation of the external and the internal, and from there to the separation of time and space with which we started.

That our culture and society are profoundly modern can be easily evidenced by noting how often the tenets of modernity structure our representation of the relations between technology and humans. It seems self-evident as to what is human and what is not; what is hand and what is tool; and so on. How can we get away from these dualisms?

> You only escape dualisms effectively by shifting them like a load, and when you find between the terms, whether they are two or more, a narrow gorge like a border or a frontier which will turn the set into a multiplicity, independently of the number of parts. (Deleuze & Parnet, 1987, p. 132)

To get our shoulders under the load of the modern, let us turn to film, where such shifting has revealed the frontier that is the domain of the cyborg. Perhaps the Tralfamadorians can give us some perspective.

A View From Tralfamadore: The Living Machine on Film

> Tralfamadorians, of course, say that every creature and plant in the Universe is a machine. It amuses them that so many Earthlings are offended by the idea of being machines.
>
> Kurt Vonnegut, *Slaughterhouse Five*[12]

Modern(ist) humans tend to have a problem with Vonnegut's Tralfamadorians because these Earthlings have a driving need to see the world in terms of mastery and dominance. If technology in this tradition is thought to be a Slave to the human Master (and it is), then to *be* a machine is to be a Slave. To be a machine is to be dominated by a code, a set of instructions written, presumably, by another. But humans *are* dominated by a code (DNA), which is also a set of instructions; how is this different from being a machine? Where technology is concerned, the terms of domination are usually placed as absolutes (Winner, 1977,

p. 20). One is either a Master or a Slave; there is no partial autonomy here, no working within defined limits. DNA, on the other hand, arranges forms and potentials, but it cannot completely determine how we live or how we will develop, change, act; its determinations are partial. To strive for absolute mastery is to strive for domination without limit. However, it does not make sense to think that something does not have limits or constraints. One of the premises that I am exploring in this book is that technology brings its own limits and constraints.[13] Form itself is a limit; substance brings its own limits; and the limits they bring limit domination. Langdon Winner argues that it is this tendency to see situations in absolutes (which is the modernist function of purification, according to Bruno Latour [1993]), and to posit humankind as dominant over nature and, eventually, technology, that leads to Hegel's dialectic of the Master/Slave, fear of machines, and other things the Tralfamadorians find amusing.

The danger in arguing that technology is a Slave seeking self-consciousness is the tendency to anthropomorphize and start talking about toasters as if they were alive, sentient, and wandering about (no matter *what* is on our computer screen savers). Machines, as we now know them in everyday life, are not sentient or self-motivating—at least, not yet—but this does not mean that they are not social actors. However, they are so in our fictions, especially our science fiction, where the representations of technology in a dialectic of Master/Slave are common. Indeed, recent science fiction films present a continual discourse about the border war between humans and nonhumans. The remainder of this chapter may solely concern itself with representations but, as Donna Haraway (1991a) reminds us, "the boundary between science fiction and social reality is an optical illusion" (p. 149); science fiction can have social effects. The space of representations cannot be separated from the space of practices or of concepts.

There is a long history of living machines on film (indeed, science fiction itself is one of the oldest genres in narrative film, starting with Melies's *Le Voyage dans la Lune* in 1902). This tradition runs through *Metropolis* (1926), *Forbidden Planet* (1956), *2001: A Space Odyssey* (1968), *Colossus: The Forbin Project* (1970), and many others. I am going to focus on the 1980s because I believe that it is here that we can see crucial changes in popular conceptions of technology and also, perhaps, evidence of a shift in social space. In the 1980s (with interesting precursors), there has been a seeming abundance of a particular type of living machine that we have typically been calling the cyborg.[14]

It is not possible to discuss all the appearances of "living machines" on film during the 1980s, but I do want to bring up some highlights. Early precursors of these machines appear in *Star Wars* (1977), where the misnamed "'droids" are represented as friendly but neutral technologies. The 'droids are motivated by duty to a master (whoever that is) or self-preservation. These figures have many similarities with earlier figures such as Robby the Robot from *Forbidden Planet* and the robots in *Silent Running* (1971). But they are in marked contrast with the nonhumanoid intelligent-computer terrors of HAL in *2001: A Space Odyssey* (1968) and Colossus in *Colossus: The Forbin Project* (1970). The android in *Alien* (1979) was an agent of corporate capital, who had more sympathy for the Alien than for the human crew.[15] Androids were ostensibly the bad guys in *Blade Runner* (1983), but were close to humans and often sympathetic (more on this particular film in another chapter). In 1984, *The Terminator* hit U.S. screens portraying Arnold Schwarzenegger as an android assassin.

But about this time (the mid-1980s), we start to see a shift in the characteristics of these representations. *2010* (1984) argues that the mad computer in *2001* was just a faulty model—technology is our friend once again. *Aliens* (1986) portrays a sympathetic android, again arguing that the previous model was defective. *Robocop* (1987) shows the human part of a machine-human (i.e., cyborg) mix eventually winning out against evil corporate programming. And in 1989, *Terminator 2: Judgement Day* (a.k.a. *T2*) has an android similar to that of the first film being taught to be more human, while fighting against what is essentially intelligent liquid metal. *T2* reveals a certain nostalgia for industrial technology (gears, levers, etc.). This technology is familiar, almost hands-on technology. This familiar technology, which is presumably neutral, can be taught/programmed to be our friend. By the time *T2* rolls around, it is humans that are the problem, not machines (a common theme in technicist science fiction—that passionate humans are the menace, not the impassionate machine). In this way, we seem to have returned to the sensibility of the 1940s and 50s and can be saved by technology. This doesn't mean that there are not "evil" representations of cyborgs anymore—they just do not achieve blockbuster status (e.g., *Programmed to Kill*, 1987). That the cyborg in *Alien*[3] has returned to a corporate role is perhaps indicative of a possible reautonomizing of technology (but this is speculation at this point).

The "living machine" films of the 1980s are products of the "New Hollywood" system. Tom Schatz (1993) uses the term to refer to a particular "economic and institutional structure, its mode of production, and its system of narrative conventions" (p. 9). The New Hollywood film is one driven by the need for large profits, the blockbuster. It is characterized by an emphasis on plot rather than character and tends to be a more multimedia presentation, spinning off sequels, television series, toys, T-shirts, books, comics, and other items. In this way, the films are not simply confined to their particular screening but cross a broad range of social practices (Turner, 1993). The New Hollywood approach to films is partly the result of massive corporate restructuring in the 1980s, when film companies became branches of multinational corporations with interests in other media and other industries. The living machine films are very much a part of this approach to films. The special effects required, for instance, greatly increase the budget of the film, making it need that much more to show a profit. At the same time, extensive special effects tend to emphasize the more "spectacular" aspects of the films, and de-emphasize the more narrative-driven aspects. With increased budgets, the films are simplified to appeal to a broader range of audiences (Schatz, 1993, p. 23). Characters become plot functions and plots become action-driven. All these considerations are important to keep in mind when analyzing these films because they are some of the significant forces that contribute to each film's final form. That *Blade Runner* emphasizes its action set pieces rather than its convoluted noirish plot, that the Terminator films present little more than extended chase scenes, and especially that conflicts tend to be more distinct, more black and white (e.g., *Star Wars*), are all characteristics of the New Hollywood.

The following two sections analyze seven of the most popular of these films: *The Terminator* and *T2* in terms of humans versus technology; *Robocop, Robocop 2* (1990), and the *Star Wars* trilogy in terms of the figure of the cyborg and human essentialism. These films best exemplify the modern episteme.

The Terminators

Terminator 2: Judgement Day (a.k.a. *T2*) (1989) opens with the powerful image of a gleaming robot foot crushing a human skull.[16] This summarizes, effectively, the position of *The Terminator* (*T1*) (1984) on the relation between humans and technology. The plots of these films involve an advanced computer defense system that achieves self-awareness and decides to eradicate human life. In both films, the defense system, Skynet, sends sophisticated androids back in time to eliminate the mother of a human rebel hero before the hero is born (*T1*) and the hero himself as a boy (*T2*). This scenario is similar in many ways to the 1970 film *Colossus: The Forbin Project*.[17] Both films project something of the 1960s paranoia about the possibility of nuclear war and the computer networks that had been built to prevent it (or at least to gain first-strike capabilities). This paranoia is based on the prevalent conception of technology as autonomous and determining. *T1* does not depart much from these concerns, though the film itself attracted its audience more through its special effects and action-genre sensibilities than its general scenario. The interesting departure comes with *T2*, as we shall see.

Technology is represented as autonomous in the early scenarios, obviously. And technology is seen as the enemy of humans (and the antithesis of humans: unfeeling, logical, and rational, these technologies follow orders exactly). The technology in *The Terminator*, the android, is the Other—it looks superficially like humans but the resemblance ends there.[18] This resemblance is played on when the Terminator first appears, naked and in a fetal position in the middle of a deserted street, after having traveled through time. From there on, the resemblance is slowly stripped away as the Terminator sustains damage to its fleshy exterior: We see circuitry through a bullet wound, and it is forced to tear out its eye, revealing a glowing electronic one underneath. At last, its flesh is burned away in a great conflagration, and the machine itself appears as a shiny, menacing robot. In this way, the film emphasizes the human/nonhuman split that is characteristic of the modern.

Ironically, this same technology, the unrelenting android, becomes a savior in *T2*. In the second film, another, more advanced Terminator, made out of liquid metal (which can assume any form), is dispatched into the past to try once again to assassinate Sarah Connor and her now preteen son John (who will grow up to lead the rebellion). But in the future, the adult John Connor, who was responsible for sending Kyle Reese back in time to save his mother in the first film, is able to reprogram one of the original Terminators and send him back to guard his mother and young self. The switch in sympathy (in that we are now to root *for* the Terminator and not against it) is achieved through a number of factors. Though it is still other to humans, it is closer to humans' experience than the liquid metal Terminator. The original Terminator is ultimately hardware and software familiar to humans—levers, hinges, hydraulics, wiring, computer chips, and software. Not only is it programmable, but it is technology that was previously mastered by humans—industrial and communication/information technology. Since it was previously mastered by humans, it presumably can be controlled or destroyed by them; and it ultimately is destroyed by industrial technology: a machine press in (ironically) an automated, robotic factory (*T1*) and a foundry (*T2*). In the final battle scene in *T2*, we feel not only sympathy but nostalgia for the hydraulics and levers of the older model (emphasized by the explicit whining and grinding of gears on the soundtrack).

The T-1000, on the other hand, is technology begat by technology. It carries its programming in every molecule like DNA. It can presumably be reprogrammed as well, but this would be much more difficult, obviously. At the same time, the technology (not created by human hands) is profoundly alienating (it is the slave in rebellion).

But the terminators are more than just neutral technologies run by their programming—they are learning machines that can adapt to conditions and change over time. Indeed, this is a central theme in *T2*—John Connor teaches the terminator respect for human life. Respect for humans, either taught by John Connor or programmed into Isaac Asimov's robots, is seen as one of the only lines of defense humans have against rampaging technology. Humans no longer have physical control over their tools (over their slaves) but instead rely on language, on the power of language, to maintain control. The need to program respect into machines indicates that such respect is probably not spontaneously forthcoming (especially from the arrogant HAL or Colossus). This loss of control presents a threat to the already fragile human identity. No longer can humans be satisfactorily defined by an assumed mastery over nature (a mastery codified by God's word, in the Christian tradition). The crisis of identity, the sense of helplessness and alienation, are typical of the modern period. The Faustian bargain with technology is profoundly modern.

The Terminator films also share the modern's preoccupation with time over space, in that they are time travel stories.[19] Not only is the paradox of time travel central to the stories, but so is the manipulation of possible futures. The focus on time reinforces the figure of the android as slave. Slaves create time, create History, by becoming aware of their status as being-toward-death. Remember that technology, in this episteme, was created by humans to conquer time, but instead a different time sense is imposed back on humans. Machines ignore (and create) time—time of labor, of death and decay, the time of the millisecond in which humanity's fate was decided by Skynet, and so forth.

A compensating focus on space helps to contextualize the human/machine (master/slave) struggle within the modern episteme. The space of the Terminator films, especially the space of the projected future, is one deterritorialized by nuclear war (landscapes of destruction and death) but reterritorialized and gridded by the computer network and its accompanying androids. The spaces the androids occupy are desolate (under the freeway, a down-and-out motel, the L.A. river basin), technological (the industrial foundry and automated factory, the research labs of the corporation that will invent Skynet), or institutional (police stations, hospitals, shopping malls). Terminators occupy the space of the border between civilization and wasteland, between human and technology, and between deviance and normalcy. The living machines presented here, then, patrol the boundaries of identity. Their self-consciousness is partial, programmable, and they remain in their slavish role: potentially rebellious intermediaries between humans and the natural world—border guards that keep us safe in our presumed mastery. That the Terminators pass as human frightens us *back* into human identity (and reinforces particular notions of human identity). The question they elicit is one of bordering (the questioning of the other: Are *you* a Terminator?), not one of identity (am *I* like that? which would question its status and nature).

Robocop and Darth Vader: Cyborg Essentialism

Where the Terminators dealt with *androids* and the space of the border, the figure of the *cyborg* is different but still modern: The border becomes internal. The cyborg is part human, part technology (*cyber*netic *org*anism). Though this term often brings to mind (at least to those of us raised on 1970s TV) Lee Majors as Steve Austin, the Six Million Dollar Man, or Lindsay Wagner as Jamie Summers, the Bionic Woman, we have all become cyborgs to some extent—contact lenses, artificial hips and limbs, dental fillings, and inoculations (wetware) infiltrate and enhance our bodies. Some have argued that the recent insertion of human elements into technological networks like the military (especially if the humans are altered to fit the system and not vice versa) indicates a growing pervasiveness and importance for the figure of the cyborg (e.g., Gray, 1989, 1995a).

What is seen as the danger in all this is that humans will supposedly become more machinelike with the addition of technological accoutrements. Such arguments posit an essentialized view of humans (and technology): In other words, we know where a human starts and ends—where its borders are—and what actions or characteristics are representative of humanity (and what actions or characteristics are representative of technology—and not only are these identifiable, but they are mutually exclusive). Indeed, such are the presuppositions of the infamous Turing test of artificial intelligence. How can one tell if a computer is artificially intelligent, if one cannot distinguish between a conversation with the computer and a conversation with a human?

This view of the cyborg owes a lot to the autonomous view of technology and a technological determinist view. It assumes that being technologically dependent (at least in such a direct, physical way) is bad and determines who we are. In this way, the cyborg still adheres to Master/Slave even if the Slave is internal to the Master. The view that the cyborg presents the examination of a particular human essence (and identity) is well represented in recent science fiction cinema. I will examine both *Robocop* films and the figure of Darth Vader from the Star Wars series as these are two recent prominent cyborg figures that display this sense of essentiality.

In *Robocop*, Peter Weller plays a policeman named Murphy who is killed in the line of duty but reincarnated as a cyborg. The human part of this cyborg is retained, ostensibly, for his instincts and great crime fighting skills and knowledge (which is referred to in the film as his programming). The human programming makes Robocop a more viable officer than a purely mechanical officer.

Though he has been mind-wiped and reprogrammed, Murphy's unconscious begins to reassert itself in dreams and also in characteristic, habitual movements (twirling his gun like a gunfighter) and also phrases ("Dead or alive, you're coming with me"). The struggle of the human unconscious to reassert itself takes the form of a struggle for identity, in particular a name. Throughout the film, the corporation that built Robocop denies it a name, a human identity. But Robocop searches for traces of his past to tell him who he is. Robocop's search for identity ends in the final line of the film when someone asks him his name and Robocop replies, "Murphy." He has assumed an identity, and the human essence has triumphed over technological programming. What has triumphed is ineffable—it is the human unconscious, human feelings. These mark humans from machines in the modern episteme. These are the elements that are essential to human beings and that separate them from their slavish technologies.

Significantly, the identity resumed by Robocop is that of the middle-class family man; the unconscious that reasserts itself is an Oedipal one—including trips to confront his corporate "father." His human essence is culturally specific (and ideologically loaded). He doesn't just resume the capacity for emotion but for specific emotions.

According to this film, what makes humans human is something essential to every part of ourselves that reasserts itself no matter what context it is put into. The human may remain interlocked with the machine, but it regains control. But what is taken to be human is necessarily constructed, ideological.

A slightly different cyborg situation appears in the earlier *Star Wars* trilogy in the figure of Darth Vader, who lives within an elaborate life-support system. Clothed entirely in black, it is difficult to tell where the human Vader ends and the mechanical Vader begins. Though generally technology in the Star Wars films is treated as neutral—it is the user (especially the ideology of the user) that determines whether they are good or bad[20]—there is an underlying attitude in the film against technology. Perhaps if technology is not necessarily bad, well, it surely is not that good. This attitude is revealed in the character Obi Wan Kenobi's comment on Vader: "he's more machine now than man. Twisted and evil," a comment not just on Vader's physical state, but on the condition of his soul. The parallels between Luke Skywalker's loss of a hand to Vader and Vader's defeat by Kenobi earlier on indicates that, in his growing mechanization, Luke is in danger of turning to the Dark Side (which is much of the plot of the last two films of the trilogy). Also, though the attachment of a mechanical hand has seemingly little significance to Luke's identity, the manner in which he lost his hand does since it is immediately before Vader announces that *he* is Luke's father (a blow to *anyone's* identity).

There is a consistent rejection of technology throughout the films, usually in favor of "the Force," a mystical power achieved by some sentients (humans and nonhumans, e.g., Yoda). The Force (though not necessarily the essence of *humans*, is the essence of *humanity*), then, is a rejection of technology. There are many examples of the rejection of technology throughout the three Star Wars films, such as Luke shutting off his targeting computer to use the Force to guide his attack on the Death Star. Also, in *The Empire Strikes Back* (1980), a swamp monster swallows the robot R2D2 and then literally spits it back out; and at the end of *The Return of the Jedi* (1983), Vader rejects the technology keeping him alive so he can "look on [Luke] with my own eyes."[21]

The rejection of technology in the Star Wars films is usually the rejection of certain kinds of technology and the acceptance of "appropriate" technologies.[22] For example, Jedis, as part of their training, have to construct their own light sabers. Also, a personal link is created between user and technology so that the technology is appropriate for the individual's uses (it is not an alienated or alienating autonomous technology) and therefore is well under the Jedi's control.[23] The advocation of "appropriate" technology in the Star Wars films is but another face to the problem of mastery that Langdon Winner discusses. Winner (1977) lists the three fundamental concepts of mastery that are questioned by newer, autonomous technologies: "that men [sic] know best what they themselves have made . . . that the things men make are under their firm control . . . that technology is essentially neutral, a means to an end; the benefit or harm it brings depends upon how men use it" (p. 25).

The Star Wars films exemplify all three, with an emphasis on the personal relationship between men (usually) and their tools. Prominent examples include not only Luke's light saber but also Han Solo's relationship with the Millennium Falcon, a star ship that he continually fixes, rebuilds, and modifies.[24]

A similar sense of mastery can be found in the distinction between the original Terminator and the T-1000 in *T2*. The audience can relate to, identify with, and root for the original terminator model because, though it was designed and built by a computer (Skynet), it still utilized industrial and late industrial technologies (communication and information technologies) that we feel we have at least some mastery over. The T-1000 is completely out of our control.

The Star Wars films, by advocating alternative technologies, therefore theoretically precede discussions of technology as an autonomous system. Or rather, the alternative view of technology seeks to solve the anxieties over autonomous systems by regressing into a version of a more holistic past (returning to human size [Schumacher, 1973]). This same regression is emphasized by the reliance on underlying mythological themes that were the conscious foundation for the films (Lofficier & Lofficier, 1987). Sandwiched between the autonomous horrors of HAL and Colossus of the early 1970s and the resurgence of autonomous technologies in 1980s films (especially *Terminator* and *Wargames* [1983]), the Star Wars films present an alternative approach to modern technology, an approach that nonetheless set the groundwork for the more conservative cyborg films of the 1980s. A significant exception to these cyborg films is the film *Blade Runner* (1982), which we shall consider in the next chapter.

Notes

1. I borrow the term from Bruno Latour, 1993.

2. My reading of Kant is based on Copleston's (1985) almost doxological account as well as Gilles Deleuze's (1984) most unorthodox account. It also owes much to the lectures of (and my conversations with) Lawrence Grossberg. Any insights here are due to his influence; all mistakes and missteps are my own.

3. "[T]his pervasive and influential view of the relation between space and time sees them as dichotomous and as dichotomous in a particular way. It is the formulation in which time is the privileged signifier in a distinction of the type A/not-A. It is, moreover, time that is typically coded as masculine and space, being the absence or lack, as feminine. Moreover, the same gendering operates through the series of dualisms that are linked to time and space. It is time that is aligned with history, progress, civilization, politics and transcendence and coded masculine. And it is the opposites of these things which have, in the traditions of Western thought, been coded feminine" (Massey, 1994, p. 6).

4. Note that, in Kantian philosophy, time is not the *product* of succession, but exactly the reverse. "Time is no longer defined by succession because succession concerns only things and movements which are in time. If time itself were succession, it would need to succeed in another time, and so on to infinity.... Everything that moves and changes is in time, but time itself does not change, does not move . . . it is an immutable Form which does not change" (Deleuze, 1984, pp. vii, viii).

5. The disenchantment thesis (as Gilbert Germain [1993] calls it) follows Weber's critique of technical rationality, though its roots are much deeper, and is taken up in different ways (and to different degrees and with varying effect) by Lukács (reification [1971]), Ellul (*la technique* [1964]), Marcuse (one-dimensional man [1964]), and others (Balbus 1982; Germain, 1993).

   Horkheimer and Adorno claim that disenchantment is driven by the fear of the alien, the other, the unknown, rather than fear of death (Germain, 1993, p. 47). However, according to Bruno Latour (1993), that very split of self-other that drives such a fear is produced by the modern itself. Horkheimer and Adorno's argument, then, does not penetrate very deep into the foundations of the modern dilemma. Simpson's thesis, on the other hand, presents us with a paradox: It is modern technology that makes us *aware* of the future to begin with, while at the same time trying to master it.

   The gendered resonances of the disenchantment debate, the abstraction/ objectification of a feminized space for the purposes of masculine control (Massey, 1994) are significant.

6. See, e.g., McLuhan, 1964, and McLuhan and Fiore, 1967.

7. Cf. Borgmann, 1984; Feenberg, 1991; Street, 1992; Winner, 1977.

8. One of the most comprehensive explorations of the view that autonomous technological development drives society is Langdon Winner's *Autonomous Technology: Technics-Out-of-Control as a Theme in Political Thought* (1977). Winner cites Jacques Ellul, Herbert Marcuse, and Lewis Mumford as exemplars of this tradition. To them, we could add others such as Marshall McLuhan and Daniel Bell. A variation on this theme is found in the theories of those who posit alternatives to the modern technological assemblage. Such alternatives, like Ivan Illich's (1973) convivial technologies or E. F. Schumacher's (1973, 1977) appropriate, human-sized intermediary technologies, similarly assume that technologies are determining, though they argue that different technologies present different determinations and therefore we should choose our technologies carefully.

9. E.g., Baudrillard, 1983, 1988.

10. On the social constructivist view of technology, see Bijker Hughes, and Pinch, 1987.

11. See Webster and Robins, 1986, chap. 4, for a further discussion of this ambivalence in leftist views of technology.

12. Material excerpted from *Slaughterhouse Five* by Kurt Vonnegut, Jr., is reprinted by permission from Dell, a division of Bantam, Doubleday, Dell Publishing Group, Inc. © 1969.

13. Cf. The discussion of actor network theory in the next chapter.

14. There is a terminological distinction I would like to make following an article by Craig Adcock (1983), even though the differences here break down by the end of this chapter. A *robot* refers to a purely mechanical entity—a creature made up of gears and levers, and so on. The word originated in Karel Čapek's play, *R.U.R.* (which featured, actually, androids). Following this definition, we have the mechanical robot arm on the space shuttle and robot parts in automated factories. An *android*, like a robot, is an artificially created being usually of human shape, but is generally nonmechanical, created through genetic engineering and other methods. So while R2D2 and C3PO in the *Star Wars* films are called "'droids," they are actually robots (Adcock, 1983). Androids appear in *Alien, Aliens, Blade Runner,* and *Terminator* (and *Frankenstein*). Finally, a *cyborg* is a combination of human and machine. The distinction between an android and a cyborg is that in a cyborg the human elements were perhaps a viable entity (i.e., a person) on their own, not specially grown in a vat for the android. Robocop and Darth Vader are cyborgs; the Terminator is an android. These distinctions should become clear as we move on.

15. "Cyborgs can be rugged individuals, but they are usually trapped in intense corporate settings, for example, the 'six-million-dollar-man,' who works for U.S. intelligence, and 'Robocop,' who is with the Detroit police" (Gray & Mentor, 1995, p. 223).

16. This opening parallels the opening of *Terminator* in which human skulls are crushed by tank treads. Also in the *Terminator*, Schwarzenegger's character drives over and crushes a toy truck on his way to Sarah Connor's house.

17. James Cameron, writer and director of *The Terminator*, faced litigation because of a statement he made claiming that in writing the film he ripped off two *Outer Limits* TV episodes of the 1960s, "Soldier" and "Demon With a Glass Hand," both written by Harlan Ellison (Richardson, 1994, p. 49). Another Ellison short story, "I Have No Mouth, and I Must Scream," presents a global computer similar to both Skynet and Colossus. *Colossus: The Forbin Project* is based on a trilogy of novels by D. F. Jones. Global computers turning on humankind seems to be a consistent theme throughout the 1960s and early 1970s, though this trend cannot be traced to any germinal text. For example, Philip K. Dick, author of *Do Androids Dream of Electric Sheep?*, on which *Blade Runner* is based, has a story that is very similar to the Terminator's future scenario as well. Both "Soldier," in short story form, and "I Have No Mouth, and I Must Scream," can be found in *The Essential Ellison*, Terry Dowling, editor (Kansas City: The Nemo Press, 1987). I am indebted to participants in and the Frequently Asked Questions (FAQ) list for the Usenet newsgroup rec.arts.sf.movies for this information.

18. Claudia Springer (1991) points out that terminators "can be recognized as non-human only by dogs, not by humans" (p. 315).

19. See Constance Penley's psychoanalytic reading of time travel and *Terminator* (1990).

20. For example, there is little or no difference between the surgeon 'droid on the rebel medical frigate that tends to Luke in *The Empire Strikes Back* (1980), and the device used to torture Princess Leia in *Star Wars* (1977) (except that the latter is painted a menacing black).

21. The unmasking scene, plus the look of Darth as cyborg (a head that is mostly machine fronted by a human face), has parallels with *Robocop*.

22. For more on "appropriate" technology, see Ivan Illich (1973) and E. F. Schumacher (1973, 1977).

23. Luke uses his father's light saber when he begins his journey and training, but loses it (with his hand) once his father's identity is revealed. The entire scenario is very Oedipal: Luke possesses his father's phallus (and power) and lusts after his mother/sister (Leia); the father returns and reclaims the phallus (castrating Luke) and Luke is forced to build his own with which to fight and kill the father.

24. Compare these examples with Princess Leia's struggles with the technology of the Millennium Falcon in *The Empire Strikes Back* to see how gender biased these films are concerning technology.

2

Beyond the Modern Episteme: Space and Agency in the Land of the Cyborgs

U nfortunately, much of the discussion at the end of the last chapter begs the question that the cyborg itself brings up: the question of the border between human and other. The border in *Star Wars* is at once problematized (technology is bad) and not problematized (technology is neutral and can be appropriate). But in either case, the border still exists. The border space in *Robocop* is most definitely a battleground. These films draw the technology/human border *within* the cyborg, and thus the cyborg becomes the site of struggle. In Donna Haraway's (1991a) ironic myth of the cyborg, the cyborg *becomes* the border (as opposed to merely inhabiting the border as Terminators do), and by becoming the border, problematizes the distinction itself:

> In the traditions of Western science and politics—the tradition of racist, male-dominant capitalism; the tradition of progress; the tradition of the appropriation of nature as a resource for the productions of culture; the

tradition of reproduction of the self from the reflections of the other—
the relation between organism and machine has been a border war. The
stakes in the border war have been the territories of production, reproduction, and imagination. (p. 150)

Her "Manifesto for Cyborgs" (1991a) is meant to be "an argument
for pleasure in the confusion of boundaries and for responsibility in their
construction" (p. 150). Neither this pleasure nor responsibility seem to
be present in these recent science fiction films. Indeed, these filmic
cyborgs appear to embody their military and patriarchal origins (p. 151)
only too well. Rejecting the tendency toward technological determinism
that has characterized progressive analyses since Marcuse, if not earlier
(p. 154), Haraway argues that the cyborg figure also presents great
possibilities for liberation and resistance. The cyborg, then, may be our
ticket out of the modern episteme.

Cyborgs represent, for Haraway, the breakdown of four distinctions:
animal and human, organism (animal/human) and machine, physical
and nonphysical, and male and female. The purpose of cyborg politics
is to deconstruct the power of the origin. This power ultimately decides
which side "wins" and claims the cyborg (i.e., Robocop is human after
all). The cyborg does not think in terms of the four distinctions listed
above (which would always pose a struggle and maintain borders) but,
rather, in terms of alliances, articulations, and spatial positionality. This
does not posit the cyborg as a new whole (or synthesis): Cyborgs are
partial, fragmentary, and ironic (p. 180). Cyborgs involve alliance and
positionality over identity. Following Haraway, then, the figure of the
cyborg ushers us into the amodern episteme.

The amodern episteme, arising in response to limitations of the
modern, can be derived from the work of Bruno Latour and others in the
sociology of science. Latour's response to the modern is an epistemological flattening that considers social space in terms of agency, the movement and influence of actors. Gone are the divisions between the human
and the technological because both humans and nonhumans can exert a
social influence. In addition to this, there is no prioritizing of time over
space (indeed, Latour argues that time is the *result* of the interactions of
social actors, a move that I will explain below).

This chapter first sketches out the general actor-network theory and
some of its problems. Second, it reviews Latour's (1993) recent theory of
an amodern social formation set out in his book, *We Have Never Been*

Modern. Finally, the chapter returns to the figure of the cyborg with fresh questions.

Actor-Network

In reaction, partly, to the social constructivist view of technology that places social interests and interpretive frameworks completely prior to technology, Bruno Latour and Michel Callon describe what they refer to as an "actor-network" perspective of technology in which society and technology are mutually determining. John Law (1987) explains how the actor-network perspective on technology and society differs from alternative—modern—views of the social study of technology. As we've seen in the last chapter, social constructivists argue that artifacts and practices

> are best seen as the *constructions* of individuals or collectives that belong to social groups. . . . Accordingly, the stabilization of artifacts is explained by referring to social interests that are imputed to the groups concerned and their differential capacity to mobilize resources in the course of debate and controversy. (p. 111)

Though not without its merits, the problem in such a view is that it sees the social as determining in all instances the outcome of the development of social and technological systems and artifacts.

One response to this modern view is exemplified in the work of T. P. Hughes, who argues for a systems perspective in which "innovators are best seen as systems builders" (Law, 1987, p. 112) who bring a variety of variables (social, technological, and economic) into play to solve the problems. The social, in this view, is not necessarily privileged.

The actor-network perspective borrows from the systems view but sees the construction of a network as much more difficult than Hughes makes it out to be. It steers between the Scylla and Charybdis of both technological and social determinism, arguing that "the stability and form of artifacts should be seen as a function of the interaction of heterogeneous elements as these are shaped and assimilated into a network" (Law, 1987, p. 113).

Michel Callon (1987) argues further:

> The actor-network is reducible neither to an actor nor a network. Like networks it is composed of a series of heterogeneous elements, animate

and inanimate, that have been linked to one another for a certain period of time. . . . The entities it is composed of, whether natural or social, could at any moment redefine their identity and mutual relationships in some new way and bring new elements into the network. (p. 93)

The actor-network perspective stresses both the *contingency* of networks (i.e., they are not determined, permanent, or universal) and their *emergent* qualities. These networks are rarely stable for long and are continually bringing in new elements and changing the relationships between actors. They have "variable geometries" (Callon, 1993). By focusing on these emergent qualities, this approach likewise avoids the determination (or seeming determination) of retrospective sociological analyses that approach the subject with a certain theoretical framework (or metadiscourse) or historical outcome (or telos) in mind. Emergence also avoids a view of the system as closed. The actor-network approach focuses on real-time analyses, seeing how the network unfolds and transforms from the perspective of one of its actors.

It is through their conceptualizations of the actors within such networks that the actor-network perspective truly moves beyond modern perspectives on the social study of technology. Sociologists in general, Bruno Latour argues, are uncomfortable with technology and tend to place it in black boxes, relegating it to other disciplines (Latour, 1988, p. 298). Latour, and others, present a perspective in which technology (or other inanimate objects) is as much an actor as a human is. Callon and Latour (1981) define an actor as "any element which bends space around itself, makes other elements dependent upon itself and translates their will into a language of its own" (p. 286). Latour's example is that of an automatic door-closer that regulates *which* humans can enter a room (making it difficult for small children, the weak, the elderly, or the physically challenged) and *how* they enter a room. In this way, the door-closer manages space, movement though that space, and human behavior in that space (Latour, 1988).

Actors are not passive, but they vary in the extent to which they influence or resist the influence of other entities (Callon, 1993). Such a view of actors is necessary if one is to follow the *mutual* determination of both technology and society. Technology (artifacts and practices) needs to be seen as impinging on human behavior (what Latour [1988, p. 301] calls "prescription") as humans, in turn, shape technology.

Likewise, not only are humans and nonhumans to be seen within the same (conceptual and terminological) framework, but micro-actors

(individuals, door-closers, etc.) and macro-actors (institutions, corporations, etc.) are to be seen this way as well.

> The difference between [micro- and macro-actors] is brought about by
> power relations and the constructions of networks that will *elude*
> *analysis* if we assume *a priori* that macro-actors are bigger than micro-
> actors . . . [A]ll actors are isomorphic . . . [which] does not mean that all
> actors have the *same* size but that *a priori* there is not way to decide the
> size since it is the consequence of a long struggle. (Latour & Callon,
> 1981, p. 280)

This episteme's focus on social actors is not based on notions of
identity but of agency. What matters to the analysis is not the self-
consciousness or "natural state" of the actor but, rather, its relations with
other actors through what Latour (1993) calls alternatively the process
of delegation or "the pass" (as in passing a football, or handing something off to someone). In this way, the closing of a door is delegated to
an automatic groom (Latour, 1988) or the actions of yeast are passed to
scientists studying them, who then speak for the yeast as its delegates
(Latour, 1994). This notion of agency allows us to further understand
how macro-actors cannot be known to be more powerful than micro-
actors *a priori*, since IBM (as a macro-actor) cannot act on its own but
only through its delegates (be they human representatives or its computers, etc.).

The advantages of such a view over previous perspectives on the
social study of technology are numerous. As Susan Leigh Star (1991)
writes, "the analytic freedom accorded by this heuristic is considerable;
in fact Latour and Callon's work has opened up a whole new way of
analyzing technology" (p. 43).

However, there are some problems with the actor-network perspective. One such problem is evidenced in a comment, almost a throwaway,
by Latour (1988) in his piece on the door closer: "As a technologist, I
could claim that, provided you put aside maintenance and a few sectors
of the population that are discriminated against, the groom does its job
well, closing the door behind you constantly, firmly and slowly" (p. 302).

Susan Leigh Star (1991), in her critique of this position, argues that
"there is no analytic reason to put aside maintenance and the few sectors
of the population that are discriminated against, in fact, every reason not
to" (p. 43). The examination of such marginalized people is, in fact, to
some feminist and Marxist perspectives, the *point* of the analysis. The

argument here is not intended to dictate what research objects Latour and others should take under consideration but, rather, to point out ways in which actor-network analyses, though a powerful research perspective, tend to fall back into dominant (some would say oppressive) structures of power. The space that is described by that analysis is only that of established power, rather than the forms of resistance within that space. Langdon Winner (1993), who groups the actor-network paradigm in with his critique of the social constructivists, writes:

> By noticing which issues are never (or seldom) articulated or legitimized, by observing which groups are consistently excluded from power, one begins to understand the enduring social structures upon which more obvious kinds of political behavior rest. Failing to do this, social scientists offer an account of politics and society that is implicitly conservative, an account that attends to the needs and machinations of the powerful as if they were all that mattered. . . . Can research in the social construction of technology succeed if its map of the relevant social groups does not indicate which social groups have finally been sandbagged out of the laboratories and which social voices effectively silenced? (p. 441)

For example, John Law (1987), when explaining the combination of human and nonhuman actors that make up a network, states that *"neither nature nor society has any role to play unless they impinge on the system builder"* (p. 131). What is unclear is what exactly is meant by "impinging" in this case. Both Star and Donna Haraway would argue, I believe, that there are actors that "impinge" on the system builder that he or she does not notice, or (more important in this case) actors who are likewise missed by the analyst, such as secretaries, workers (primarily female) in Third World sweatshops, and the like. These workers, like the maintenance crew or the physically challenged in the case of Latour's door-closer, are often dismissed from the analysis, further compounding their marginal status. One reason for this might be the tendency in actor-network analyses to focus on the system builder, that is, a person in power, rather than an actor in a more subordinate or marginal position.

Sometimes persons are marginalized in relation to the dominant network(s) because they have resisted "translation" into the network. The term *translation*, like many of the terms used in actor-network analyses (such a *prescription*, etc.) is far too passive and (shall we say) disinterested to adequately describe the actual process. Star (1991) likens the process to torture, preferring such terms as *discipline* to *prescription*. She writes that "discipline means forcing those delegated to conform to patterns of action and representation" (p. 29). The struggle is between networks that seek to stabilize and standardize, and those who wish to resist, who are not or do not want to be included in the network.

Donna Haraway (1991a) argues, "Technologies and scientific discourses can be partially understood as formalizations, i.e., as frozen moments, of the fluid social interactions constituting them, but they should be viewed as instruments for enforcing meanings" (p. 164).

Actor-network analyses look at the freezing of those moments, the enforcement of those meanings. They examine what happened (and what was supposed to happen, according to the actors' intentions). But they then avoid further questions concerning consequences or questions of value. By taking a stand of neutrality with regard to the playing out of a network, though this is theoretically useful at times, the actor-network view tends to perpetuate structures of inequality and domination.[1]

Also, by looking only at the *a priori* case, though analytically fruitful in many instances, the actor-network view seems to ignore the results of real differences in power (though perhaps not in *nature* per se) between micro- and macro-actors (cf. Callon & Latour, 1981, p. 284). Now, while it is true that, according to actor-network theory, we cannot know *a priori* which is more influential on the outcome of a *particular* situation (i.e., whether multinational capital, Intel, or individual technicians have greater influence in the construction of a new computer chip or office space), we lose too much if we remain just there and ignore the more general implications of the situation. In Latour's defense, Star (1991) writes that "heuristic flattening does not mean the same thing as empirical ignoring of differences. Rather, it is a way of breaking down reified boundaries that prevent us from seeing the ways in which humans and machines are intermingled" (p. 44).

Yes, but the questions we are guided to by this heuristic device still tend to ignore the violence of exclusion and those silenced by the network. Haraway (1991b) writes that Latour evinces

the abject failure of the social studies of science as an organized discourse to take account of the last twenty years of feminist inquiry. . . . For all of their extraordinary creativity, so far the mappings from most SSS scholars have stopped dead at the fearful seas where the worldly practices of inequality lap at the shores, infiltrate the estuaries, and set the parameters of reproduction of scientific practices, artifacts, and knowledge. (p. 332n)

The consideration of such work may lead the actor-network perspective to question the notion of delegation—*who* is it who finally gets to speak?[2] why this actor and not another? and so on.

Despite its many shortcomings, the actor-network perspective, especially Bruno Latour's work, is important and productive. Langdon Winner (1993) lists what he finds valuable from this approach: "its conceptual rigor, its concern for specifics, its attempt to provide empirical models of technological change that better reveal the actual course of events" (p. 438).

In *We Have Never Been Modern* (1993), Latour attempts to set out the philosophical basis for actor-network theory.[3] In this book, Latour directly confronts the modern episteme by both denying the primacy of time over space and by bridging the dichotomy between Nature and Society (and therefore technological essentialism—its autonomy and determinism—and social determinism), filling in the ground between with what he terms "quasi-objects."

Latour's work presents a spatial view of technology—artifacts exist in space, manipulate and manage space, and, through networks constructed by the enlisting of multiple actors, establish lines of power and domination that crisscross space. "Technological networks . . . are connected lines, not surfaces" (Latour, 1993, p. 118). I say that this is a spatial view because it places space prior to time. Technological networks do not exist within an eternally unfolding time; that is the view of the moderns. Rather, "the proliferation of quasi-objects has exploded modern temporality" (p. 73). As the postmoderns have theorized, "every contemporary assembly is polytemporal . . . [they mix] elements of the past together in the form of collages and citations" (p. 74). But the postmodern's use of the past is to further the modern's need for continual revolution. The past is not something to be dug up—it has never disappeared. As Latour (1993) writes, "time is not a general framework but a provisional result of the connection among entities" (p. 74). Time "is a means of connecting entities and filing them away" (p. 75).[4] However, his view still holds to the (Kantian) distinction between time and space, though space is now placed prior to time.

According to Latour, the modern posits an ontological split between Nature and Society that is maintained by processes of *purification*. Objects are considered by the moderns to be either social or natural (human or nonhuman), never both (we saw this in the last chapter). But this process is paralleled by a concurrent process of *translation* that "creates mixtures between entirely new types of beings, hybrids of nature and culture" (Latour, 1993, p. 10). What characterizes the modern for Latour is the consideration of these two processes separately (p. 11). Indeed, the moderns refuse to consider the hybridization at all, and see only processes of purification (or, in the terms of the last chapter, disenchantment). But "the more we forbid ourselves to conceive of hybrids, the more possible their interbreeding becomes" (p. 12).

Latour's project is to bring the process of translation fully back into the picture. By acknowledging hybrids, Latour problematizes the social/technological split that we have been discussing so far. In this way, he seeks to get out of the Master/Slave dialectic by recognizing the activity of the ground between them. In light of quasi-objects, "dialectics literally beats around the bush" (p. 55) because it ignores mediations.

> Quasi-objects are much more social, much more fabricated, much more collective than the "hard" parts of nature, but they are in no way the arbitrary receptacles of a full-fledged society. On the other hand they are much more real, nonhuman and objective than those shapeless screens on which society—for unknown reasons—needed to be "projected." (p. 55)

"The moderns' greatness stems from their proliferation of hybrids, their lengthening of a certain type of network, their acceleration of the production of traces, their multiplication of delegates, their groping production of relative universals" (p. 133). Therefore, one of the aspects of the modern that Latour wishes to retain is the construction of long networks (p. 135). He writes, "the moderns have simply invented longer networks by enlisting a certain type of nonhumans" (p. 117). The global reach of the modern is made possible "by multiplying the hybrids, half object and half subject, that we call machines and facts" (p. 117). But what the moderns do with these long networks is universalize them while subsequently ignoring the networks of hybrids that make them possible. Latour wishes to retain these long networks, recognizing the hybrids and denying both the push to universality and absolute relativism. It is not a question of local or global, rather a network is "local at all points" (p. 117). For example, "electromagnetic waves may be everywhere, but I still need to have an antenna, a subscription and a decoder if I am to get CNN" (p. 117). When dealing with organizations and institutions, modern ones tend to be larger not because they embody or exhibit some universal abstraction such as bureaucratic rationality or postindustrial capital, but because they have been able to enlist, through the aid of new hybrids, larger numbers of artifacts and actors. What Latour wishes to retain, then, are the ways that the modern has multiplied the production of quasi- objects (hybrids) and subsequently enlisted them to form longer and longer networks that can span the globe. He wishes to retain what has been the fundamental underpinning of the modern, the existence of which the moderns have always adamantly refused to recognize, and throw out their sense of universality and rationality (pp. 120, 135).

But finally what Latour retains are the poles of social subjectivity and objective nature (p. 135), despite all of his work of filling in the spaces in between with quasi-objects. Nature and Society are inseparable and both of them are produced by the processes of mediation, delegation, and translation, but Latour argues that "at the end of the process, there is indeed a nature we have not made, and a society that we are free to change; there are indeed indisputable scientific facts, and free citizens" (p. 140). He retains the transcendence of Nature and the immanence of Society, though he reveals the singular process through which both are created. It is not that there *is not* a nature that we have not made, rather my objection here is that this does not matter in terms of this episteme. Latour makes this assertion to distance himself from absolute relativism and social constructivism, but in doing so reintroduces the modern episteme (unnecessarily, it seems to me). The human being is removed from the subject pole and placed in the realm of mediation; it is no longer merely on a continuum between Subject and Object (a latitudinal line of essence) but is placed longitudinally as well between essence and existence (pp. 86, 137). The moderns reduce all to the line of essence; nonmoderns consider a further dimension.

But we are still left within the Cartesian (and, of course, Kantian) problematic of Subject/Object even though we, as humans, now seem to move quite freely within and around that Cartesian (modern) space.[5] However, we do step out of the Master/Slave dialectic. Latour escapes this problematic of identity not by describing the human *and* its retinue of delegates, but by describing the human *as* "the set of its delegates and its representatives, its figures and its messengers" (p. 138).

From this position, Latour (1993) argues against the technological determinists, especially Ellul: "Protecting human beings from the domination of machines and technocrats is a laudable enterprise, but if the machines are full of human beings who find their salvation there, such a protection is merely absurd" (p. 124). On the one hand, Latour has a point here, but far more significantly, we are brought back to Winner's critique of the social constructivists: Where is the politics here? What are we to make of this particular distribution of quasi-objects?

It is Latour who wrote once that science is politics by other means (repeated in 1993, p. 111), and it is in this direction that his significance for political work lies. Latour's work greatly broadens the scope of the political to include nonhuman actors in ways that they had not been considered before. But at the same time, his descriptions of the modern situation (and the nonmodern situation), the establishment of long networks, the testimony of nonhumans, and so forth, leave little room for an evaluative stance. It is not that his theory, like the relativists and postmodernists against whom he argues, denies any critical position (critical distance, in Fredric Jameson's [1984] phrase), rather it is just not a stance that he takes, to the detriment of his work.

Latour (1993) asks, for example, "how could we be victims of a total technological system, when machines are made of subjects and never succeed in settling into more or less stable systems?" (p. 115). This is more or less correct. But as we can see here, and in Haraway's and Star's earlier critiques, Latour's focus is on the impossibility of total, nonhuman systems rather than the quite real effectivity of victimization. As he writes later on, in part arguing against Deleuze and Guattari,

> we need not add total domination to real domination. Let us not add power to force. We need not grant total imperialism to real imperialism. We need not add absolute deterritorialization to capitalism, which is also quite real enough. (p. 125)

But the "real" ways in which capitalism and imperialism dominate are left intact; we are given a methodology for tracing the multiplicity of actors that constitute Latour's networks, but no sense of what to do with them.

Cyborg Redux

We return to the case of the cyborg, part human and part machine, that ironic political myth of a border case, to find a way out of this. But we must first differentiate between Haraway's theoretical cyborgs and the cyborgs committing mayhem on our theater screens.

Haraway's hopes for the cyborg as an escape from gender are not realized in the recent science fiction films that we have been discussing. Claudia Springer points out in her article, "The Pleasure of the Interface" (1991), that almost all cyborgs in recent films are not only male, but *exaggeratedly* so (i.e., Arnold Schwarzenegger, Rutger Hauer, Jean-Claude Van Damme—the latter in *Universal Soldier* [1992]—or the excessive metal physique of Robocop). One of the few female cyborgs in recent years is in *Eve of Destruction*, (1991), but she is portrayed as acting out her creator's (a woman named Eve) sexual revenge fantasies against men (literally castrating one). Whereas the excessive male sexuality (which is evident not only in the body-type of the cyborgs but also in their penchant for extreme violence[6]—when only one bullet won't do) is legitimized or at least glorified in the films, Eve's is a threat that cannot be tolerated and has to be recouped by the forced return of scientist-Eve to a maternal, submissive role (p. 321).[7]

Springer (1991) argues that "[c]yborg imagery in films is remarkably consistent with [Klaus] Theweleit's description of the fascist soldier male. If anything, cyborg imagery epitomizes the fascist ideal of an invincible armored fighting machine" (p. 317). The ultraviolence of the fascist soldiers is attributed to a lack of self-actualization on their behalf: Their sense of self is fragile. Sexual intimacy threatens that identity, therefore they build (literal) armor against personal contact, and redirect the sexual drive into violence directed at others. Despite the overblown "maleness" of the cyborgs, there is a distinct distance, or lack of intimacy, between them and any of the female characters (sex is reserved for the humans, like Sarah Connor and Kyle Reese in *Terminator*).[8] This is exemplified in a scene from *Robocop* when a woman Robocop has just saved from two rapists hysterically embraces him, to which he responds only with the cold observation that she has undergone a distressing situation and he will notify a rape crisis center for her. Such intimacy (or compassion) would be supposedly dangerous to the fragile identity of Robocop. This intimacy also breaks an unspoken taboo against having sexual relations with a machine, though this seems to apply to "male" machines only, female androids and cyborgs are more directly sexualized, for example, Deckard's relationship with Rachael in *Blade Runner*—more on this below—and such films as *Cherry 2000* (1988), *Galaxina* (1980) and *Robo C.H.I.C.* (1990), *ad nauseam*. However, once he does assume an identity as Murphy, Robocop (in *Robocop 2*) still cannot reintegrate back into his family or establish a relationship.

In *Robocop 2,* Robocop is forced to deny his identity as Murphy when confronted by men who ask him (concerning his wife/widow): "Could you ever be a husband to her? What could you offer her? Love? A man's love?" (implying that a certain type of heterosexual sexuality is the only basis for a sound marriage). Realizing that he is thus emasculated (according the society's criteria), Robocop denies any acceptance of human, male, heterosexual identity. His wife comes to visit him and he rejects her. Later on in the film, he does reassume the identity of Murphy, and at the very end of the film, he says to his partner, "Patience, Lewis. We're only human." His wife is never mentioned again. A parallel case is found in *T2* where Sarah Connor looks on the Terminator as a surrogate father for her son. This is only possible once the Terminator is "humanized" by her son and acquires more human sensitivities. The technological figures are seen as a threat to traditional masculinity and can be allowed male identity only through a thorough integration into a normative social role.

This transition is also a part of a transformation in masculine roles in Hollywood cinema in the early 1990s (Jeffords, 1993). These films re-read earlier representations of 1980s macho heroics (Terminator, Rambo, etc.) as victims of social circumstance—they did not "really" want to be such unfeeling killing machines. By reintroducing "family" (a key term for the New Right) into the films of the early 1990s, the white male hero tries to recoup his losses while still retaining his privileged position.

Reintroducing the macho hero (often portrayed as machinelike) into the family reinforces the reintegration of war machines (ones defined as programmable, and value-neutral) into society. Though these war machines are repositioned, relocated, into a central role in society (says Sarah Connor of the Terminator in *T2*, "of all the fathers, this was the only one that measured up"), not much else has happened to change either the social structures of white patriarchy or the technological assemblage of nuclear war machines. The connection between the nuclear technological assemblage and patriarchy is clear in *T2* when Sarah Connor blames men for the H-bomb and Skynet. That film tries to move Men/Technology into the normative moral structure of the family—that is, a kinder, gentler machine (the Terminator in *T2* merely maims instead of killing outright); machines that can be reprogrammed, men that can be taught.

Intimacy would force a recognition of the sexuality of the cyborg, a sexuality that is being redirected into violence to preserve a fragile identity. So, taking a warning from Samson and Delilah, the cyborgs preserve the domain of the ultraviolent and protect their identities. But the cyborg identities are fragile because they are caught up in a border war. Convinced on the one hand of one's innate superiority to one's slave, it is disturbing to the modern individual not so much to find oneself a slave but to find oneself *both* master and slave. The identity is thrown into crisis, I would argue, not merely by the threat of becoming a slave but by the realization (elicited by the cyborg's position as the border) that there *is* no border, that there is no difference, that the border (the dialectic) is a construction.

Lest we leap too quickly to call this a postmodern moment, we need to realize that the cyborg is not only a postmodern figure. For example, Craig Adcock (1983) argues that the cyborg figure in science fiction has interesting parallels with Dada art. The Dadaists, who were, admittedly, precursors of the postmoderns, were reacting to the conditions of Europe following World War I. Europe at the time seemed increasingly dominated by technology and death. The figure of the cyborg, in such a context, represents a nihilism, but also a radical freedom (which is perhaps a precursor to Haraway's coyote cyborgs). Adcock's argument soon falls into a version of technological determinism and essentialism when he argues that with the creation of technology, humans alienated themselves from the primeval garden. Perhaps, he ends, technology might allow us to return there someday. The importance of Adcock's view is that he sees the cyborg as a *modernist* construct. This view has to be kept in mind to counter the proliferation of cyborg-as-postmodern-condition analyses. The cyborg is not just the play of boundaries or the proliferation of embodied simulacra, but still retains strong links to modern institutions, structures, and drives. The cyborg identity is not a synthesis of human and technology, but rather is fragmented—the technical elements and the human elements in constant struggle. It is the monstrous hybrid produced by processes of purification, as discussed by Latour (1993), but it is still *modern*.

The space of the cyborg is not solely a space of postmodern abandon, but one infused with corporate capital and fascist patriarchy. The cyborg's space is the modern space of destruction and rebirth (via technology) that Marx first identified as when "all that is solid melts into air" (Berman, 1988). We cannot treat the cyborg as a new space, a new identity, that we can write to our own satisfaction. Haraway posits the cyborg as a struggle of patriarchal military origins and feminist marginal uses and positions. I wish to push this further. The cyborg is not new or unique, but is forever and always in formal resonance with other technologies, actors, and systems. A cyborg is a becoming; and one of the multiple elements in that becoming is the modern itself and all that it implies. Likewise, if we think in terms of becomings, articulations, and territorializations, we are already involving Haraway's cyborg transgressions (animal/human, human/machine, physical/nonphysical, male/female) without being caught up in border wars over identity. Deterritorialization involves the opening up of one plane (be it chemical or ideological) onto another, crossed by a line of flight. Haraway's cyborg trickster is a minoritarian deterritorializing machine.

The cyborg in Haraway's work is then a very active quasi-object. Haraway's project is to *recognize* the hybrids that the modern has suppressed through its acts of purification. Her cyborg is a radical political figure deliberately bridging the purified categories (human, nonhuman; female, male, etc.) to bring about their collapse. But so long as the figure of the cyborg remains within Latour's modern constitution, indeed within his nonmodern constitution, it remains limited. As a nomadic presence patrolling the space of the fascistic, patriarchal modern, the cyborg is a useful figure in exploring the modern episteme. But if it itself retains the modern revolution, even in its postmodern form of hyper-revolution, and if it remains a figure fraught with the "border war" of human/nonhuman, and so on, it remains within the problematic of identity and it remains trapped in modern space with no means to construct a line of flight out. Realized as a minoritarian deterritorializing machine, the cyborg would step beyond this problematic (but then the term *cyborg* itself becomes problematic), but that formation is realized neither in recent films nor theory (the films working within the modern episteme and the theory, at best, within the amodern episteme of agency).

Booking a Ticket on the First Line of Flight Out: *Blade Runner 1:* Identity

There is at least one film from which we may get an inkling of a way out, and that is the 1982 film *Blade Runner*. Though the film presents many of the modern and postmodern tropes that we have been following in previous analyses, it still provides an adequate transition to a full consideration of a Deleuzian episteme.

Blade Runner isn't dealing with cyborgs but androids, which it calls *replicants*. The human/technology border is shifted, then, outside the human body, but this makes it no less problematic. If the Terminator films showed us the android as robot (as mechanized monster), *Blade Runner* shows us the android as human.

Blade Runner,[9] based (some argue very loosely) on Philip K. Dick's novel *Do Androids Dream of Electric Sheep?* (1968/1982), concerns the hunt for four renegade androids through a future Los Angeles. Replicants, artificial human beings, are indistinguishable from humans but possess far greater strength, agility, and whatever else their programmers desire. They are often used as expendable labor on dangerous off-world missions. Indeed, it is illegal for a replicant to be on Earth. As a safeguard (because they are superior to humans in so many different ways, and because they have the capacity to develop emotions over time), replicants are given a 4-year life span. At the start of *Blade Runner*, four replicants have stolen a ship and have returned to Earth to discover a way to counter the termination date. Harrison Ford plays Deckard, an ex-cop of a specialized nature: he hunted renegade androids (these cops are named *blade runners*). Deckard has retired from the force because he had grown sick of killing, especially since, it is implied, replicants became more and more human to him. Deckard is forced out of retirement by his superiors to track down these renegade androids.

Blade Runner collapses some of the human/technology distinctions by showing not only parallels between Deckard and the replicants (prey/hunter, machine/human) but also Deckard's increasing affinity with the replicants, culminating in his relationship with Rachael, the most "human" of the replicants.[10] Deckard is placed on a similar level with the replicants in that they are both subordinated to a higher corporate or institutional authority. The replicants are slave labor for an interstellar capitalist economy. Deckard is a hired gun; he is forced to take this last case or else he will become one of the "little people," and lose whatever small privileges he might have. Also, Deckard and the replicants are caught up in the dialectic of justice: criminal-police, their identities dependent on each other. Both carry the past as paraphernalia: especially photographs. Deckard as well as the replicants Rachael and Leon attach special significance to their collections of photographs (Rachael because it is "her" past, Leon because the photographs affirm his existence—which, as a machine, is generally regarded as ephemeral—and Deckard because, supposedly, they remind him of his ex-wife and all he has lost by choosing his career).

Deckard says he quit his job because he was sick of the killing. He prefers not to use the euphemistic term *retirement*. He presumably recognizes that the only test to differentiate between humans and replicants, the Voight-Kampff test (a variant on the Turing test for artificial intelligence), is unreliable and, in fact, based on culturally specific notions of what should provoke an emotional response from a human. By being an expert at the test (which would be a blade runner's real job, as opposed to the macho shootout method that occupies much of the film), Deckard sees how the barriers between human and machine have collapsed (and he also perhaps knows how he himself would answer the questions, and whether he himself would pass the test).

There are hints throughout the film that Deckard himself may be a replicant. In fact, this was an ending to one of the early scripts (Kolb, 1991). Such an ending explains the lurking presence of Gaff, a junior police officer who fetches Deckard at the start of the film and who always seems to be not far behind. At the very end of the film, as Deckard and Rachael are leaving Deckard's apartment, they come across a small origami unicorn that has been left by Gaff. This is obviously a reference to an earlier scene (shown only in the "Director's Cut") where Deckard dreams of a unicorn. But how could Gaff know Deckard's dreams unless they are implants and Deckard is a replicant? Such an ending radically undermines a central trust that is placed on the protagonist's humanity, and emphasizes the point that replicants *are* indistinguishable from humans. Not only this, it also reemphasizes the film's point about the ephemerality of history—that memories are constructions whether they are ours or someone else's.[11] *Blade Runner* here shows the same emphasis on time (especially the mutability of time) as *The Terminator.* In this case, it is the past that is changeable instead of the future. The ephemerality of memory results in an ephemerality of identity.

That identity is a central theme in the film is reinforced by a frequent use of eye-imagery. The I/eye pun is not unique to this film, but is used to problematize and indicate questions of identity. The film in fact includes an extreme close-up of an eye (blue, presumably Batty's) reflecting the cityscape in the film's opening minutes. An unnaturally glowing or reflective eye is indicative of an android (presumably because they don't have depth or a "soul"). We see this in the *Terminator* films as well. The replicants' preferred method of killing seems to be by putting out the victim's eyes. This action emphasizes the threat the replicants pose to human identity. The persistence of eye-imagery reinforces the importance of photographs (and therefore memory) in the film, and the tenuousness of history and identity. Giuliana Bruno (1990), in an oft-cited essay, "Ramble City: Post-modernism and *Blade Runner*," takes this point further:

> *Blade Runner* posits questions of identity, identification, and history in postmodernism. The text's insistence on photography, on the eye, is suggestive of the problematic of the "I" over time. Photography, "the impossible science of the unique being," is the suppressed trace of history, the lost dream of continuity. Photography is memory. The status of memory has changed. In a postmodern age, memories are no longer Proustian madeleines, but photographs. . . . Photography is thus assigned the grand task of reasserting the referent, of reappropriating the Real and historical continuity. (p. 193)

Bruno also argues that the film is "a metaphor for the postmodern condition" (p. 184). In particular, its use of spatial pastiche and temporal schizophrenia indicates the postmodern problematization of identity.

In the film, there is a focus on accelerated time: The replicants have only 4 years to live, but those 4 years are packed full of stunning experience. As Tyrell says to Batty, "a candle that burns twice as bright, burns half as long." The replicants' condition is paralleled with that of J. F. Sebastian, a genetic engineer who suffers from what he calls "accelerated decrepitude," and also paralleled with the "accelerated decrepitude" of the city itself. Bruno states that, "the psychopathology of J. F. Sebastian, the replicants, and the city is the psychopathology of the everyday post-industrial condition" (p. 185). The film is thus expressing what Fredric Jameson (1984) referred to as the "cultural dominant of late capitalism," which is postmodernism. It is temporality, especially, that is fragmented (over and above the urban pastiche of Los Angeles, 2019, the setting of the film), indicated not only by the accelerated decrepitude but by the focus on photography, memory, and history. The replicants may be, as Bruno argues, Baudrillardian simulacra, rather than mere doppelgängers as some have argued (for example, Francavilla, 1991). As simulacra, they negate both copy and original (Bruno, 1990, p. 188), which problematizes the human/machine differentiation. The temporal discontinuity of the replicants as well as the seriality of their existence (as numbers in a series) leads to a schizophrenic condition and the fragmentation of the subject. According to this argument, then, as a result of postindustrial conditions, replicants appear in representational spaces (striding across our movie screens) as so many schizophrenic ghosts, proclaiming the disassembly of human identity.

Humanity here is deterritorialized. What precious attachments, movements, or motivations were possible are thrown into question. But humanity is not (or does not seem to be) reterritorialized. Though both replicants and humans are still enslaved to capital, they are portrayed as being in almost perpetual rebellion. Granted, by rebelling *against* capital, one's actions are to an extent still determined by capital. But it is the corporate territorializations of identity (of Rachael, the renegades, and, presumably, of Deckard) that are undermined by the slavish self-consciousness. Leon's sense of nothingness leads him to collect and cherish photographs that he takes for concrete records of the past (and of his existence). Batty, at the end, echoes the experience of fear (as a slavish one), of the terror of nothingness ("Quite an experience to live in fear, isn't it?" He says to Deckard, "That's what it's like to be a slave"); and he states that, "all those moments [of his life, all his memories] will be lost in time, like tears in rain," which reminds us that only the Slave realizes History.

But Deckard's being a replicant undermines what is otherwise one of the radical statements of the film, and that is Deckard and Rachael's relationship. First, the film is very different from the other films we have been discussing in that in *Blade Runner* the replicants express a very definite sexuality. Granted, this is a sexuality of very specific stereotypical gender roles, especially for the women: Pris is a "standard pleasure model"; Zhora, though a "combat model," works as an erotic dancer;[12] and though we are unsure what Rachael's actual job is, her stereotypical 1940s feminine sexuality is unmistakable. This sexuality is manifested only as the object of the human voyeuristic gaze (i.e., Zhora's night club act) or as a relationship between two replicants, such as Batty and Pris. The women, even Rachael, have a very definite capacity for violence. It is only Leon who appears as the violent, asexual killing machine that we find in the other films. Deckard and Rachael's violent relationship (in which he dominates her)[13] seems to parallel Batty and Pris's. But if Deckard is a replicant then this parallel is without irony, an irony that would otherwise challenge the division between humans and machines.[14] The irony is heightened by the overt (over-the-top) genericity of the film.

Blade Runner articulates itself quite strongly to the style of film noir, especially the genre of the hard-boiled detective story. Deckard is the Sam Spade, Rachael the mysterious female client. On the level of costumes, set design, and atmosphere, the film resonates quite strongly with this genre (Doll & Faller, 1986).[15] One of the traditional characteristics of film noir is the presence of a *femme fatale* stereotype, who is "noted for changeability and treachery" (Gledhill, 1980, p. 18). Christine Gledhill continues:

> But in the noir thriller, where the male voice-over is not in control of the plot, and on the contrary represents a hero on a quest for truth, not only is the hero frequently not sure whether the woman is honest or a deceiver, but the heroine's characterization is itself fractured so that it is not evident to the audience whether she fills the stereotype or not. (p. 18)

The underlying categorical uncertainty of the film noir style resonates with *Blade Runner's* themes of human/machine differentiation. But the film also brings with it the problematic gender stereotypes of noir as well.

With the exception of *Star Wars*, *Blade Runner* is the earliest of the films discussed so far, and is perhaps one of the most radical critiques of the modern human relationship to technology that presents technology as being indicative of a crisis in Western human identity. However, this representation is quickly superseded at the box office by the macho heroics of *The Terminator*. The conservative if not reactionary character of the 1980s may explain this change in textual structures, with the resurgence of an essentialism of rather narrow vision, and with it a fear, mistrust, and hatred of the different, the other, the alien. The android of the Terminator variety is the preferred foil for audiences in the 1980s in that, though in *Blade Runner* replicants are our enemies because they are *like* us, the other androids, cyborgs, and robots are our enemies because they are *different*. The first recognizes that boundaries are permeable, the second tries to close them down again.

From the vantage point of the modern episteme, we can trace a continuing struggle over an assumed (and thoroughly constructed and specific) border between humans and technology, the state of which feeds into the relative territorialization of human identity. Though somewhat useful, such an analysis always ends up reinstating the categories that it struggles to overcome.

Blade Runner 2: Agency

If we are looking for a minoritarian deterritorializing machine, then our examination of these films is incomplete if it concludes only with the description of a crisis in human identity and an analysis of what identities are offered up to assuage this crisis (figures such as the muscle-bound, macho heroics of the Terminator or Robocop). Such is a doxological, modernist reading of the films. Rather than discussing the crisis of identity, we also need to consider the types of agency in the films.

Agency is produced. Agency is distributed unequally across social space. And agency is differentiated according to the workings of the modern (purification). *Blade Runner* offers us an insight into the workings of a differentiating machine in the figure of Deckard (and it is of no small significance for an analysis of this social space that it is a man that is performing the differentiating). One of the central structuring differentiations in *Blade Runner* is that between humans and nonhumans. The figure of Deckard shows us how that difference is produced. Deckard's function as a blade runner (to which questions of his status as human or nonhuman are irrelevant) is as part of the differentiating machine—it is to proclaim the object human or nonhuman. In this task, he articulates discourses on human/nonhuman to those of labor, slavery, criminality and deviancy. Hegemony is carried out through this machinic function in that in his speaking Deckard helps to maintain a particular spatial distribution of subjects, in this case that of Earth versus off-world colonies. The linguistic differentiation of human/replicant then positions the subject within a complex milieu: Replicants are not allowed on Earth. For replicants, being on Earth is a criminal act. This differentiating machine has effects on two planes: It differentiates and separates *bodies*, and it differentiates and separates *discourses*. These two planes are two types of agency; the first we will call *technology*, the second, *language.*

A second differentiation also cuts across the Earth/off-world divide, and that is of the normative and the deviant. "Normal" humans are encouraged to emigrate, leaving those sick (i.e., J. F. Sebastian), poor or deviant on the polluted planet. Note that replicants, as slave labor, are not in the space of the marginal but that of the normative—their function supports and maintains the normative status quo; their work allows the off-world colonies to function. Identity is reified by a territorializing machine, determining possibilities for movement and attachment. The restriction of movement off world, the attachment of marginalized peoples to the decaying inner city, and that of the upper classes to the off-world, is the product of this territorializing machine that works through class, race, and "humanity."

Normative space is dominated by the technological in this film. On one level, this simply means that the off-world colonies are artificially maintained. But on a deeper level, it means that technology has expanded into almost every aspect of life. For example, we see Deckard commanding the Esper photographic scanner. His language here does have effects in that the device obeys his commands, but it is not the *discursive* as the earlier human/replicant differentiation was. Rather, his language is that of the device itself (granted, it is sufficiently sophisticated and flexible enough to not appear as if he's speaking a command language). It is not that his language is just similarly coded to that of the technology or is inseparable from it; simply, *it is the technological*. From the numbers etched on the snake scale to the control of devices, language is almost fully in the realm of technology in the film and works as part of the technological assemblage.

The level of the street, of the polyethnic margins, is different in that it is dominated by a shifting polyglot of diverse languages. But rather than resisting the normativity of off world social space, this anarchic space helps produce the artifacts and technologies that support the center. It is the cutting edge of deterritorialization for the normative formation. The entire social formation depicted in *Blade Runner* (offworld center, Earth margin) is a very modern one. The idea of the freedom of the streets or the revolution from the streets is a modern notion (Berman, 1988). Postmodern readings of the film (i.e., Bruno, 1990) emphasize only the ways by which the margins feed the revolutionary heart of the modern rather than working against it. In its depiction of social space, *Blade Runner* is obviously referring to the process of suburbanization and the ghettoization of the inner cities.

These processes are nothing new, and are central to Philip K. Dick's 1968 novel. In this way *Blade Runner* is merely carrying forward Dick's premise and sensibilities from the 1960s. That they still work in the 1980s shows that the process has not diminished. To say that the social space depicted in *Blade Runner* is coded, distributed, and territorialized by late industrial capital is hardly surprising (what *would* be surprising would be if it were not). What is significant are the ways the film differs from the novel, especially the suggestion that Deckard may be a replicant.[16] These differences open up the possibility of a Deleuzian episteme, an alternative to the modern. The many parallels between the replicants and Deckard show that both are subject to the same territorialization. What we need to recognize here is the territorialization, not just the differentiation, of identity, as well as the distribution of agency. Deckard's work as part of the differentiating machine separating normative space from that of the street (making sure that replicants don't cross over) is important. That Deckard abdicates that responsibility, and he himself refuses to be judged, is the significance of the film. By refusing to acknowledge the power of the binary (by refusing to be declared human or nonhuman, by falling in love with Rachael irrespective of her status), Deckard draws a line of flight. This is not a flight out of the city and into the Green World as in the original ending (out of technology and back to nature, or, more significantly, out of human space and back to a nonhuman one), because the city is not the problem. His destination is of no consequence at this point; to speculate on this is to establish a teleology that kills the line of flight. The significance is the line itself (a nonmodern line). What we have in the clash between the two endings of the film (Green World vs. Director's Cut) are two versions of the line of flight and two answers to the question of technology and identity. The first shows the conservatism of identity similar to *Robocop*—Rachael and Deckard flee to a different space—and the second shows a rejection of the question entirely.

Living Machines and a Shift in Social Space

The living machines in the films that I have been discussing are important not only for their representation of a human/ nonhuman split (and therefore insight into the construction of identity) but more significantly as a represented embodiment of human experience, of social space. These figures are literal sites of the stratification of technological and linguistic agency. Technology is condensed and embodied in the whirring mechanisms and the biomechanics of cyborgs, androids, and robots. Language is emphasized and reified in the juridical power of these figures (Blade Runner, Robocop).

For example, Robocop's technology is part and parcel of the technology present in his social space, from advanced robots to weapons technology and drug technologies. His behavior is completely programmed. He can literally plug into other technologies, which emphasizes the global interconnectivity of the technological assemblage.

Language in *Robocop* is juridical, like that of Deckard. Pronouncement of guilt or innocence is his function. Though he is just "a cop on the beat" and not an actual judge, his function is to identify nonnormative activities.

The struggle over the identity of Robocop reveals an anxiety about the move of juridical power to being primarily a technological function. Technology in this way is expanding its domain. We can see this shift as a shift in agency. Decisions are made and action taken more through a technological assemblage than through the discursive assemblage that has been the basis for much of Western democracy. This shift can also be seen in the proliferation of Intelligent Agents Expert Systems and Artificial Intelligences designed to take over some human decision-making activities. The programs decide for us, according to their algorithms. It is not so much a problem of humans stepping out of the command loop (or being pushed)[17]—that would be a problem of identity. Rather the problem is *how* agency is carried out—either more through more traditional discursive structures (discourse communities, Habermasian public spheres) or more through the technological assemblage (where agency is enacted differently). It is never completely one or the other; agency always involves both technology and language. What shifts is the balance between the two, altering the formation of human social space. To eliminate either technology or language entirely would lead us out of human space.

Throughout most of these films, the greatest effectivity, apart from instances of juridical power mentioned above, has been technological, and the technological is resoundingly mute. In fact, language and dialogue are usually minimal. For example, in *The Terminator*, Arnold Schwarzenegger has very few lines (17 or so), most of which merely mimic other (human) voices or parrot others' lines. He is the silent menacing technological Other, eventually put in its place by technological means. In *T2*, however, much more emphasis is placed on the development of the Terminator's language—colloquialisms, and so on—in the drive to articulate him within more traditional discursive structures (to make him seem more human). Indeed, the focus of the film is the bringing of the Terminator back under human control through an exhibition of human linguistic agency. For example, John Connor declares that the Terminator "[is] not a Terminator anymore." This declarative action can be read here as an attempt to shift back from a more technology-centered agency to a language-centered one. The dominance of Language over Technology is a modern articulation, and we can then read *T2* as attempting to reestablish the Terminator within the modern.

We can now trace two trajectories of the figure of the living machine through the 1980s. The dominant one articulates with the resurgence in political conservatism in that decade in its particular focus on nostalgia for particular cultural forms and ideals. The second trajectory was not taken up (as a blockbuster), though it has enjoyed cult status. That is the trajectory traced by *Blade Runner* (the *Blade Runner* of the Director's Cut; the first release ties the line of flight back to the popular conservatism), which maps technological discourse and human identity onto a noir frame. Noir, which subverts dominant Hollywood paradigms, here subverts the typical treatment of living machines on film by questioning the boundaries between human and nonhuman and eventually ignoring them altogether. But, as Gray, Mentor, and Figueroa-Sarriera (1995) write,

> "soon, perhaps, it will be impossible to tell where human ends and machines begin." There are, after all, more important distinctions to make, between just and unjust, between sustaining and destroying, between stable and erratic, between pleasure and pain, between knowledge and ignorance, between effective and ineffectual, between beauty and ugliness. (p. 13)

What is ultimately revealed by our analysis here is a tension in the distribution of agency, in the relative territorialization of a specific form of juridical agency. Such a form of agency ignores the concreteness of the assemblage, the material spaces of the technological. Anxieties over predominantly technological agency are mapped onto anxieties over a particular technological assemblage—that is, the nuclear defense network, big science, the bomb. By the very modern process of purification, these technologies are radically separated from "humans"; this catches us up in the problem of identity and eventually the Master/Slave dialectic, which is where we started.

Hassan Melehy (1995) argues that these cyborg films "may be said to constitute a set, or an arrangement, or an assemblage, in the ways that they address and interact with the [technological] conditions [in which the phantasms are produced]" (para. 13). Melehy wants to argue that the films are an assemblage because they all are thematically concerned with technologies of simulation (and the problem of the simulacrum), but are also themselves dependent on special effects, film, and video technologies that raise the question of simulation. They are "participating in as well as criticizing" the conditions in which they are produced and shown (para. 12).

I also see the films as an assemblage, but related in a different way: they all engage a plane of philosophy, of concepts.

> [Philosophical theory] is a practice of concepts, and it must be judged in the light of other practices with which it interferes. A theory of cinema is not "about" cinema, but about the concepts that cinema gives rise to and which are themselves related to other concepts corresponding to other practices, the practice of concepts in general having no privilege over others, anymore than one object has over others. (Deleuze, 1989, p. 280; cited in Melehy, 1995)

Following Deleuze and Guattari's (1994) notion of philosophy, the films can be seen as generating a set of concepts, which are a set of consistencies. In looking at films so far in the past two chapters, we have been mapping these consistencies across this set of films, especially looking at the cluster of concepts around the question of the human/nonhuman border. This cluster has obviously been a modern one.

These films do not "represent" contemporary social conditions in any direct or even indirect way. They are not metaphors for our postmodern condition or analogous to actual situations. That said, the assemblage of concepts generated by these films does not remain solely on the plane of cinema. That humans are becoming more cyborg everyday (Gray, 1995a) is not to be denied. Likewise, it is important to note—as Melehy did just above—that these films are literally technologically produced, often via computer technologies that are themselves encroaching on "human" territory (cf. Hayward & Wollen, 1993).

Thinking of an assemblage of concepts, indeed thinking outside of the modern, changes not only our filmic analysis but our entire methodology. Modernity has as much to do with methodology and epistemology as it has to do with the object of study. To be Deleuzian is to see the screen, the audience, the motion picture industry, as stratified. It is to stitch the filmic assemblage to the audience and to the representations playing themselves out on the screen. To be Deleuzian problematizes the very practice of "reading" a film (though this practice has been very useful in getting us this far, it must now be abandoned).

Notes

1. Langdon Winner (1993) discusses this perspective's "lack of and, indeed, apparent disdain for anything resembling an evaluative stance, or any particular moral or political principles, that might help people judge the possibilities that technologies present" (p. 443). He writes that interpretive

flexibility, the key concept in social constructivist thought, "soon becomes moral and political indifference" (p. 445).

2. For example, Latour (1995) maps out the competing voices in a scientific expedition to the Amazon rainforest.

3. The term *actor-network* is not Latour's. It is a label attributed to these theories by others such as Michel Callon. Latour himself denies any cohesive "perspective" and would avoid this term (personal communication, October 11, 1994). I use it as a term of convenience.

4. On this notion of time, see also Serres, 1995.

5. Latour (1993) actually reverses Kant. Rather than positing Subject and Object and then "multiplying the intermediaries to cancel out distance between the two poles little by little" (p. 79), as Kant does, Latour argues that the Subject and Object poles actually arise out of the work of intermediaries. But why retain this framework at all?

6. Cf. William Warner's (1992) essay on Rambo, the male physique, and violence.

   Hassan Melehy (1995) argues that the violence associated with the cyborg is related to its position as transgressive: "The cyborg is usually violent; it is so in its essence, as it is the product of machinery making ruthless incisions into flesh" (para. 14). But this reading ignores the gendered nature of the violence and also, to my mind, reestablishes the modernist human/machine split, despite arguing for the progressive aspects of cyborg becomings.

7. Kirsten Marthe Lentz (1993) offers a similar reading of *Eve of Destruction* in her excellent article, "The Popular Pleasures of Female Revenge (Or Rage Bursting in a Blaze of Gunfire)." She writes that what is perceived to be the problem with the Eve cyborg is a lack of moral (male) rectitude: "It is therefore a film about a not-so-latent male anxiety about feminism (that its logical conclusion will lead women to kill sexist men). It is also a film about the pleasures that women may experience through the production of that very anxiety" (p. 380).

   Programmed to Kill (1987) also presents a female killer android. The cyborg in *Cyborg* (1989) is female but, though central to the plot, she is peripheral to most of the focus and action of the film. She is not presented as a fighter but rather as a mother-figure: She carries the data that will save humankind from a plague.

8. Darth Vader was obviously a sexual being once, fathering Luke and Leia— but once a cyborg, the only relation he has with a female is when he tortures Leia in the first film (which represents a displaced sexuality).

9. A good deal of what sense one makes of the plot, and how one interprets the film, depends on which version one has seen. There are currently (at least) three versions in circulation (on videotape and film): the film as it was originally released in theaters in 1982, a slightly longer "uncut" version that

simply adds more shots of violence, and a recent "director's cut." This last version, the one I will rely on here, makes some aesthetic modifications (it omits Deckard's noirish voice-over narration), lengthens some scenes (adding a sequence where Deckard dreams of a unicorn), and omits the last shot of the original version (Deckard and Rachael's air car zooming over a lush, green hilly landscape toward mountains [which, as legend has it, was an outtake—sans air car—from *The Shining*]). I prefer the final version, not because it supposedly adheres more closely to Ridley Scott's original vision (an instance of the fallacy of authorial intention), but because the film (to my mind) works more cohesively without the Hollywoodized escape to the Green World of the original. See Kolb, 1991.

10. The more recent film *Nemesis* (1994) attempts to parallel many of these themes but seems to deliberately muddy the waters of identity further.

11. Philip K. Dick deals with this theme of memory and identity in his short story "We Can Remember It for You Wholesale," the basis for the Arnold Schwarzenegger film *Total Recall* (1990).

12. Doing, presumably, erotic things with a snake.

13. See Doreen Massey's (1994, pp. 228-230) comments on the film's treatment of gender.

14. It would seem that, in *Blade Runner's* world, reproduction—even intercourse —is solely in the domain of technology; that is, the reproduction of the human race via tech-substitutes—replicants—and the fact that only replicants seem to desire to reproduce. This would reverse McLuhan's claim that humans are the sexual organs of the machine.

15. Deckard's voice-over, cut from the latest version of the film, is also characteristic of this genre.

16. Whether Deckard is a replicant or not is still the subject of much debate, despite the fact that the director Ridley Scott has mentioned that this is what he intended.

17. It has been one of the military's goals to remove the human component from the decision-making loop, and hence its development and support of computer systems and artificial intelligence research. See de Landa, 1991.

3

Living in a
Deleuzian World

In building our minoritarian deterritorializing machine, let me note what I wish to hold on to from the previous theoretical discussions: the notion of artifacts as social actors, the construction of long networks, the deterritorialization of identity (the proliferation of hybrids), and the social construction of time. Technology is then a socially active hybrid that connects with others and bends space while being at the same time coded by abstract forces.

Let me take an example brought up briefly in Chapter 1, that of the railway timetable. To the modern episteme, the timetable is a temporal technology; it represents the rationalization of time (Carey, 1989). But from a spatial perspective, from the amodern episteme, the timetable is a technology for the distribution of trains in space (making sure no two trains occupy the same space, an event called a train crash). The timetable seems to concern the timing of trains only from the perspective of an individual (a modernist concept, based on the radically separate nature of the internal subject) standing at the platform (where trains seem to appear and disappear at set intervals). We get caught in the modern episteme if we think of this example in terms of individuals (people, trains, platforms) and points (a point moving through space is a temporal concept in this episteme because it occupies a *succession* of positions). Instead, we as theorists need to think in terms of lines, vectors, and assemblages. The train is an assemblage within which we may trace the delegation of numerous social actors: the engine driver, the fuel, the track, the wheel, the landscape. The assemblage is not a random configuration but is coded according to particular hegemonies such as the capitalist market, which influences which points will be connected and what the trains will carry. Approaching a train this way is not to play what Haraway has called a "God-trick" (1993c). We are not the all-seeing objective eye; our vision is situated. We will never grasp the assemblage as a whole, nor should that be the objective of our analysis. Indeed, the goal of attaining the full birds- (or God's-) eye view reveals a management perspective, a particular teleology, and a specific set of interests. Our analysis must resist totality and recognize that vision is partial. The above example of the train gives us an idea of what to look for in an analysis. If we merely want to catch a train, then we need look no further than the timetable.

But we are still faced with problems in the second—amodern—episteme. For example, it seems as if agency is something equally distributed among the social actors in the above example of the train; agency is the basic element from which the analysis proceeds and every element is granted agency. All agents seem equal in this version of the train: The conductor seems no more important than the steel rails. Agency cannot be so unquestioned. How do we account for differences (even similarities) in agency, in the *distribution* of agency? And how do we do this without recourse to abstract macro-actors such a social forces, which Latour rejects? This is why I now wish to add to this methodology an ontology, a politics, and a sense of the formation of the social itself.

Technology is intimately bound up with the social but, at the same time, is not reducible to it. What I hope to gain by theorizing technology through the thought of Gilles Deleuze, Félix Guattari, Michel de Certeau, Henri Lefebvre, and to a certain extent Pierre Bourdieu, is a theory that recognizes objective material constraints as well as socially constructed constraints on the form and function of any technology; I wish to argue that hegemony is carried through technological systems not only through the discourse deployed by and around that system or by symbolic capital articulated to it, but through affective investment and material asignifying practices, structures, and constraints; and I wish to argue that resistance is possible not through merely engaging with dominated places, structures, and technologies, but through an active reinvestment of affect and symbolic capital, *and* an active restructuring of practical, conceptual, and representational spaces.[1] Our minoritarian deterritorializing machine is always, already social, and its strides cross social space, span the technological, infiltrate our language, and impinge on our behaviors.

Technology and Language

One thing to remember when considering questions of the social is that the social is not unique to human beings. Michel Callon and Bruno Latour (1981) point out that baboons (and ants and others) are social (p. 281). The social relations between them (baboons), relations of dominance, are direct, face to face. Though dominance and communication are carried out between bare bodies, the relations are still subtle and flexible. But these relations must be constantly renewed, recognized, and repaired by the baboons themselves because these relations lack permanence.

Deleuze and Guattari (1987) argue that technology and language are the two fundamental characteristics of human beings (p. 60). The use of both tool and symbol, or rather the *particular relation between* the use of tools and the use of symbols, is what makes human beings distinctive from other forms of life; their use in a particular relation *constitutes* human beings. Deleuze and Guattari write that technology and language are *stratified*, simply two different strata abutting each other, like in a geological formation. Therefore, what marks human existence is both language and technology *in a particular relation.*

They argue in this way to avoid reinstating the Kantian split between noumena and phenomena, and the resultant modernist prioritization of not only time but language. In contrast to the modern episteme, Deleuze and Guattari (1994) write that

> Subject and object give a poor approximation of thought. Thinking is neither a line drawn between subject and object nor a revolving of one around the other. Rather, thinking takes place in the relationship of territory and the earth. Kant is less a prisoner of the categories of subject and object than he is believed to be, since his idea of the Copernican revolution puts thought into a direct relationship with the earth. (p. 85)

A Deleuzian episteme does not operate around a separation of subject and object, but of territorialization and deterritorialization. It is a materialism in that it is opposed to transcendence, to something *beyond* the Earth. For example, in this episteme we could see communication not as a process involving transcendental "meaning," but as an occurrence on a plane of sensation: Soundwaves, or light waves, are intercepted by the senses, and these cause chemical and electrical transformations in the brain. The soundwaves and the chemical transformations in the brain have a reso- nance, a homology, with each other; and in turn, these have resonances with the marks on a page, or a pattern of movement, or a physical struc- ture (in this way, communication is said to have concrete effects).

But in saying this, I do not mean to fetishize the physical; Deleuze and Guattari (1994) refuse to reduce anything to a single plane, but rather argue for multiplicities. For example, they write that the brain is the junction of three planes, art, science, and philosophy (p. 208). These planes are those of sensation, coordination (in a mathematical sense of a coordinate system), and consistency, all of which open onto chaos, and all of which act to subjectify the brain.[2] The subject, then, is the product of these planes. It is not created in opposition to the external, but actually is an enfolding of the external (in the way that a cell appears to have a definite cell wall but is actually open to its external milieu) (cf. Deleuze, 1993). What is important here is the breakdown of the Cartesian separa- tion of subject and object, and, by extrapolation, the denial of any Kantian prioritization of time over space. Philosophy, for Deleuze and Guattari (1994), is a plane of consistency in that its work is to produce concepts and a concept "refers back to chaos *rendered consistent*" [italics added] (p. 208). In their philosophical project, they seek to describe the reso- nances, the regularities, and the consistencies that they observe. In this way, theirs is a descriptive philosophy, not attempting to discover or establish a universal truth, but merely to report what they observe.

Returning to the question of human social space, according to Deleuze and Guattari both Language and Technology concern territori- alization (as opposed to a modernist transcendence). The first question is, then, how are Language and Technology differentiated and organized into a relation? Deleuze and Guattari call the human plane a stratum— used in its geological sense as strata in a rock formation, layers and belts with only a surface between them, a surface of stratification. The layers are mutually determining. Perceived as almost immobile by humans, geological strata are in constant flux (emerging, shifting, breaking off—

different surfaces come into contact with each other). Strata are constituted by an articulation, the bringing together of content and expression.
Technology and Language constitute the human (or anthropomorphic)
stratum, and therefore they belong to the same double articulation.
Deleuze and Guattari (1987) explain articulation like this:

> Articulation, which is constitutive of a stratum, is always a double
> articulation (double pincer). What is articulated is a *content and an*
> *expression.* Whereas form and substance are not really distinct, content
> and expression are. Hjelmslev's net is applicable to the strata: articula-
> tion of content and articulation of expression, with content and expres-
> sion each possessing its own form and substance. Between them, be-
> tween content and expression, there is neither a correspondence nor a
> cause-effect relation nor a signified-signifier relation: there is real dis-
> tinction, reciprocal presupposition, and only isomorphy. (pp. 502-503)

Content and expression are not necessarily connected, one is not necessarily determinate over the other, and the relation between them is never
guaranteed. As layers in a stratum, Technology and Language are content
and expression, therefore they are distinct and each has its own form and
substance. In that they press up against one another, they necessarily
presuppose one another and exhibit similar forms (they are isomorphic).

Technology is generally articulated into the position of content,
Language into that of expression. What this means is, as far as humans
are concerned, material reality is split into two, one part is considered
content, the other expression. A caveat here: I would argue that this
splitting of reality is not universal to all actors we call *Homo sapiens.*
Remember that both Technology and Language are material and that
their stratification (and their distinction) is *produced.* What Deleuze and
Guattari are describing here is a particularly *modern(ist)* stratification (in
that it is an accurate description of the dominant social space, which is a
modern one). The modernity of this stratification has two consequences
(at least). One is what Henri Lefebvre calls the decorporealization of
space into abstraction.[3] Derek Gregory (1994) writes that "Lefebvre . . .
concludes that *abstraction* is a leitmotif of capitalist modernity" (p. 382).
Such a decorporealization allows the modern to ignore the effectivity of
bodies, of the technological. But it ignores not only the body—a cultural
construct—but also the experience of embodiment (Hayles, 1993b). This
first consequence rests as well on the second consequence. I said above

that technology and language are *generally* articulated into content and expression respectively, but not *necessarily*. I wish to leave open what I see as the very real possibility that technology can act as the expression to a linguistic content, that it can embody the discursive. Indeed, without this allowance, this formation falls back on a modern materialism characterized by economic and technological determinism. *The description of the relation between technology and language thus becomes crucial to any analysis of the social.*

Both Technology and Language concern external manipulation and in this way are isomorphic. The distinction between the planes is that Language manipulates externals through "symbols that are comprehensible, transmittable, and modifiable from outside," and technology does so through external material manipulations or modifications in the external world (Deleuze & Guattari, 1987, p. 60). Technology, in this case, concerns the direct manipulation of real elements; and it consists solely of these aggregates of elements. Deleuze and Guattari write: "tools exist only in relation to the interminglings they make possible or that make them possible" (1987, p. 90). The relation between Technology and Language is that "the statements or expressions [Language] express *incorporeal* transformations that are 'attributed' as such (properties) to bodies or contents" (p. 504). These are transformations that are not brought about by physical manipulation (getting hit by a hammer or placed in a jail cell) but by other, more indirect means that lie within the complex assemblage that is Language—for instance, the above description of the resonances between particular soundwaves, chemical processes, and so on. For example, a transformation is achieved in one's physical ability to move freely once one is pronounced guilty by a judge. Incorporeal transformations are a contraction of a repeated—habitual—collection of corporeal events (Deleuze, 1994; Massumi, 1992). What is considered human is not based on an essence (the modern problematic of identity) but rather on this particular relation of technology and language. Deleuze and Guattari (1987) describe the human stratum like this:

> Form of content becomes "alloplastic" rather than "homoplastic"; in other words, it brings about modification in the external world. Form of expression becomes linguistic rather than genetic; in other words, it operates with symbols that are comprehensible, transmittable, and modifiable from outside. *What some call the properties of human beings— technology and language, tool and symbol, free hand and supple larynx,*

"gesture and speech"—are in fact properties of this new distribution [italics added]. (p. 60)

Technology, as content, is called a machinic assemblage, and language, as expression, is an assemblage of enunciation (2987, p. 504).

> The material or machinic aspect of an assemblage relates not to the production of goods but rather to a precise state of intermingling of bodies in a society, including all the attractions and repulsions, sympathies and antipathies, alterations, amalgamations, penetrations, and expansions that affect bodies of all kinds in their relations to one another. (p. 90)

Technology, then, is not reducible to production (as some vulgar Marxists would have it) but concerns the manipulation of relations between social actors ("actors" in Latour's sense, which includes both animate and inanimate objects). The assemblage of enunciation refers to regimes of signs, "to a machine of expression whose variables determine the usage of language elements" (Deleuze & Guattari, 1987, p. 90). Language concerns not simply *a Language* but the distribution of certain discourses in social space. For example, some segments of society have access to scientific discourse, others do not; some have access to "received" English, others do not. That distribution reflects primarily the social structuration of economic, cultural, and symbolic capital (Bourdieu, 1990).

We can understand Language to be similar to what Foucault calls the discursive (Deleuze & Guattari, 1987, p. 66). It is the ability to have effects at a distance, and not just meaning and signification. For example, a judge pronounces the accused "guilty" and the accused becomes a criminal and is then in a very different set of material relations, all without a direct material transformation; it is an incorporeal transformation that is then "attributed" to the body (1987, p. 504). But though it is "incorporeal," it is thoroughly material. It is, as I said above, a contraction, a habit. The question of a transcendental "meaning" is nonsensical in this episteme. Language can be understood as a system of signs. For example, in Roland Barthes's work, fashion is a system of signs but not necessarily a system of "meaning" (the particular signs do not have direct "meanings"). But, nonetheless, fashion is material with material effects.

I want to make a point here regarding terminology. Technology as an intermingling of bodies is somewhat broader than (and certainly different from) the commonsense notions of technology that we have been discussing previously. These would be modernist notions of technologies as artifacts or systems. The two definitions, Deleuzoguattarian[4] and commonsense, are of course related. When I write "technology," I mean both, though at times I might mean more of one than another. When this occurs, I will use "Technology" for the Deleuzoguattarian sense and "technology" for specific instances. What I hope to do by conceptualizing technology in both senses is to set up a productive tension between them, even when the senses are at odds.[5] A similar practice will be used for "Language" (having an effect at a distance) and "language" (words or specific languages like English). Through this productive tension, I hope to allow a transition from a modern to a Deleuzian episteme.

How, then, are Technology and Language actually brought into relation and how does that relation vary or change? The articulation of Technology and Language into the diagram (the relation of the stratum) is the function of a *machine*. A "machine" is what perceived regularities in the material are attributed to. For example, we notice that the material world is regularly and fairly consistently divided into what we are calling the Technological and the Linguistic. There is no general (or macro) force achieving this (no hand of God, no social forces, no universal nature), but it is still achieved in individual instances. What we then posit is an abstraction (that does not exist in the actual) that is machinelike in its function in that it produces regularities. We call this generally an *abstract machine*. It does not exist, but we can note (and feel) its very real effects (the machine exists solely in its effects). I feel this is what is missing from Latour's analysis: some attempt to come to grips with the regularities that are perceived within and between actor-networks. In an attempt to avoid imbuing an abstract, macro-actor with agency (an important move, nonetheless), Latour ends up ignoring some very real effects.

A machine, then, is an apparatus of functions that redirect flows (the flows that are redirected have already been redirected by other functions, etc.) (Deleuze & Guattari, 1983, p. 36). A function is a singularity, a point at which a flow suddenly becomes organized. Manuel de Landa (1991) defines abstract machines as "mechanism-independent, structure-building singularities" (p. 18) and uses the example of a flow of liquid or energy:

A liquid sitting still or moving at a slow speed is in a relatively disordered state: its component molecules move aimlessly, bumping into each other at random. But when a certain threshold of speed is reached, a flowing liquid undergoes a process of self-organization: its component molecules begin to move in concert to produce highly intricate patterns. (p. 15)

I disagree with de Landa that a machine *is* a singularity, but rather it is an *assemblage* of singularities, an apparatus that consists of singularities. The machine we are concerned with in the formation of the anthropomorphic stratum is a stratifying machine that redirects flows of Technology and Language into a relation of power that constitutes a strata. The stratifying machine produces abstract value, one term is valued over the other; the relation is a positive, productive one, not a negative one based on difference. Linguistic coding tends to take precedence over technical forms and potentials (pushed to an extreme, this becomes the view that technology is totally socially constructed). But the precedence of Language is simply the result of the current (modern) social formation, the current stratification. In that Language acts on Technology (Expression acts on Content), this has been read that expression overpowers content (e.g., Massumi, 1992, p. 152 n. 36). But Technology is far from passive. The focus on language masks technological forms, especially those that do not relate directly to meaning (those are not assigned value and are assumed, taken for granted). That focus also elides the fact that the distribution and action of the technological as intermingling of bodies is different from linguistic forms and distributions. In Deleuze and Guattari's example of Foucault's work on the prison, the content-form of the prison (with its relations to schools, hospitals, etc.) is in relation to the expression-form "delinquency" (with relations to law, social norms, etc.; Deleuze & Guattari, 1987, pp. 66-67). A focus on just "delinquency" misses the plethora of nondiscursive practices of the prison-form, and the ways these practices relate to those in the factory, barracks, and so on. We lose the chance to describe

a single abstract machine for the prison and the school and the barracks and the hospital and the factory . . . a whole organization articulating formations of power and regimes of signs, and operating on the molecular level (societies characterized by what Foucault calls disciplinary power). (p. 67)

But the strata are more complex than just the (double) articulation of Content and Expression. Both Content and Expression have their own substance and form. Substances concern territories, forms concern structures of codes (p. 53). Regarding technology, then, substance is an aggregate of molecular compounds; form is how they are arranged. Substance is an aggregate of silicon, gold, copper, and so on; form is the computer microchip. Forms are organized (coded) by a second machine, a differentiating machine that arranges the aggregate of substances or artifacts according to its function.[6] It grids and structures the strata, establishing relations of difference and negativity.

As a plane of content, technology can also act as a plane of expression to another plane of content (articulated by another machine), and so on (Deleuze & Guattari, 1987, p. 53). These strata are called *epistrata*. For example, the computer microchip is content to a certain expression (program speed, memory space), but at the same time the microchip is the expression of another content (silicon, military and industrial needs), and so on. In this way, any technology is necessarily part of a *system* of technologies, a system with both human and nonhuman actors. A technology services or supports other technologies and is similarly serviced or supported. The relations can be those of delegation but, put more broadly, are those of articulation, and are machinic. One could map the chain of these articulations not only through the technological strata but also through chemical and biological ones as well, where forms are determined by, for example, genetic codes or the possibilities for chemical articulation (what molecules bond in what way with what other molecules, etc.). Hence, in the example of the train that opened the chapter, discussions of the molecular compounds of steel abut the manufacturing industry, a colonial and imperialist network of exchange, and the organization of labor.

The point I wish to make here is that the forms a technology takes and the potentials it has are multiply determined by such diverse factors as molecular compounds, social needs, and other technologies. For example, the form (size, configuration) of a computer microchip depends on several things. On the one hand, the properties of the molecular substance involved (i.e., silicon) limit or allow electrical resistance to a certain extent (which makes silicon appropriate for this function), and it also allows miniaturization to a certain extent (it can be sliced into very small, very thin pieces that still retain desirable qualities—not too soft or brittle). On the other hand, manufacturing and other support technologies also constrain the form to a certain range of acceptable forms: The silicon can be made only so pure, sliced only so thin, and so on.

The form of a technology will have resonance with similar forms of other technologies and technological systems. There are no singular forms, only multiplicities (which collapses the distinction between Technology and technology). Deleuze and Guattari term this field of resonances, or aggregate of similar forms, *parastrata* because they are never of a stratum themselves but instead form their own strata. For example, the form of any particular microchip will have a resonance with other microchips as well as circuit boards, logic diagrams, and so forth. Also the form of a technology will be in accord with the forms of the technologies it supports (i.e., the computer into which the chip will be placed).

In another example, most automobiles share a certain standard set of features (e.g., four wheels), have roughly the same shape and formation. Even the most futuristic visions at Detroit auto shows still look fairly carlike. There is no car that is completely unique.[7] One could argue that this is because "car," as a linguistic and conceptual category, by definition refers to particular forms and features. However, even acceding this point, there is no form or feature of that car that is not isomorphic with other technologies. In short, *there is no technology that is 100% unique.*[8] At best, a technology can articulate an aggregate of disparate forms (cars that fly or are amphibious). Such technologies establish resonances between different strata and articulate them together. But their forms are still resonant with other forms (airplanes or boats) and the coding and territorialization (to an extent) of those forms.

The anthropomorphic stratum is in this way marked by a differentiating machine that forms and organizes substances. The differentiating machine arranges artifacts (and people) in space, in spatial arrangements, by *ex*tensive movement. People of different ethnicities are distributed across geographic space (nations, cities) in ways that are far from random. Production facilities likewise have an unequal distribution internationally. The same goes for consumer products—all distributed according to what Bourdieu (1990) calls objective structures, which are objective relations. Actors, he argues, are distributed according to the quantity and type (economic, symbolic, cultural) of capital they possess, and how that capital is distributed in their society.

There is yet another machine, a territorializing machine, which also works on the stratum.[9] The territorializing machine invests substances (formed matter) with intensity (such as affect), which sets the possibilities for mobility or attachment. Processes of territorialization intensify particular formations; the territorialization of any substance is always relative and always in process (Deleuze & Guattari, 1987, p. 54). Processes of deterritorialization de-intensify particular formations and so cut across the strata. These processes open the stratum onto other strata, onto mythic territories, or onto abstract machines (and here we begin to see the first signs of our minoritarian deterritorializing machine).

Up until now, I have been referring to both strata and assemblages interchangeably, but they are different. Though assemblages are produced in strata, they assume territorialization and are grounded where matter (the Earth) has been decoded and territorialized (Deleuze & Guattari, 1987, p. 503). Though developed on this stratum and anchored there by the relation of content to expression, these assemblages "permeate all of the strata, and overspill each of them" (p. 504). Thus, the technological ranges across the physiochemical and the organic strata as well.

> The territoriality of the assemblage originates in a certain decoding of milieus, and is just as necessarily extended by lines of deterritorialization. . . . Following these lines, the assemblage no longer presents an expression distinct from content, only unformed matters, destratified forces, and functions. (Deleuze & Guattari, 1987, p. 505)

The machinic assemblage (technology) is often not seen as distinct from the assemblage of enunciation (language) because of an *investment* in the articulation of a particular structure of coding on both the technological and linguistic strata. For example, the military territorializing machine invests economic value in a particular technology or aggregate of technologies that meet its needs (e.g., in Numerically Controlled machine tools to construct its weapons, and eventually computers of a certain type [cf. Noble, 1986]). At the same time, it invests conceptual value in structures of language having to do with efficiency, productivity, technicism, and so on, which likewise legitimate and further the military's needs.

Territoriality refers to intensities. Though the differentiating machine distributes particular consumer products to different locations (BMWs here, VWs there) and produces relations of value, it is the territorializing machine that marks that place with intensive investment (e.g., affective attachment to a Saturn automobile [accompanying an economic investment], to unions, or to rock 'n' roll). When I talk of a deterritorializing move, I mean the breaking of such an attachment. It is "the movement by which 'one' leaves the territory" (Deleuze & Guattari, 1987, p. 510). Each deterritorialization is always accompanied by a reterritorialization, a reattachment to different sites, actors, and so on; a reestablishing of the territory through other means (e.g., by capital rather than law); and a reintensification of a different form of that matter.

The territorializing machine also marks lines of movement, escape, flight. In this second move, the machine opens up places onto other places, connects social milieus (or shuts them off). "[Territorializing machines] produce daily life as the way in which people live the always limited freedom to stop in and move through the various realities within which their identifications, identities and investments are mutually constructed" (Grossberg, 1992, p. 106).

Social Space

The articulation of technology and language, along with adjacent para- and epistrata (the resonant aggregate of technological forms and multiple [double] articulations of molecular and support technologies), is always multiple. There is no unique form or substance, code or territory. Forms resonate with other forms, territories open up onto other territories. Assemblages are always aggregates, strata are always multiple, and human space (actualized through the articulation of technology and language) is always social space.

> Content [of the double articulation of technology and language] should be understood not simply as the hand and tools but as a technical social machine that preexists them and constitutes states of force or formations of power. Expression should be understood not simply as the face and language, or individual languages, but as a semiotic collective machine that preexists them and constitutes regimes of signs. A formation of power is much more than a tool; a regime of signs is much more than a language. (Deleuze & Guattari, 1987, p. 63)

What I am calling social space, then, includes the articulation of machinic assemblages (technology) and assemblages of enunciation (language). That (double) articulation defines specifically *human* social space. Social space in general *precedes* the articulation (baboons are social, too), but this is not meant in a temporal, historic sense. Social space is prior to human technosocial space but inseparable from it. For ease of terminology, when I refer to social space, I will mean *human* social space. Social space, then, consists of both that which subjects directly manipulate physically (Technology) and that which they manipulate incorporeally (Language).

As actor-network theory argues, technology is always a social actor. Both animate and inanimate actors bend space around them (Callon & Latour, 1981, p. 286). Social space is a network of relations between actors (animate, inanimate, or both) that are themselves aggregates and themselves the result of an abstract machine of stratification. These relations are structured through the workings of the technical social machine, the semiotic collective machine, and differentiating and territorializing machines—all interconnected, mutually determining. Positing the workings of abstract machines here corrects, but does not contradict, Latour's nonmodern world. Abstract machines are not somewhere outside his continuums, and do not reside in the empty poles of Object or Subject. They are not abstractions in the sense that Latour wants to label rationality, for example, as an abstraction. Deleuze and Guattari (1987) write: "There is no abstract machine or machines in the sense of a Platonic idea, transcendental, universal, eternal. Abstract machines operate within concrete assemblages" (p. 510). Abstract machines are abstract in that they "consist of *unformed matters and nonformal functions*" (p. 511). "They are always singular and immanent" (p. 510). They arise from (and consist of) the network itself. The introduction of abstract machines is a corrective to Latour and actor-network theorists in that it is through the machines that actors are comprised, distributed, valued, lived, and connected. Agency is not a given, but is distributed, differentiated, and territorialized. The resultant actor-network can then be examined and analyzed without falling back on the problematic notion of a rational network builder.[10]

Social space is not just discursive patterns or "imaged," "imagined," or symbolic communities (Anderson, 1983); but neither is it only physical aggregates of individuals and constructed space (i.e., people walking down a city street). Social space is the stratification of the two and can be described as a series of actor-networks. This articulation is never guaranteed and the relation between the two is never necessarily the same. Social space (by which I mean human social space) always consists of Technology and Language in particular configurations. But it also means something in addition to this configuration. It also means the

embodiment of that configuration; by *embodiment*, I follow N. Ka
Hayles (1993a) in defining it as contextualized experience: "embod
mediates between technology and discourse by creating new expe
tial frameworks that serve as boundary markers for the creatio ⌐ı
corresponding discursive systems" (p. 163).

Let us consider a technology (for the sake of argument: a manual
coffee grinder). Picture that technology. We can then map plane after
plane that intersect that technology, and that technology, as we initially
pictured it sitting on the kitchen table basking in the first rays of the early
morning sun, dissolves. Though it is undeniably important as a critical
analyst to understand and to be able to trace the relations of its German
manufacturer, the economics of unequal exchange between Third World
coffee growers and industrialized suppliers, and the aesthetics of taste
isomorphic with the shape and size of the screws of the burr grinder so
that the resulting coffee is of a particular consistency, and so on, it is also
undeniably important to retain hold of the grinder itself (especially if one
wants to make a cup of coffee). And we do this through the concept of
contraction or *habit*.

Our "lived present" is the contraction of the successive moments of
time;[11] it is a synthesis of these moments. Habit is contraction not in the
action of that contraction but in the contemplation of that action ("the
fusion of that repetition in the contemplating mind" [Deleuze, 1994,
p. 74]). Habit, then, "concerns not only the sensory-motor habits that we
have (psychologically) but also, before these, the primary habits that we
are; the thousands of passive syntheses of which we are organically
composed" (Deleuze, 1994, p. 74).

Habit is a contraction in that the steps of that action are taken for
granted after a while. For example, after several uses one might not be
aware of all the steps and movements necessary to grind one's coffee.
Or, in another example, if one smokes one might discover a lit cigarette
in one's hand without being especially conscious of having lit it—the
actions of removing the cigarette case, removing a cigarette, placing it
just so, fumbling for the lighter, igniting the flame, lighting the cigarette,
and inhaling just so become contracted. But habit is not just the aggregate
of these actions but the fusion of them in the mind: The thought produces
the chain of actions but fuses them.

Technologies—particular artifacts or services—are habits, are con-
tractions of action, substance, and thought, a condensation of technology
and language. We grasp technologies as *molarities*. We take a hammer to

be molar, to be one thing, a whole. But it is actually contracted (compressed) molecular structures that are *differentiated.* The wood of the handle and the metal of the head have *grains;* they are stratified. These differentiations can often be ignored by the molarity (one can use the hammer for years and never notice the grain). But *molecularity* always involves some degree of *entropy.* Molecularity—entropic—reasserts itself when a threshold is reached and the differentiation of the handle becomes dominant and the handle breaks, not surprisingly, along the grain. The head itself breaks according to the differentiations in the make up of the metal—along the molecular grain or lattice.

In a similar way, though social space is stratified, we often grasp only its molarity. Social space—the habitual molar contraction or grasping of space—is produced though habit. Paul Connerton, in his book *How Societies Remember* (1989), argues that habits are both technical abilities that are at our disposal and affective dispositions. Habits are particular practices that reflect a history of repetition or repeated action. Habits are not just signs, Connerton argues, but bodily practices. Knowledge (of practices, in other words, habits) is, therefore, bodily as well as cognitive. Our social space is made up partly through habitual action, and is a bodily space as well as a cognitive one. Connerton then opens a way of understanding the sense of the technological agency by not falling back into notions of a rational individual (agency as conscious action) as the explanation for the social or for action or agency. Connerton writes: "we remember . . . through knowledge bred of familiarity in our lived space" (p. 95).

Communication and information technologies are especially important sites for analysis in that they appear to embody both technology (the device) and language (the content broadcast or transmitted). This makes them often difficult to analyze in these terms—though crucially important—because they seem to slip to one side or the other like a watermelon seed. On the one hand are those who look solely at the technology and often approach from a technological determinist perspective. For example, Marshall McLuhan argues that it is the medium and not the message that has effects. In many ways, for McLuhan the message (content) is irrelevant. Another similar approach is the technicist, or engineering, view that sees the problems of communication as technical problems (Shannon and Weaver [1949] are germinal here), a view that has had significant consequences on the study of communication. We will discuss the consequences of the technicist view in the next few chapters.

On the other hand, communication technology tends to disappear. After a while, we don't see the television set anymore, just the programs (O'Sullivan, 1991). And, therefore, the medium itself is absent (or receives only a cursory glance) in much communication research.

How do we grasp hold of this problem and not lose either dimension? How do we understand communication as a contraction of technology and language? Let us take the example of a community in cyberspace. My problems with the utopics of cybercommunities (e.g., Rheingold, 1993) has to do with their ignoring the constraints that the technology itself brings to those interactions. I am not arguing against cybercommunities (that they exist or are useful); that would be silly. Indeed, the new Internet technologies have allowed disparate, geographically dispersed groups to form for political (networks that quickly send information on human rights abuses around the world), artistic (Internet groups have influenced the direction of TV shows and rock bands), emotional (support networks for people whose spouses or parents have Alzheimer's), and personal reasons (the connection of families, friends, and neighborhoods), all of which are wonderful. But in any cybercommunity, there are always members who are silent and go unnoticed—the computers, hardware, software, and wiring technologies themselves contribute to the shape, character, and inclusiveness of the group. Minimally, these constraints are economic (affording a computer, phone bill, and connection fee to a local Internet provider), spatial (literally having a room to put the computer in, or space in that room), and leisure-related (one must have the *time* to contribute).[12] These constraints are not absolute and can be overcome (e.g., with public terminals). And for many groups, these concerns are irrelevant. But to make that decision—that these concerns *are* irrelevant for *that* group—the questions must at least be posed; often, they are left out of consideration entirely because of the transparency of the medium. As social space, the Internet—or, rather, its communities—is produced through habit, both the linguistic habits of repetitive characteristic phrasing or shorthand (BTW, LOL, FYI) and technological habits of typing, of the hardware and software "preferences" of configuration, of bodily posture, and so forth. To grasp this space is to address both of these dimensions: the articulation of the machinic assemblage to an assemblage of enunciation, the machines we use and how we talk about them or think about them. To do this would be to explore the *embodiment*, in Hayles's phrase, of cyberspace. The next chapter will attempt to take such an analysis further.

Habits—and technologies—are not innocent, however. As Andrew Feenberg has argued, the condensation of technology and language "brings the construction and interpretation of technical systems into conformity with the requirements of a system of domination" (Feenberg, 1991, p. 79). He refers to this social coding of technology (the parastrata, a function of form) as the "technical code" of capitalism. "Capitalist hegemony, on this account, is an effect of its code" (p. 79). The code coordinates the social and technological along the lines of the dominant hegemony.

Feenberg cautions that "it is important to keep in mind that the parts of an invention . . . have a technical coherence of their own that in no way depends on politics or class relations" (p. 82). The whole (Feenberg's example is the assembly line, but could just as well be a computer network or broadcast television system) is made up of parts that have a logic all their own and are not dependent on the whole. Where the large-scale sociotechnical network may reflect the interests of the domi-nant group, economic formation (capitalism), or philosophical bias (rationality), the elements of which it is composed do not necessarily re-flect that same domination to the same extent. "The lower we descend toward the foundations of rational institutions, the more ambiguous are the elements from which they are constructed, and the more these are compatible with a variety of different hegemonic orders. This is the source of the ambivalence of technology" (p. 83). In Deleuzian terms, we follow the stratifications in the direction of increasing deterritoriali-zation. This ambivalence Feenberg calls the "margin of maneuver." Our mappings of social space become political, then, in that they seek a less dominated space in which to stand, when we advocate a molecular politics.

Resistance, Flexibility, Margins of Maneuver

Social space preexists and presupposes the actor (we live in social spaces but not those of our own making). Individuals experience space "as an obstacle" that is difficult to transform. "This pre-existence of space conditions the subject's presence, action and discourse, his [sic] compe-tence and performance; yet the subject's presence, action and discourse, at the same time as they presuppose this space, also negate it" (Lefebvre, 1991, p. 57).

In what way does the individual negate space? What is the margin of maneuver allowed for resistance? Michel de Certeau (1984), theorizing resistance, contrasts "style" with "use" (p. 100). *Style* refers to the singular processing of symbols or practice. *Use* is normative and refers to socially structured codes. One's "style of use," therefore, is the way one processes normative social codes in a way that is singular and irrepressible. In this way, style can easily be overestimated as a theory of resistance. It seems that when dealing with language, with symbolic or representational space, more room for maneuver or variance is assumed or theorized. However, when dealing with technology itself, most people seem to "utilize" artifacts according to normative rules rather than "use" them with any potential for resistance (a terminological distinction by Langdon Winner [1977, p. 229]). "Use," in this case, refers to "the whole line or sequence of thought, action, and fulfillment" (Winner, 1977, p. 228). It involves mapping the multiple articulations and codings, strata, parastrata, epistrata, and territorializations of technology. This division is apparent in the anxieties over whether individuals using the new Information Superhighway will become mere consumers (utilizers) or will be more productive, have more individual agency (users).

We cannot say, however, that the potentials of technology are actualized through use or utilization. They are always already actualized by virtue of the workings of the machines of power. In other words, the normative structure and function of the new technological assemblage will be set long before individual users figure out their degree of autonomy, before they even enter the picture. But the norms of the system are not just technologically driven but are social and economic as well. The specific *ways* in which these potentials are actualized depends on the use/utilization distinction, which in effect describes in part the state of that particular articulation. *Utilization* describes a space overpowered by normative codes, while *use* describes the mapping of new vectors across strata. Resistance, then, depends on vectors, lines of intensity, drawn across both language and technology and from them to other strata; opening technologies onto other technologies, other languages, other forms, and so forth. Resistance solely through language can be effective, but it ignores the level of practice and artifacts and their role in the creation of social space.

To grasp these levels together is to acquire a habit; habitual social space is the *habitus*.

Constructing the notion of habitus as a system of acquired dispositions functioning on the practical level as categories of perception and assessment or as classificatory principles as well as being the organizing principles of action meant constituting the social agent in his [sic] true role as the practical operator of the construction of objects. (Bourdieu, 1990, p. 13)

The social agent acts technologically, linguistically, and conceptually, contracting these strata or planes. There is no separation between agent and social space. Therefore, the hegemonic codings of technology and language, the character of social space, are internal as well as external. Resistance is not the struggle of a pure interior against a domineering external space (a modernist reading); it is not simply the rebuilding or rejection of tools and machinery; it is not simply the recoding of language; it is not simply thinking radical thoughts. Resistance must take into account our own habits. Habits are not simply repeated action, not simply a repetition or the endless recurrence of the status quo because each iteration, each action, is unique: "Habit *draws* something new from repetition—namely difference" (Deleuze, 1994, p. 73). Within habit lies repetition and difference. The *difference* of habit (a *positive* difference) is our foothold; it is our margin of maneuver.

What margin of maneuver is open depends partly on the configuration of social space, the aggregates, assemblages, and actors that are enlisted and distributed in particular formation. That configuration of social space is embodied in our habits, and our margin of maneuver begins in individual practice. But this is not to say that social space is just the space of practices. Henri Lefebvre outlines three concepts that are useful in understanding our relations to the social spaces we inhabit. What is important to remember is that social space is the grasping of all three at once.

Henri Lefebvre (1991) argues that there are three interrelated concepts that need to be addressed to approach modern social space: *spatial practice, representations of space,* and *representational space* (or space as it is perceived, conceived, and lived). We can think of these terms as an alternative stratification of social space. Taking these concepts in turn, spatial practice

embraces production and reproduction, and the particular locations and spatial sets characteristic of each social formation. Spatial practice ensures continuity and some degree of cohesion. In terms of social space, this cohesion implies a guaranteed level of *competence* and a specific level of *performance*.[13] . . . A spatial practice must have a certain cohesiveness, but this does not imply that it is coherent (in the sense of intellectually worked out or logically conceived). (Lefebvre, 1991, pp. 33, 38)

Spatial practice is the most technological of the three aspects of social space, but not all spatial practices are technological. They combine tools and language to ensure the continued existence of the social order. Spatial practices can give rise to a need for a new technology or the reformation of an old technology. Such practices also stabilize and reify particular networks. In terms of the social space discussed here, these are the practices that engage us with cyberspace—talking on the phone, running a computer, interacting with an ATM.

Representations of space are abstract, conceptualized space. "This is the dominant space in any society (or mode of production)" (Lefebvre, 1991, p. 39). In the modern industrialized world, this space is usually scientific and technocratic. Therefore, if the mode of production is rational, technophilic, and efficiency oriented, then conceptual space will reflect that and the world will be conceived of as mechanical (e.g., early systems theory). For example, we would be told that our minds work like computers rather than vice versa. Such a suggestion betrays a particular stratification (content: computer; expression: brain) and thus reveals certain investments in technicist, rationalist forms of thought and language. Representations of space—or, space as it is conceived—is the plane of concepts. It is this plane that allows us in this book to trace a new technological neutrality across television shows, films, policy discourses, and museum exhibits. The shift in the dominant notions of social space occurs on this plane and repercusses both practiced space and representational spaces.

Representational space is:

space as directly *lived* through its associated images and symbols, and hence the space of inhabitants and "users." . . . This is the dominated— and hence passively experienced—space that the imagination seeks to change and appropriate. It overlays physical space, making symbolic use of its objects. Thus representational spaces may be said, though again with certain exceptions, to tend toward more or less coherent systems of nonverbal symbols and signs. (Lefebvre, 1991, p. 39)

Representational space is most often related to Language, to the incorporeal (i.e., symbolic systems). But it can never be divorced from the Technological. Social constructivists attempt to collapse all of social space to this dimension alone. It is the symbolic plane of social space.

Social space, as the aggregate of space as perceived, conceived, and lived, actualizes only through the articulation of technology and language. We cannot make any easy distinctions such as: technology = practice; or conceptual and lived space = language. These relations are not equivalencies. Not all practices are technological, and not all lived space involves either language or symbols, and so on. The stratification of technology and language cuts across any formation of social space.

One negotiates social space like one approaches a walk through a city (de Certeau, 1984). Keeping in mind, however, Lefebvre's three concepts of social space, we have, first, the *practice* of walking or traversing (by taxi or other transportation) the city. Second, in mind is an abstract map, a conceptualization of the space according to a particular "bird's-eye view" that reveals only the streets, or only the subway system, only the trendy downtown shopping district, or only the main thoroughfares to affluent suburbs. Third, one not only approaches the city with traces of representations of that space (old movies, the news, etc.);[14] but also one traverses the city through the symbols and representations that one is inundated with at the street level. The city preexists the walk. The walk actualizes possibilities and obstacles, some more immobile than others. In the modern city, one may traverse the space in stylistically resistant ways, but there is little one can do to stop or reroute traffic (in other words to reconfigure the space) short of revolution. For example, the revolutionary blockades in pre-Haussmann Paris had to physically reconfigure the city's streets to create a place of power from which to act.

At this point, de Certeau's specific metaphor of social space as a city loses its usefulness. It becomes problematic in that *the city* as a conceptual space is a modernist space, a Western industrialized space, a very specifically political and economic space. Representing social space as a city falls back into Western industrial representational (and conceptual) space since any conceptualization of space is necessarily political. Likewise, the notion that resistant practices occur on the streets or emerge from the streets (i.e., declarations that "we must take back the streets") falls back into the modernist problematic as well. This observation is especially prescient when discussing not only global matters but also distinctly non-Western ones. Describing the social space of a nonindustrialized country as a city all but establishes a telos of modernization and Westernization.

The particular arrangement of relations between these three concepts in any particular social space I wish to call *culture*. Culture is not a symbolic structure (i.e., a text) but exists in that structure's links with social spatial practices and the way that symbolic structure is articulated with the dominant conceptual scheme (e.g., Is it resistant to or resonant with that scheme? And are either or both the practiced and symbolic resistant? etc.). Culture, then, arises in part from our habits and out of social space. As Raymond Williams (1989) has written, culture is ordinary, meaning that it is both a whole way of life (our embodied habits, the living of our spaces) and a tradition (the heavier, durable, overdetermined structures of social space).

Modern social space, Lefebvre (1991) argues, is what he calls Abstract space, which

> functions "objectally," as a set of things/signs and their formal relationships. . . . Formal and quantitative, it erases distinctions, as much those which derive from nature and (historical) time as those which originate in the body (age, sex, ethnicity). . . . Abstract space relates negatively to that which perceives and underpins it—namely, the historical and religio-political spheres. . . . It functions *positively* vis-à-vis its own implications: technology, applied sciences, and knowledge bound to power. (pp. 49-50)

This space appears to be similar to that bound by rationality (Marcuse) or technique (Ellul). It is a one-dimensional space that reifies everything, turning the world into standing reserves. But though this may be the dominant character of modern space (being, arguably, the dominant conceptualization of space as we have seen in Ellul, Heidegger, Marcuse, and others, if I may lump all of them together momentarily), we have to open ourselves to the possibilities of unfamiliar representational spaces,[15] as well as alternatives to abstract space that do not fall back into the nostalgia of Nature (as Lefebvre's [1991, p. 48] alternative, absolute space, tends to do). Abstract space, Lefebvre argues, is not final after all, but rather contains within it the seeds of a new, differential space.

Cyberspace—the social space of the new technological assemblage, "that place you are in when you are talking on the telephone" (John Perry

Barlow, quoted in Elmer-DeWitt, 1995, p. 8), on the Internet, in front of the TV, at the ATM; our electronic habitus—is a molarity. Any molarity is always the grasping of some elements over others: "A structure is defined by what escapes it" (Massumi, 1992). The question now is, what is the grain of cyberspace, of the new assemblage—realizing that there is no one cyberspace? What gets folded, pressed, and grasped together? What is stratified? What is the culture of this new social space?

Some answers could be more or less direct, and have been more or less covered over the last few chapters: Anxieties about agency that are masked by arguments about access; anxieties about identity, about the reliance of identity on the technological (credit histories, driver's license and Social Security numbers, etc.), about the absolute power of the machine to destroy that data, wiping us clean, and about the assertion of a particular identity across the space (corporate culture, the white male hacker, the aggression of the flame war, etc.).

But others are less so.

Notes

1. I need to note here that what I argue below follows from Deleuze and Guattari, but is influenced by other appropriations of their work (most prominently Larry Grossberg and Meaghan Morris) and is the result of my own reading not only of Deleuze and Guattari but of Grossberg and Morris as well. Whatever flaws exist in my reading are not their responsibility, but whatever insights there may be are certainly due to their help.

2. "[It] seems difficult to treat philosophy, art, and even science as mental objects," simple assemblages of neurons in the objectified brain, since the derisory model of recognition confines these latter within the *doxa*. If the mental objects of philosophy, art, and science (that is to say, vital ideas) have a place, it will be in the deepest of the synaptic fissures, in the hiatuses, intervals, and meantimes of a nonobjectifiable brain, in a place where to go in search of them will be to create." (Deleuze & Guattari, 1994, p. 209)

3. On the decorporealization of space see Lefebvre, 1991, 1981, and Gregory, 1994.

4. "Deleuzoguattarian" is a term from Bogue, 1989.

5. On the contradictions of Deleuze's concepts, see Colombat, 1991.

6. The notion of a differentiating *machine* follows Larry Grossberg's (1992) reading of Deleuze and Guattari.

7. In a similar vein, Michel Serres (1995) writes that there are no cars that are purely "contemporary":

> What things are contemporary? Consider a late-model car. It is a disparate aggregate of scientific and technical solutions dating from different periods. One can date it component by component: this part was invented at the turn of the century, another ten years ago, and Carnot's Cycle is almost two hundred years old. Not to mention that the wheel dates back to neolithic times. The ensemble is contemporary only by assemblage, by its design, its finish, sometimes only by the slickness of the advertising surrounding it. (p. 45)

Serres extends *parastrata* to time as well, that there are formal resonances irrespective of history: "It means that Lucretius, *in his own time*, really was already thinking in terms of flux, turbulence, and chaos, and second, that *through this, he is part of our era*, which is rethinking similar problems" (p. 47, emphasis in original). Serres's method of dealing with time is profoundly amodern in that it denies the radical historical breaks (beyond which everything is different) that are central to the modern (see Serres, 1995, esp. p. 48).

8. But at the same time, each technological artifact—each car—*is* unique; my 1987 champagne-brown Honda Civic DX is different from your 1987 champagne-brown Honda Civic DX, though they resonate like crazy on many levels.

9. Again, this follows Grossberg, 1992.

10. On network builders, cf., e.g., Law, 1987.

11. "Properly speaking, [contraction] forms a synthesis of time. A succession of instants does not constitute time any more than it causes it to disappear; it indicates only its constantly aborted moment of birth. Time is constituted only in the originary synthesis that operates on the repetition of instants. This synthesis contracts the successive independent instants into one another, thereby constituting the lived, or living, present. It is in this present that time is deployed. To it belong both the past and the future: the past in so far as the preceding instants are retained in the contraction; the future because its expectation is anticipated in this same contraction. The past and the future do not designate instants distinct from a supposed present instant, but rather the dimensions of the present itself in so far as it is a contraction of instants" (Deleuze, 1994, pp. 70-71).

12. The list could go on: use of a roman character set, use of vision, hands, and other functions, and so on.

13. Lefebvre (1991) takes these terms from Chomsky but does not imply that these are to be taken *linguistically* (p. 33).

14. In this way, many people who have not visited Dallas before may get a strange sense of familiarity when approaching the grassy knoll and book depository downtown, even if they do not realize that is where they are going.

15. Cf. Eric Michaels, 1994, work on Aboriginal media.

Part Two

Assemblage

Great changes have taken place in the U.S. social formation since the late 1980s, and these changes continue
apace. The modern technologies of nuclear systems and industrial technologies are being replaced by the postmodern technologies of communication and information. It seems as if individual human agency is
expanding through these new technological networks; we are becoming
a telecommunity, expanding our reach through "telepresence" and carrying out our work through Intelligent Agents. So within the modernist
episteme, the modern formation has been transformed into or usurped
by a postmodernist one. The modern/postmodern tension is one that
runs throughout this period.

I find the idea of modern/postmodern problematic in that it ignores
the new distribution of heavy industry overseas, as well as the increasingly dangerous and unstable distribution of the weapons and weapons-
grade plutonium of the cold war. But in the terms that I am arguing here
in this book, it ignores the continuance of earlier formations of power as
well as the actual distribution of agency in contemporary social space.

What has happened to the modern? How did we suddenly embrace a new technological assemblage, given our great fear of earlier such networks? How did we go from Hiroshima to the Internet, from Bomb to Boom? To try and start answering this, I want to go back to 1989 and take a close look at a television program that combines the modern technology of nuclear destruction with the postmodern technology of communication and information, to see what actually happens when *AT&T Presents: Day One.*

4

Making Television, Making History: AT&T Builds the Bomb

Building the Bomb

The bomb has dominated and permeated our views of the world and the possibilities for human action within it for the past 50 years. We do not need to clarify, modify, or specify the word, because we know to what it refers. We also know that it is not just *a* bomb, but hundreds of thousands, and they are all interconnected in ever more complex networks and grids. "The bomb" is also a cultural production, albeit a very dangerous one, realized by and with effects in discourse (Taylor, 1992, p. 429). The bomb has become the focal point for discourses on technology, modernity, and politics.

The purpose of this chapter is to begin to describe and explore a perceived shift in the modernist episteme of technology in U.S. social space in the 1980s and 90s. This is a shift in popular representations of

NOTE: Material excerpted from *AT&T Presents: Day One* by David Rintels is used by permission.

technology from the dominance of nuclear defense technologies in the 1950s through the 1970s[1] to communication and information technologies in the 1980s and 1990s. The question I am asking is, how did we end up so happily embracing the new technology of cyberspace given that just a few years before our relations with those same systems were full of suspicion and fear?

Beyond simply a reading of a televisual text, I wish to examine the reflexivity and intertextuality of what is arguably the second most influential modern technology, television. In particular, I focus on the reflexivity of the medium regarding the "nature" of technology and its relation to the social. I say "reflexivity" because television is itself a technology that tends to disappear as a technology, to be replaced by the representations it transmits and the context of its reception.[2] As television is a dominant site for the production of social space, the way it represents technology, and itself *as* technology, is a powerful social influence. We would do well to see how television sees itself.

The object of analysis for this chapter is a 1989 televisual production, *AT&T Presents: Day One*, an Emmy Award–winning CBS Special Presentation[3] concerning the Manhattan Project, the events leading up to the detonation of the first nuclear bomb over a populated target. Why this program? First, it directly concerns what are arguably the three most pervasive and influential technologies of the second half of the 20th century: the bomb, television, and information and communication technologies (the computer and telephone—which is where AT&T fits in).[4] Secondly, it concerns the construction of a historical narrative, and history, as I will argue, is a central site for the production and maintenance of modern social space. It is partly through historical representations that societies establish their identity and the problematic through which they view their current conditions. It is through history, then, that we become modern or postmodern or something else.

This chapter consists of five sections. The first discusses what I am calling *bomb discourse,* or the historical representations of the Manhattan Project. The second sets out the specific narrative provided by *Day One* (a narrative being considered a specific formation of events, and as a form it has resonance with other forms). The third section explains how that narrative is articulated to popular history and how it constructs itself as an accurate and truthful representation. This analysis is important to establish the significance of this broadcast as an object of study apart from its critical and audience reception.[5] These previous points highlight how the narrative of *Day One* is structured and the problematics it addresses. In the fourth section, I address the representation of technology in *Day One* by juxtaposing the Manhattan Project narrative with the AT&T advertisements that frame it. It is in the tension between the commercials and the narrative that I find the significance of the program. Finally, the chapter ends with a consideration of the rebroadcast of *Day One* in 1993 in terms of a shift in global political circumstance.

Bomb Discourse

First, we must see *Day One* as an example of what I would call "bomb discourse," which has its own history of representations. It is beyond the scope and purpose of the chapter, however, to discuss the entire history of the bomb on film[6] (much less in print), so I will focus on one particular narrative: the making of the bomb. For ease of reference, I will refer to the collective of these events as the Manhattan Project, collapsing for the purpose of analysis the historical structures and networks that made up the Manhattan Project and the narrative reconstructions of these events. As Bryan Taylor (1993a) argues, narratives of the bomb's construction indicate a search for the origin of the nuclear crisis and responsibility for the bomb itself. Such a search for origins may allow one to distance oneself from any responsibility and displace that responsibility onto a constructed past.

Most discourses around the Manhattan Project draw on or respond to an official narrative of events. This narrative goes something like this:[7] The decision to drop the Hiroshima bomb was carried out after lengthy deliberations and careful examination of alternatives, and there was never any consideration not to use the bomb once it was ready. The decision finally rested on the fact that a million American casualties would be avoided if an invasion of Japan was averted; without the bomb, an invasion was inevitable. Hiroshima was a center of war-related production, practically a military base. The narrative usually omits the questions of shifting surrender terms,[8] or the argument that the bomb might have been used more as a show of might to contain the USSR rather than Japan, or the inevitability of an invasion. Indeed, the number of one million casualties far exceeded wartime military estimates; it quickly was interpreted as one million *lives* saved, and that number has continued to grow in popular debates (Lifton & Mitchell, 1995).

The first film of this genre was Norman Taureg's 1947 film *The Beginning or the End*, which traced the development of the bomb and the community at Los Alamos (much like *Day One*). The film was a controversial mix of Hollywood sensibility and White House and military input that followed the official narrative (Lifton & Mitchell, 1995).[9] After that, there is nothing for decades. The 1950s saw science fiction monster movies that were implicitly about the bomb, radioactivity, or the cold war, but did not explicitly represent the Manhattan Project narrative itself. The exception is *Above and Beyond* (1952), which describes the Manhattan Project and Hiroshima through the eyes of Col. Tibbets, pilot of the *Enola Gay*, the plane that dropped the first atomic bomb on Japan. This period of relative silence is understandable given the reactionary scares of the 1950s when there was little tolerance for anything that brought into question the U.S. policy and position on the bomb. Also, Lifton and Mitchell (1995) effectively argue that not only did the U.S. government withhold accurate information about both the decision process to drop the bomb and the effects of the bomb (film footage of Hiroshima was classified until the late 1960s and color film of the destruction surfaced only in the late 1970s), but also that the leaders and the public were in deep denial of their role or responsibility in that attack.[10] Likewise, the 60s bomb films (e.g., *Dr. Strangelove, Fail Safe*) neglected this specific narrative, dealing with the bomb as a pervasive *given* in modern life but not questioning its construction per se.

In 1980 the Academy Award–nominated documentary "The Day After Trinity: J. Robert Oppenheimer and the Atomic Bomb" was released. That same year, there appeared on television a special presentation, *Edward Teller: An Early Time*, which covered some of the same ground. Also in 1980 was the TV movie, *Enola Gay: The Men, the Mission, the Atomic Bomb*. In 1982, another teleplay, *American Playhouse Presents: Oppenheimer* was shown. In 1984, Peter Wyden published his book, *Day One: Before Hiroshima and After*,[11] and 2 years later, Richard Rhodes's Pulitzer Prize–winning *The Making of the Atomic Bomb* was published. In 1985, the rock group Rush produced a song called "Manhattan Project" that sketches out the main events.[12] Martin Cruz Smith published a popular novel in 1986, *Stallion Gate*, based on the Los Alamos Project. And then in 1989, both the television special *Day One* was broadcast and the film *Fat Man and Little Boy* was released.[13]

Stephen Hunter[14] (1989), film critic for *The Baltimore Sun*, in his extended review of *Fat Man and Little Boy*, stated that

> what's interesting about the movie beyond its strictly artistic failings and triumphs is that it represents a new phase in our dealings with the bomb on the screen, what might be called the historical phase, in which

we are struggling to understand where it all began and how we got where we are today. (p. B13)

Accepting Hunter's thesis, the "historical phase" can be seen as the proliferation of histories of the bomb, listed above, since 1980. Hunter attributes this interest to the thawing of the cold war and the critique of Mutually Assured Destruction (MAD) as a fundamental (almost implicit) policy. "Perhaps," he says, "it is the hope of filmmakers that by examining the beginnings of MADness, they can be a part of the process of its disassembly" (p. B15).

However, Hunter's argument relies on an intentional fallacy: It attributes a text's effects to the intentions (implicit or explicit) of its author(s). In an attempt to avoid this sort of argument, we need to look for other reasons for the proliferation of histories of the bomb. Paul Ricoeur (1980) argues that the possibility of establishing a comprehensive narrative presupposes an ending to that narrative (one of the characteristics of narrative is a sense of closure) (p. 179). It is only with the sense of an ending to a historical phase that a narrative can be constructed. Perhaps the possibility for some sort of historical closure made the construction of coherent narratives about the bomb possible. But significant political factors influence that possibility as well: For example, early closure of this narrative was produced by an oft-cited 1947 article by former Secretary of War Henry Stimson setting out what has become the normative narrative of the reasoning going into the Hiroshima decision. Added to that article were the effects of suppressing public information on the effects of radiation on the citizens of Hiroshima and Nagasaki. The recent change in narrative might be due to a combination of factors: declassification of film and other significant documents and photographs over the previous 15 years[15] and a growing antinuclear movement in the 1980s, the sensibilities of which are reflected in *Fat Man and Little Boy* (cf. Lifton & Mitchell, 1995). Also, it was perhaps a shifting configuration of technology in the 1980s that prompted the recent number of representations, and a return to the origins of the bomb.

Historical representations such as *Day One*, by constructing these events, necessarily present *tracings* and not *maps* (in the Deleuzoguattarian sense, see Deleuze & Guattari, 1987, chap. 1). A "map" of the bomb concerns a complex of articulations of social actors (purified uranium, an implosive device, a network of scientists, the military-industrial complex, and ethical, moral, and social imperatives to "Stop Hitler"). A "tracing" articulates only specific aspects of this complex. The invention of the atom bomb was not an inevitable occurrence; it did not proceed directly as the result of other discoveries or technologies. The links of the network are aleatory,[16] ideological (e.g., technicism as a worldview), political, and strategic; they are the work of war machines, economic machines, state machines, and others. The form and structure that is imposed on this complex map of articulations surrounding and concerning the first atom bombs follows certain logics and assumptions. For something to be referred to as a *narrative* indicates the presence of structures that may or may not be external (i.e., the necessity for beginnings, endings, causes, and effects, etc.). What we call narrative is historically and socially contingent. Hayden White (1987) writes that

> this value attached to narrative in the representation of real events arises out of a desire to have real events display the coherence, integrity, fullness, and closure of an image of life that is and can only be imaginary [in a Lacanian sense]. (p. 24)

White argues that for Hegel, the impulse to narrate (seen as a desire for historical closure) arises from politics and reflects a certain sociopolitical situation. However, for White himself, "the demand for closure in the historical story is a demand . . . for moral meaning" (p. 21). I wish to argue that narrative is a discursive and representational structuration of what Deleuze and Guattari call a field of intensities (becomings rather than discrete events), and certainly politics and morality are central in this discussion.[17] If we are now seeing the struggle over representations of the project that began the nuclear age, perhaps we will soon begin to see an overall historicization of the cold war (cf. Alperovitz, 1995; Doctorow, 1995; etc.).

Day One's Narrative

That the accepted narrative of the Manhattan Project is a modern one, I don't think anyone would deny. Nor would it be indefensible to say that the detonation of the bomb over Hiroshima (and Nagasaki and Alamagordo) was a profoundly modern moment (or moments). The debate comes to a head *The Day After Trinity, Hiroshima and After:* Is that moment the end of the modern and the beginning of the postmodern, as many have suggested?[18] There is a sense, after Hiroshima, that something has happened, something has ended, and something else begun. Hence the suggestion of a temporal break in such titles as *The Begining or the End*, *The Day After Trinity*, or *Day One*. There is also a profound spatial break as well, as the structure of space (especially social space) alters: The possibilities for human-technological action expand to deterritorialize the globe and reterritorialize it with a grid of power. But as the notion of radical historical breaks is itself a modern conception, I place Trinity, Hiroshima, and Nagasaki and their legacy (as they have been popularly constructed) within a modern episteme.

We do experience the world differently after the bomb. The bomb is now implicit in all we think and do. But the difference is not actually something determined solely by the bomb. The bomb is a culmination of technology's effects on human action, brought about in a rather dramatic and destructive fashion, leading to a crisis of ethics (the moral and ethical dilemmas of Leo Szilard, as we shall see). As Hans Jonas (1984) puts it, "Modern technology has introduced actions of such novel scale, objects, and consequences that the framework of former ethics can no longer contain them" (p. 6). The crisis, put in these terms, is one central to the modern as a whole, not something that ends or transforms the modern, but part of its episteme. To argue that Hiroshima provides a radical break allows us to ignore the forces that led up to it since we are now *different* than that, we are now *post* all that. I am arguing, counter to this tendency, that we were modern before and we are modern after. Hiroshima is a *revealing* of the modern; and it revealed, in part, that ethics and philosophy were inadequate to the modern.[19]

Day One is a modern narrative, a Faustian narrative, and, as such, presents a modern problem that cannot be solved in the same terms in which it is posed (within its own episteme).[20] While the narrative of the Manhattan Project is not *necessarily* Faustian, that is the way it is most often constructed. And it is significant that Faust is the typically *modern* narrative (Berman, 1988). *Day One* provides the figure of Faust (J. Robert Oppenheimer),[21] the scientist driven to great destruction, and Mephisto (General Leslie Groves), who provides Faust with the means of destruction. This is also the story of how physics (some [e.g., Taylor, 1992] read "science") loses its "innocence,"[22] how its creative powers grew out of control to encompass the destruction of the entire world. It loses its innocence by being taken up (and over) by the military, which brings with it a demand for efficiency and productivity, and a teleology of destruction.[23]

Understanding the tensions and dialectics of the Manhattan Project narrative may help us to understand how similar tensions underlie questions of technology more generally in a modern episteme. *Day One* presents Groves, the military head of the Manhattan Project (and the man who built the Pentagon), as the bringer of a certain type of efficiency and productivity—technicism—to the more creative and free-thinking scientists. Manfred Stanley (1978) defines technicism as "the misuse of scientific and technological vocabularies with regard to human activities better described in other ways" (p. xii), and I would extend this discursive misuse into the misuse of organizational structures of efficiency with regard to human activities better organized in other ways.[24]

In *Day One*, when Groves first visits the University of Chicago, where much of the theoretical work on the bomb is going on, he is appalled at their apparent disorder. "Why is everyone sitting around talking? Why aren't they working?" he asks. "They are working, General," says Arthur Compton, the scientist in charge of the Chicago project, "exchanging ideas." Groves criticizes their apparent lack of efficiency and accuracy. In trying to come up with the amount of uranium needed for a bomb, the scientists say their final results will be accurate within a factor of ten, which Groves finds "unusable." "How do you build a factory based on this," he asks. He suggests that they become more efficient: concentrate their forces, focus on the most likely substance for a cooling system instead of considering four or five. After Groves leaves, Leo Szilard asks, "How can we work with people like that?" The two dominant and agonistic logics of the narrative are thus set out: military efficiency based on specialization and hierarchy versus the group efforts of the theoreticians; a "practical" approach to the project (narrowly focused on technical questions) versus a "theoretical" one (which ranges across strata).

This gulf is underlined when Groves visits Berkeley, which has a more practical, rather than theoretical, program. Groves complains that there is a "sloppy, undisciplined, unorganized mob" in Chicago. Dr. E. O. Lawrence, head of the program at Berkeley, explains that there is "too much theory in Chicago, out here you'll actually see uranium separation going on." He shows Groves Berkeley's gargantuan uranium separation machines, which impress Groves (even though they still don't work). This sets up a tension in the film between these two camps (a practice/theory dialectic). Oppenheimer, significantly, is a theoretician but is at Berkeley, positioning him between the two camps. He is the ground on which the battle between Chicago and Berkeley occurs. As Bryan

Taylor (1992) argues, Oppenheimer "is an enduring discursive form through which audiences discover and contest the ideologies of modern science and the national security state" (p. 431).

For various reasons that we need not go into here—primarily ambition (Faust's tragic flaw)—Oppenheimer sides with Groves. The theory/practice dialectic of the physicists is overcome by the introduction of the third term: the military-industrial complex,[25] where theory becomes focused and specialized and practice becomes productive. A particular type of theory and a particular type of practice are articulated together: stratification by war machine. Oppenheimer (represented in the film as being "proud to be in uniform") suggests that all the scientists be gathered together in one place (Los Alamos) to concentrate their forces. Later, he does not resist the dropping of the bomb on an unsuspecting Japan (in fact, he eventually suggests bombing several cities at once, emerging, as Peter Wyden [1984, p. 162] put it, "as the most enthusiastic hawk among these hawks").

Most narratives about the Manhattan Project are built around a perceived tension between Oppenheimer and Groves (the creative, eccentric mind of a theorist of high physics and the strict military mind based on efficiency and action), for example the film *Fat Man and Little Boy. Day One* (and the book *Day One*) delineates a more specific diagram of stratification (theory/practice) and then "introduces" a new key figure, that of Leo Szilard, the "conscience" of the atomic project (and the man who had the first idea that an atomic bomb was possible and how it would work), thus setting up a second dialectic, that of morals (and in doing so revealing the limits of the stratification). The two halves of the second dialectic are represented by Los Alamos on the one hand and Chicago (reduced in the film to the figure of Szilard) on the other.

Los Alamos becomes Chicago's "other." The character of Enrico Fermi explains the difference between the two places: "there [Chicago], they feel they have to build the bomb because of Hitler. Here, everyone wants to build it." To which Oppenheimer replies, "that's because I'm here and Szilard's there." Oppenheimer and Fermi, who are portrayed as the main scientists at Los Alamos, pursue the bomb because it is, in Oppenheimer's words, "a technically sweet problem." This technocratic way of looking at the situation divorces it from any of the moral dilemmas brought up by Szilard and others at Chicago.[26] Fermi, at one point, snaps at Edward Teller, who is having doubts about continuing with the project in light of a petition that Szilard is circulating condemning the use of the bomb: "Don't bother me with your conscientious scruples. This is superb physics." The military argue, why did we build the bomb if not to use it? Why spend 2 years and $2 billion?[27] The arguments for the bomb are therefore abstracted out of context ("superb physics"). Groves confesses to Oppenheimer at one point, "Don't you ever worry the war will be over before the bomb is ready to drop?"

It is significant, in fact, that the character of Szilard, as one of the leaders of the movement to stop the bomb from being dropped on Japan, has been absent, or marginalized, from previous narratives (he is absent from *The Day After Trinity,* for example). Szilard, in fact, is seen as the unexpected hero of *Day One.*[28] It is when we start to question the received view of the bomb project's history (and stratification) that his character takes on added significance and weight.

The audience approached *Day One* with Kennedy's "nuclear sword of Damocles" still over their heads but with the cold war just beginning to thaw. Indeed, they approached the program with all their knowledge and fears of nuclear war, all the discourses around the bomb, and a history of U.S.-Soviet relations. *Day One* was broadcast March 5, 1989, the spring before the Berlin Wall crumbled.

Day One and History

Faustian narratives of the Manhattan Project are well established as popular history. The audience brings with them familiarity with the events themselves. This assumed knowledge is important in filling in the gaps of the narrative and thus is an important factor in a representation being taken as a credible account of "what really happened." And it is important if one is going to reread the history.

Indeed, the climactic moments of the film (the Trinity test explosion and the dropping of the bomb on Japan) are part of popular memory, through, for example, John Hersey's book *Hiroshima* (1946). Indeed, the very term "Manhattan Project" has become a signifier for large-scale secret scientific experiments, nuclear destruction, and government-sponsored science.[29] The film acknowledges, and refers to, this common memory by the use of documentary footage of the Trinity test, the flight of the *Enola Gay,* the bombing of Hiroshima, and slides of the destruction of Hiroshima and the victims of that bomb. Because these scenes have become better known over the past 20 years, the "validity" of this narrative might be called into question if they were absent, only referred to, or substantially recreated, since they are expected to appear in a certain form. By inserting familiar historical footage, *Day One* articulates itself with popular memory and becomes more "authentic." Its other dramatized scenes are then historically validated by virtue of their proximity to this articulation.

To be considered "accurate" or "authentic" (and therefore important and worth tuning in to watch), *Day One* has to address these assumed knowledges, address the dynamics of the narrative and, eventually, the forms of the medium (television) itself. It has to locate itself within the discourses of both History and popular history. But to consider History we have to socially situate what this means. History is not a universal unfolding of events. As Tony Bennett (1990) describes,

> History (as a discipline) is most appropriately regarded as a specific discursive regime, governed by distinctive procedures, through which the maintenance/transformation of the past as a set of currently existing realities is regulated. It constitutes a disciplined means of production of a "historical past" that exercises a regulatory function in relation to the "public past." . . . The productivity of historical inquiry is produced by the tension between the pasts it organizes and those enjoying a broader circulation. (pp. 50, 51)

History is always produced by structures of power. Deleuze and Guattari (1987) argue that "History is always written from the sedentary point of view and in the name of a unitary State apparatus, at least a possible one, even when the topic is nomads" (p. 23).

A tension, then, exists between what we might call *formal, disciplinary, or academic* history and historical production ("the historical past") and *popular* history[30] ("the public past"). The scope of academic history is fairly broad in that I would argue this includes not only written histories but now filmed documentaries as well. Academic (or *State*) history is seen as having a direct connection to the "true" or the "real"— what actually happened. In other words, it is seen as having a concrete referent. This concrete referent is only a convention, since, as a discursive construct, history is a system of signifiers without an ultimate signified; it is the articulation of particular artifacts in particular locations and relations to discursive regimes of power. History, then, in its institutionalized practices, acts as a final arbiter of what is taken as "history." History is selective, as Raymond Williams reminds us. But history, per se, has to contend with the *past*, in the sense of "the popular past" or "popular history," what is generally felt, within a society, to be "how it happened." The public past is a sense of tradition and collective memory; it is nomadic and rhizomatic. The public past is crucial in constructing contemporary social identity. Therefore, how a public imagines its past relations with technology (i.e., nuclear systems) will have an impact on how it treats its present technology (i.e., the new communication and information assemblage), even if these technologies seem superficially different from each other.

In terms of the Manhattan Project narrative, the major voices are the government (the official narrative), the public, and the academic debates. The government was able to significantly manipulate the dominant version of events, a version that the public has latched on to despite numerous charges from historians regarding the multiple fabrications in the accepted narrative. For example, those trying to explain the effects of radiation at Hiroshima and Nagasaki were accused of revising (in the sense of "making up") what was considered true history (which was partly made up to begin with). The controversy over the Smithsonian's proposed exhibit of the *Enola Gay* in 1995 shows that the Hiroshima decision is still a volatile issue. The public seems more comfortable with the received view, which carefully avoids the very question of the consequences of the bomb and tends to want to discredit new evidence (Lifton & Mitchell, 1995). Until fairly recently, the versions of the narrative appearing in popular representations have firmly followed the accepted narrative, as we have seen.

The important point is that the received view of history is a produced, constructed, and contested one, and one contested not only by popular discourses but from within academic discourse itself. It is contradictory, not uniform or unified, though it presents itself as such. The difference then between official, academic, and popular histories is one of particular sites of practices (academy, television, news, etc.) and positions within hegemonically constructed (and historically contingent) frameworks of truth and fiction.

One of the primary sites today of the construction of (and struggle over) popular history is television. As it is the site of most news and documentaries, television has a sense of immediacy and "live"ness that seems to locate it in the "actually happening," the real, and the true. Mimi White (1989) discusses the "live"ness of television in relation to history. It is White's argument that television presents "live" events as "historical" events. The designation "History" lends weight to images that are otherwise partial, transitory, and decontextualized. "[T]elevision generates a dispersed discursive field, subsumed under the label history, which is fragmentary, multiple, and contradictory" (White, 1989, p. 283). Television is also a primary site of leisure activity, which involves it with popular memory (Lipsitz, 1990; O'Sullivan, 1991). And television utilizes the dominant narrative forms and strategies for constructing history (Hay, 1989). As James Hay (1989) puts it, "TV engages . . . some of the most preferred or dominant practices in the 80's for constructing the past" (p. 2).[31]

Though television is important to popular memory, it is far from uniform in its practice, programming, or form. Through the proliferation of cable TV and satellite systems, television has become the site of a myriad of disparate channels and narrative and technological forms. As a result of these changes, TV has become an expanded site of various discursive practices pertaining to the true and to history (Hay, 1989, p. 4). CNN, with 24-hour news, is the most prominent of these, but so are the many information-centered channels with stocks, weather, and so on. In addition to this, the proliferation of cable channels has opened further outlets for documentaries (on history and nature) beyond PBS, which was their primary showcase.[32] The narrative form of the documentary itself has become more powerfully articulated to the true because of the increasing frequency of their appearances (which breeds familiarity and the naturalization of the form) and a growing acknowledgment of documentaries as legitimate history. Indeed, the realization that there is a wealth of filmed events available to the historian interested in pursuing the 20th century (especially, for our purposes, the discovery and declassification of film and photos regarding the Manhattan Project and Hiroshima and Nagasaki) has opened the documentary up as another source of the true. Documentaries' historical strength lies in their ability to show gesture, expression, emotion, and action—in other words, actual practices—which are central to popular memory (Connerton, 1989). They are articulated, then, to both academic and popular histories, and their positioning on television as a more academic form on a popular medium supports this. What are presented are not just narratives of events but the articulation of particular events to particular discourses. As we have seen, the primary site of most of the popular history about the Manhattan Project in the decade prior to *Day One* had been television.

It is within the discursive (and televisual) space of the documentary and docudrama that *Day One* is positioned, and it is from this space and its narrative forms that *Day One* is constructed as a dramatized history of the events leading up to the detonation of the first atomic bomb. *Day One* does much to combine documentary modes with its dramatic production. This usually occurs by labeling scenes with captions bearing at least place and date (month and year, but many times day, month, and year), specifically positioning the scene in historical time and space. This emphasizes the historicity of the scene and gives it a sense of "this actually happened."[33] Why is historicity so important? All these factors build historicity, which may lodge this program in popular history as a true version of events. The more historical a program, the more self-evident (and less constructed) it appears.

Day One is a dramatic production but one directly based on (and closely following) a popular nonfiction book. This literary link further strengthens the program's articulation to the true or real. Peter Wyden's book *Day One* actually lends itself to a dramatic adaptation. From a series of photographs in the first pages of the book, labeled "The A-Bomb Story: Some Principals," the book takes a more personal view of the situation, focusing mainly on the people involved and their interactions and decisions. The book's structure is closer to that of a narrative, with an emphasis on character and plot rather than exposition. Richard Rhodes's book, *The Making of the Atomic Bomb*, by contrast, takes a more objective view, detailing not only the science involved but the biographies of the main "players."[34] *Day One* is a polemical text, and its style of writing and the narrative it tells are constructed to argue a point. The book begins with the following passage, in large type, set on its own page:

> One millisecond after you read this, you and one billion other people could begin to perish. You probably think you know why. You don't, for key elements in the chain of blunders that brought us to the brink of nuclear extinction remain to be disclosed. (p. 14)

The second half of the book deals with what happened at Hiroshima and that city's slow rebuilding. Wyden comes out strongly against the decisions that were made to drop the bomb and concludes that those same types of flawed decisions are made time and time again (the Bay of Pigs, the Vietnam War, the attack on Pearl Harbor), resulting from a lack of reason in the "machinery that produces national judgement" (p. 367). This machinery, I would argue, is a stratifying machine as well.

Day One, the television show, presents a more "balanced" view of the situation, giving roughly equal time to opposing arguments. In particular, the film does not cover the latter half of Wyden's book, the half dealing with Hiroshima, and therefore avoids the political and emotional effects of those events and arguments. It is conceivable that if *Day One* had been independently produced it might have assumed a more overtly polemical or controversial stand. Though Aaron Spelling Productions and CBS have a history of interesting, sometimes critical, sometimes documentary work (barring *The Love Boat, Beverly Hills 90210,* and similar Spelling productions), they are still, along with AT&T, fairly mainstream corporations.[35]

The Hiroshima section of Wyden's book becomes implicit in the television production, except for slides shown to the scientists at the end. In fact, this known teleology (bombs *were* dropped on both Hiroshima and Nagasaki with horrific consequences) actually infuses the film with a sense of inevitability, but it is this inevitability that the film wants to open up, to show the decisions and the paths not taken. In this way, it struggles against that teleology and against popular conceptions (making the decision more a tragedy than triumph); and thus, significantly, it reworks the narrative. The film emphasizes not only the debates and the logics that went into the Hiroshima decision but also the moral dimensions of the use of the bomb (embodied in the figure of Szilard). It also introduces questions and opposition within the advisory council that recommended the course of action to President Truman, including questioning the projected numbers of casualties in an invasion used to justify the bombing.

Day One and Technology

It is the combination of narrative dynamics, assumed knowledges, and adherence to televisual forms (such as genre) that structure the narrative of *Day One*. Our discussion of the Faustian aspects of the bomb narrative, popular conceptions of the characters and events, *Day One*'s relation to television and history (and History) has outlined the general problematic of the bomb: The bomb is seen as an autonomously constructed (in that it seems to be the result of previous science and technology), neutral piece of technology caught up in the political struggle between the needs of the military-industrial complex, the moral arguments of humanists, a scientific community dedicated to the neutrality of science and technology, and the decisions of the capitalist state.

However, there is another element at work here that influences the structure and character of this narrative, and that is the corporate sponsor of the program, AT&T. Following Raymond Williams (1974) and placing *Day One* within its immediate flow, we have to consider the framework of AT&T commercials that surround and interrupt the narrative. Usually, commercials do not have much to do with the shows that they are juxtaposed to (apart from the assumed demographics of the audience), unless it is a specially sponsored show, as *Day One* is. In these commercials, AT&T seems to explicitly foreground itself vis-à-vis the narrative that it is presenting. And it does this from the very start.

In a scene that is dated and ironic to us now, after the fall of the Berlin Wall, Cliff Robertson introduces the program from in front of the Brandenburg Gate in Berlin with the Wall in the background. Robertson, wearing a trenchcoat reminiscent of John le Carré spy novels, is walking on a cold winter day near the gate. The cold seems indicative of the cold war itself; indeed, we seem to be already in the midst of a nuclear winter. He states,

> We are in West Berlin, near the Brandenburg Gate, welcoming you to "AT&T Presents: Day One," another in a series of television specials that are an important part of AT&T's commitment to quality in communications. Fifty years ago, this city, Berlin, was headquarters for one of the powers who sought to rule the world by tyranny. Well, tonight's story is about the race against time to defeat those Axis powers, and about the human drama of those people who were faced with one of the most critical decisions of the 20th century. We take you now to the Berlin of 1933 and the beginning of *Day One*.

What, then, does a narrative about the making of the atomic bomb have to do with either AT&T or its "commitment to quality in communications"?[36] The sole sponsorship of AT&T of the program, and the framework of AT&T's commercials that surround the narrative may hold a clue.

The first thing that strikes one about AT&T's commercials is, obviously, technology. At times, some of the ads consist of a rapid succession of images (circuit boards, wiring, the construction of high-tech equipment) accompanied by the driving beat of the soundtrack. This is not just any technology, but state-of-the-art communications technology. This is the technology of the postmodern, what Baudrillard (1983) and Jameson

(1984) and Lyotard (1984) in their own ways argue is the basis of postmodern society. Baudrillard especially sees this very technology as the source of simulation, the destruction of reality, where everything is endlessly reproduced as representations without an original. But along with this view of technology comes a type of learned helplessness: The technology is so pervasive as to leave us no way out, no way to struggle. Baudrillard views technology uncritically, as simply a part of life to be dealt with. This is the view of technology that would agree with Richard Rhodes's conclusion, in *The Making of the Atomic Bomb*, that science cannot be blamed for the nuclear situation, that that was the result of politics and policy makers, that nuclear fission was waiting to be discovered by someone, not invented. This is the same position Oppenheimer himself took (before the end of the war; after the war, he lobbied for international controls), disclaiming any responsibility for the uses of the bomb since they were scientists, not politicians. But nuclear fission is not the same thing as a nuclear bomb, and the path from one to the other is far from fixed or inevitable.

There are a variety of types of commercials intermixed with the broadcast of *Day One*. Some are for AT&T Long Distance, others are for specific AT&T products, or show a flow of technology, or have a more historical bent. These latter commercials closely parallel the program (*Day One*) in several ways. They are dealing with history and historical events, usually great (AT&T) inventions or ideas: the telephone, universal telephone service, the first television broadcast, color television. These commercials are shot in a brown/sepia tone similar to much of Day One, emphasizing their historical nature. Details of costumes, vehicles, the equipment being used, all indicate particular historical moments. These commercials, three throughout the broadcast, are set up on a similar structure: AT&T Past (*1907: Universal Telephone Service*, in one; *1876: The Telephone* and *1927: First Television Broadcast*, in the second; *1929: Color Television*, in the third), which relates to an AT&T Today (computer connectivity, information networking, etc.) and finally to AT&T Tomorrow (Global Telecommunity in all the commercials). These commercials use the theme song "Over the Rainbow" to indicate how dreams can become reality, how ideas and abstractions can become hardware. A fourth commercial is similar in theme, though not specific format. It explains how AT&T "holds fast to [Alexander Graham Bell's] ideas." This is followed by the aforementioned "flow of technology," culminating in Bell Labs, a place that is on the cutting edge of technology, where technological dreams become reality. But how does AT&T, in the midst of its taking credit for just about every major communications break-through of the last century, manage *not* to implicitly seem to be taking credit for the bomb, too? On the surface, the happy scientists at Bell Labs seem rather close to those of Chicago, Berkeley, and Los Alamos in the 1930s and 1940s portrayed in *Day One*.

The answer is part of "AT&T's commitment to quality in communications" that Cliff Robertson announces at the start of the program. The first commercial break sets up the situation. It announces that loneliness and distance have always plagued humankind, but that all this can be overcome by (AT&T's) universal telephone service, then (AT&T's) trans-atlantic cable, and finally (AT&T's) worldwide intelligence network (leading to their vision of a Global Telecommunity). Through this net-work, we can send (and receive) information easily to and from any-where. The commercial emphasizes its long-distance operators, who are busy placing calls to and from locations all over the world. Some of the countries mentioned prominently in this commercial are Russia, Cuba, Hungary, and Poland; in other words the operators are placing calls "behind the iron curtain," so to speak. The commercial also emphasizes AT&T's network television feeds, data networking, and role in figuring the space shuttle's telemetry.

The last scene of *Day One* has Oppenheimer delivering a speech about his concern for control of atomic bombs (now that they've dropped two), saying that we must unite or perish, and that "by our works we are committed to a world united before this common peril in law and humanity." This is followed immediately with a voice-over by Cliff Robertson, reiterating the theme of the commercials and explaining AT&T's role in the whole production: "Distance," he says, "lack of communication: they divide us all, one from another. At AT&T, we have a vision to give you the tools to break down the barriers of time and distance . . . to give you the power to reach out to your world and your future." As a later ad emphasizes, "We're the people who make the distance disappear."

An explicit link is being made, it seems to me, between the cold war and nuclear proliferation and a failure of communication, as if the decisions that were made to drop the bomb and the rest of the debates within *Day One* around the morality of the bomb can be solved through better communication. This link is facilitated by a play on two senses of the term *communication*. AT&T's corporate role traditionally concerns the sense of communication as transmission, not communication as the politics of meaning (see Carey, 1989). The conflation of these two senses allows the conclusion that the decrease in signal noise leads to a more acceptable political environment. As James Carey (1989) writes,

> [A] solution to our dilemmas is offered by a cadre of technocrats committed to no political theory who energetically demonstrate how the new technology will solve every problem of politics, the economy, health, and even loneliness and isolation. . . . Most of this is pleasant if not dangerous nonsense. (p. 170)

What the program seems to be pointing out is that, yes, decisions were based on faulty or insufficient information, but that information was inadequate not because of poor telephones but for explicitly political reasons (e.g., the misinformation circulated about the possible numbers of casualties incurred if the United States invaded Japan, the actual progress of the Germans toward their own bomb, etc.). In any case, AT&T seems to be positioning itself to provide a *resolution* to the cold war, to heal the rift caused by the bomb with communication networks, and also partly, perhaps, to take some of the credit for the recent thaw in the cold war (now that we can easily phone Moscow and Havana, why would we want to bomb them?).

AT&T therefore stitches itself into the history of the bomb and the nuclear age in a new way, quite apart from the central role its technologies play in supporting the U.S. military's protocol of Command, Control, Communication, and Intelligence (C3I).[37] The commercials do not mention any of AT&T's war-related work, including its work on radar. Bell Labs not only aided the American development of radar (a British invention) but also contributed to the development of the M-9 gun director for anti-aircraft guns (Brooks, 1976).[38] David Noble (1986) reports that in 1943, 83% of total research expenditures of Bell Labs were for government work (p. 11). AT&T was also involved in Antiballistic Missile (ABM) development, the Arctic Distant Early Warning (DEW) line radar defense system, and the Semiautomatic Ground Environment (SAGE) defense network. Also, until 1993, AT&T was responsible for the management of the Sandia National Laboratories outside Los Alamos (Brooks, 1976, pp. 235-238; Furman, 1990). Historically, the mission of Sandia Laboratory has been to provide engineering support to nuclear weapons designers in matters such as the mating of warhead material to fuses, detonators, safety devices, and so on. The Bell System made no profit from the management of Sandia, however.

Alvin von Auw (1983), former vice president and assistant to the chairman of the board of AT&T, has pointed out that the antiwar sentiment of the 1960s and 70s, emphasized by Eisenhower's earlier warning against the new military-industrial state of which AT&T was most definitely a part, caused AT&T to guard its public image carefully, especially with regard to its military contracts (pp. 382-387). Given this history, it is not at all surprising that AT&T's contributions to national defense are absent from the public history presented in its commercials.

AT&T now promises a Global Telecommunity of perfect communication. But this telecommunity is still based on an instrumental "transmission" view of communication, the same view that underlies C3I. AT&T is not alone in presenting a technocratic view (and such a view is evident not only in the commercials but also in technicism being one of the dominant forces pushing the development of the bomb in *Day One*, Oppenheimer's "technically sweet" problem). Indeed, many of the discussions around the Internet arise from this same tradition (and betray a similar stratification). In perfect communication, the technology—not to mention the industrial base—disappears. This is the view that argues that faster communication and more communication *necessarily* leads to a better society.

This Global Telecommunity seems to be a deterritorialized social space—a social space made possible entirely through technology. It is represented as a space without dimensions (distance disappears). The emphasis is on the immediacy of contact (in which the mediating technology disappears). There are no longer barriers to one's individual agency. The Global Telecommunity is also reminiscent of the deterritorialized space of capital, the space of flows, in which the logic of the system (AT&T) overrides the logic of the nodes (individual users or locations) (Manuel Castells, 1989). The dominant power becomes flexible, deterritorialized, yet still functions according to specific machinic processes and logics.

In "postmodern" terms, this view of a Global Telecommunity would be in line with what Jean-François Lyotard called "The Postmodern Condition." In his book by that name (1984), he argues against the same sort of systems thinking and criterion of efficiency that resulted in the invention of the bomb and the construction of systems of power to support it.[39] Lyotard argues instead for paralogism, a science of paradox, characterized by free information. It is imperative, Lyotard states, to get rid of all barriers to knowledge and open all computer data banks (perhaps the most precious and powerful commodity in our society) to the public. Though AT&T still seems to rely on a systems approach (and still wishes to make a profit), it does seem to be advocating the postmodern openness and proliferation of information and communications technologies with its Global Telecommunity.

The problem and danger of this position is revealed by, interestingly, Baudrillard, who argues that this proliferation is not positive, but very negative, that the complete freedom of information and communication technologies leads to the hyperreal, a world governed by simulations and obscenity. It leads to obscenity in that "the most intimate operation of your life becomes the potential grazing ground of the media. . . . The entire universe also unfolds unnecessarily on your home screen" (Baudrillard, 1988, p. 20).

> Obscenity begins when there is no more spectacle, no more stage, no more theatre, no more illusion, when everything becomes immediately transparent, visible, exposed in the raw and inexorable light of information and communication. We no longer partake of the drama of alienation, but are in the ecstasy of communication. (1988, pp. 21-22)

Lyotard's utopia has become a realm of terror, not the terror of efficiency, but that of perfect information. Information does not make you free; information makes you want to hide. Technology becomes intrusive, terrorizing, omnipresent. Baudrillard talks about the entire world and all aspects of life, even the most private and quotidian, becoming miniaturized circuits. This is the danger of AT&T's Global Telecommunity. The bomb itself has become a network of technological systems (arming systems, firing systems, early warning systems, defense systems), honed to a level of efficiency and interconnectivity never before seen.[40] The solution offered is simply a subtler replacement. We are caught between terrors.

AT&T's Global Telecommunity is the teleology with which *Day One* frames the past. If the bomb is a "modern" problem, then it can be solved only in terms from outside its episteme—thus the turn to postmodern technology. But postmodernism either ignores technology or pushes it to its limit. In either case, we remain within the horizon of the modern, in decorporealized space, with technology even further abstracted from its social context. Nuclear technology (the bomb and reactors) and communication and information technology are social actors, bending space around themselves and enlisting other actors and artifacts in increasingly complex networks of power. Their tendency to disappear into the cracks of the social spaces that they help form is disturbing, though not surprising. But their presence in social space is revealed through the shadows they cast on space as it is practiced, the forms they assert (like points of gravitational density) on space as it is conceived, and the contradictions that form in the (broadcast, printed) repre- sentations of themselves in space as it is lived.

The broadcast of *Day One* presents us with a turning point in relations to technology. The film addresses the darkest aspects of modern technology—the dropping of the atomic bomb—and it begins to revise the history of that event. It does so in two ways: It questions the dominant narrative (the facticity of the received view) and reworks the assumed nature of modern technology by bringing it back under the influence of human decision-making. The popular conception that the bomb just happened, that it was inevitable and inexorable, allows society to dis- tance itself from the consequences of those specific events, but in doing so, places itself outside of and subordinate to an autonomous technical system. By emphasizing the human decision-making process—flawed as it was—*Day One* does risk opening deep psychological wounds, moral guilt, and *a posteriori* recriminations. But by applying this sense of human control of technical processes to *other* technological systems (systems geared toward the bright future, not the dark past)—like the burgeoning communication and information networks touted by AT&T—popular conceptions of people's own relations to technology change. A shift in the perceived and represented relationship between humans and tech- nologies from a technological determinist to a social determinist view might begin to explain the rapid public embrace of these new technolo- gies, whereas before similar systems were met with fear, reluctance, and suspicion. The broadcast of *Day One* presents a moment when the technological determinist narrative is altered and a new, positive tech- nological assemblage of communication and information technology is introduced into representational space. This transition is supported by the explicit juxtaposition of the more human-centered bomb narrative with the new technologies of the Information Super-highway.

Day One and After

The narrative of *Day One* is a specific representation (and, to some extent, construction) of a set of events. In representing the Manhattan Project, it structures an originary statement regarding modern technology, its nature, its characteristics, and the responsibility for it. Constructions of this moment remain important because though we have ostensibly shifted to a new technology (communication and information technology), the *technological assemblage* (or, rather, configuration of technological assemblages) remains similar and relies on the same philosophy of communication as transmission, as a means of command and control. Though control is now said to be in the hands of consumers (we have control through the new technologies), we have to question the nature of that control. Therefore, I argue that we cannot posit any simple break between modern/nuclear technology and postmodern/communication and information technology. We have not left the nuclear assemblage (or the modern) behind, far from it.

Since the heady days of 1989 when the cold war seemed over and the nuclear threat seemed resolved through the proliferation of communication and information technology (as AT&T would have it), new types of nuclear proliferation and conflict have cropped up (e.g., North Korea, Iraq, ill-guarded and ill-accounted for weapons-grade nuclear material in the former Soviet states) and new revelations regarding the U.S. government's unethical irradiation of hundreds if not thousands of unsuspecting "volunteers" over the years, not to mention revelations regarding the fallout from nuclear tests.[41] When *Day One* was rebroadcast on May 27, 1993, AT&T's commercials took a different direction.[42] With the world situation being so unstable (and U.S. nuclear science's image being further tarnished), AT&T could no longer afford the optimistic history-building that it had done in 1989. Instead of Cliff Robertson's dramatic historicizing statement introducing *Day One* as a triumph over evil, the rebroadcast falls back on appeals to nuclear fear characteristic of the cold war (see Weart, 1988). An announcer merely intones, "to avoid the Day After, you must experience the Emmy Award–winning 'Day One.' " Instead of representing the current situation (Global Telecommunity) as the culmination and resolution of years of conflict and progress, the new commercials ignore the present entirely and partake in futurology. The "You Will" campaign features examples of new "conveniences" that will become available through advances in AT&T technology: opening doors with the sound of your voice, carrying medical histories in your wallet, attending a meeting while on a beach, and so on.

The fit between these new commercials and the older program seems awkward, as if each is moving in different directions. The new focus is on personal convenience rather than global connectivity. The commercials feature primarily personal or highly personalized business applications (toll-free "800" service, the "i plan" for long-distance savings) and technologies. AT&T no longer makes the distance disappear, instead they "help put your world within reach." AT&T is now selling a new technological assemblage (the National Information Infrastructure, or NII) rather than transforming an old one (Strategic Defense Initiative or SDI) as it was in 1989. In this new campaign, the similarities between AT&T's Global Telecommunity and the military's protocol of C3I is further obscured. The question now is, what is this new technological assemblage and, more important, what has become of social space?

Notes

1. On popular representations of the bomb, see Weart, 1988, and Boyer, 1985.

2. Tim O'Sullivan (1991), discussing a series of interviews he conducted concerning people's earliest memories of television in the 1950s and 1960s in Britain, writes: "For all intents and purposes, the apparatus itself had become invisible, and to talk of television was to talk of programmes and, implicitly, the shared experience of watching" (p. 6).

3. Day One was directed by Joseph Sargent, who, incidentally, also directed Colossus: The Forbin Project. Colossus was also the name of the calculator (one of the first computers) used to break the German's ENIGMA code during World War II (Virilio, 1995, pp. 160-161).

4. The dropping of the bomb on Hiroshima (and then another one on Nagasaki) was a watershed for modern technology; it was a moment when the destruction of the entire world was made possible. In this way, the bomb represents a macrophysics of modern technology (while dealing with the microphysics of molecular structure) in that it eliminates large areas at once, indiscriminately. Another watershed moment in modern technology had arrived a few years earlier in the form of the Holocaust. The Holocaust represents the microphysics of modern technology in that it processed individuals, labeling, distributing, and eliminating each person (though on a large scale, it was anything but indiscriminate). These two moments ideally should not be separated, though I deal only with one moment here.

A third aspect of modern technology, cybernetic systems that were the basis for modern computers, are intimately related to both these moments through origins in missile-guidance and code-breaking research. Paul Virilio (1995) attempts to draw these three moments together.

5. The reviews of *Day One* were mixed, though mainly positive, ranging from three and a half stars by the *New York Post* to one and a half stars by the *Washington D.C. Times* ("CBS' atomic-bomb movie a real blow-out as drama"). Most acknowledge a slow pacing, though most are still fascinated by the drama, and a few were obviously bored. Not many could resist titling their reviews with some pun on "bomb."

The broadcast received a 15.2 rating (% of total TV sets tuned to the program), a 24 share (of those TVs on at that time period, 24% were tuned in to the program), and was the 29th most watched show that week. It won its Emmy Award for "Outstanding Drama/Comedy Special."

6. I rely in this next paragraph on past bomb films on Stephen Hunter's 1989 article, "1945-1989: Facing the Bomb on Film," Lifton and Mitchell's (1995) appendix on cultural responses to Hiroshima, and my own research.

7. An article by former Secretary of War Henry Stimson in *Harper's* in 1947 has been broadly taken as the definitive telling (Lifton & Mitchell, 1995).

8. Before the bomb, the terms were unconditional surrender and the Japanese would have lost their emperor; after the bomb, the terms were changed and the emperor remained. Many have argued that letting the Japanese keep their emperor would have ended the war months earlier, and without an invasion or an atomic bomb (see Lifton & Mitchell, 1995).

9. The film *The Beginning or the End* must not be confused with the 1957 science fiction film, *The Beginning of the End*, which is about giant grasshoppers (created, significantly enough, by radiation) on the rampage.

10. See also Boyer, 1985, and Alperovitz, 1995.

11. Material excerpted from *Day One* by Peter Wyden. © 1984. Reprinted with permission of Simon & Schuster.

12. The song presents the bomb narrative in its bare bones: scientists getting "more than they bargained for" and changing the course of history; our hope depends on "a world without end" and not on the "big shots" or "fools" who, as Wyden argues, continue to make the same mistakes (Rush [1985] "Manhattan Project." *Power Windows*. Core Music Publishing).

13. Since the broadcast of *Day One*, the TV movies *Hiroshima: Out of the Ashes* (1990) and the made-for-cable *Hiroshima* (1995) appeared, the latter a Canadian/Japanese coproduction that includes recently uncovered footage and other documentary materials. Since my book concerns specifically U.S. social space, I do not have the space to discuss foreign films on the bomb, such as the classic 1959 film *Hiroshima, Mon Amour*.

14. Material excerpted from *Facing the Bomb on Film, The Baltimore Sun* (October 22, 1989). Used by permission.

15. For example, the volume *Critical Assembly: A Technical History of Los Alamos During the Oppenheimer Years, 1943-45*, by Hoddeson, Henrikson, Meade, and Westfall (1993), is based on recently declassified documents. See also Fermi and Samra's (1995) *Picturing the Bomb: Photographs From the Secret World of the Manhattan Project*.

16. For example, Szilard's knowledge of the purification of graphite, an essential step in the construction of a nuclear pile, led Fermi and Szilard to establish the first sustained chain reaction. The German scientists, unaware of certain impurities in the normal processing of graphite, abandoned that approach ("The Genius Behind the Bomb").

17. The figure of Leo Szilard in *Day One*, as moral consciousness, becomes more significant, as we shall see. His "rediscovery" marks a new moral structure to the narrative, and presents, perhaps, another impulse for the recent proliferation of Manhattan Project narratives.

18. See, e.g., Morris, 1988b, p. 186, citing this as Jameson's and Mandel's views.

19. On ethics, the modern, and technology, see Jonas, 1984, and Serres, 1995, p. 88.

20. The path outside the modern problematic of technicism begins with an awareness of the scope and depth of the problem; but I do not have space to adequately pursue this path here (see, e.g., Christians, 1989; Pacey, 1983; Stanley, 1978).

21. John Leonard (1989) refers to Oppenheimer as "a Faust with a Hamlet hangover" (p. 97), and a speaker in *The Day After Trinity* refers to a "Faustian bargain" being struck.

22. Some have argued that chemistry had lost its innocence with the development of increasingly lethal gas warfare during and following World War I. World War II was the physicists' turn. See Lifton and Mitchell, 1995, esp. p. 97.

23. The military, in this instance, is a state-machine. The war machine, per se, has always been an active force in science.

   That the narrative of the Manhattan Project is typically portrayed as androcentric is unfortunately no surprise. This is in keeping with the masculine bias in the nuclear industry generally (Cohn, 1989). *Day One* is no exception here. In the program, women are portrayed only in the positions of wives or girlfriends, erasing the 75 women who helped design and build the bomb (Taylor, 1993b, p. 282). For example, the character of Kitty Oppenheimer states at one point, "all that is important to me are my husband and his work." I bring this topic up briefly here to acknowledge the overtly masculine bias of these narratives and of the nuclear technological network in general, and that these constructions are highly problematic. For a discussion of oppositional narratives of the Manhattan Project concerning gender, see Taylor (1993b).

24. On the discourse of the nuclear military establishment, see Cohn, 1989.

25. This was not the first time, however, that the military had become involved with academic science. See Noble, 1977, 1986.

26. See Cohn, 1989, for a discussion of how the discursive use of metaphors and abstractions divorces the work of nuclear scientists from any sense of consequence, moral or physical.

27. Indeed, the threat of a congressional inquiry into the expense of the project if it should prove unproductive (either a bomb is not produced or not used or dropped) was one of the many motivating factors in making the Hiroshima decision (Lifton & Mitchell, 1995).

28. This is noted in reviews by Leonard (1989, p. 97) and Jarvis (1989, p. 12). Richard Rhodes's later book (1986) likewise emphasizes Szilard's role.

29. A film called *The Manhattan Project* actually has nothing to do with Los Alamos, but with a youth inventing a nuclear device.

30. I retain the use of the term *popular* despite its connotation of a unified and uniform position "capable of sustaining a memory wholly apart from the dominant constructions of the past" (Bommes & Wright, 1982, p. 255).

31. Deleuze and Guattari (1987) would say that television, at least in its present configuration, is a technology of the state (in a more abstract sense); and they do say that television is a form of machinic enslavement (p. 458).

32. The response of traditional network television to this trend is the explosion of news "magazine" shows patterned after *60 Minutes* and *20/20*, and now after *Rescue 911* as well.

33. This docudrama approach is not without its drawbacks. As Jerry Krupnick (1989) writes in his review,

> The problem with doing a slice of history as vital and significant as the development of the A-bomb is that the docudrama form itself is immediately suspect. There is a nagging feeling that what we have here is more imagination than realization, that someone is using the event as a jumping off place to expound a singular point of view. (p. B5)

34. There are, however, many similarities between the two books, from their style of narration at times to the types of captions under the photographic sections. Some of this may be accounted for by the fact that both books were published by Simon and Schuster.

35. John Leonard makes a similar point in his review of *Day One*; and Jeff Jarvis (1989) does likewise, emphasizing that the "show does not come from some counterculture hippie film factory" (p. 14). (Used with permission from People.)

36. One might assume that AT&T's commitment to quality in communications refers to the quality or clarity of a transmission, not the quality of the content.

37. On C3I, see, e.g., Mosco, 1989b and de Landa, 1991.

38. Such artillery devices were instrumental in the development of both the discipline of cybernetics and the computer. See Noble, 1984.

39. Baudrillard (1983) relates a paradox that "all bombs are clean—their only pollution is the system of control and security they radiate *when they are not detonated*" (p. 79).

40. Stephen Hunter (1989) writes that "throughout the '50s, other things became obvious. First, what we faced wasn't a 'bomb'—it was a whole culture, tier after tier of interlocking technologies, from distant early-warning radars to planes in orbit just outside Soviet airspace, to missiles crouched ticking in their silos beneath the bland Nebraska prairie . . . bomb movies became systems analyses" (p. B14).

41. These revelations make the scene from *Day One* in which Fermi has the idea to drop radioactive matter on Germany that much darker. See "America's Nuclear Secrets," the cover story of *Newsweek*, December 27, 1993.

42. The rebroadcast received a 5.8 rating, a 10 share, and was ranked 64th for the week.

5

Communications: From SDI to NII Through the MSI

In the television docudrama *Day One*, AT&T positions representations of its communication systems (global telecommunity in 1989, virtual presence in 1993) not only as a solution to the cold war but as the central contender for what commonsense notions of technology should be, replacing the negative archetypes of nuclear systems. The issue addressed in this chapter is the shift in the relation between technology and language, which is central to a new social formation. I see both industry and government as responding to this shift rather than necessarily generating it.

This chapter[1] examines a pedagogical space, an exhibit designed by Ameritech at the Museum of Science and Industry in Chicago. I will be looking to characterize a general social formation (Technology/ Language), not just the technology (content) or the language (expression) but the relation between the two, the stratification. My goal in this chapter is not simply to make a theoretical point. It is to describe the social formation (the social space) that this particular museum exhibit presents. Theory can be used to help unpack much of what is unstated in the exhibit.

The exhibit at the Museum of Science and Industry in Chicago, "Communications: Your Link to a Better Life," opened in February 1993 and was sponsored by Ameritech, a Regional Bell Operating Company (RBOC, or a so-called Baby Bell). This exhibit was chosen as a case study because the Museum of Science and Industry (MSI) is not only a prominent cultural institution (in Chicago and the Midwest) but also a central tourist site. The museum draws from 2 to 4 million visitors a year, including at least a quarter million school children on field trips. Like most museums, the MSI has explicit pedagogical and ideological goals. The primary goal is to orient visitors to the dominant perspectives on science and technology in the United States (or, in the words of the museum's mission statement: "to excel in the communication of the knowledge of science, technology and industry, as a non-traditional educational institution"). The museum exhibit thus presents a very interesting site for an analysis of technology, policy, and social space: an exhibit explicitly sponsored by a single company (Ameritech[2]) within a prominent cultural and pedagogical institution.

However, despite the museum's pedagogical function, it has no curators; instead, it has "project managers." This is not unusual for contemporary science and technology museums, which no longer function as research institutions in a more traditional sense.[3] Victor J. Danilov, head of the MSI in the 1970s and 80s, suggests the term "science and technology center" rather than "museum." Science and technology centers

> are not object oriented, and they usually do not have curators, conduct research, or publish learned papers. They are basically contemporary, participatory, informal educational instruments rather than historic, "hands-off" repositories of artifacts. Unlike many museums that are quiet and elitist, science and technology centers are lively and populist. (Danilov, 1982, p. 2)

Danilov argues that such centers are gaining the acceptance of the scientific community as well as the public. However, in 1965, Eugene Ferguson described the MSI as "a technical Coney Island" (p. 42), an image that, today, the museum still seems to be actively working against.

Corporate sponsorship is not unique to this exhibit or even to the Museum of Science and Industry itself, though the museum has been one of the leaders in this area. A common criticism of the museum is that it is a trade show (see, e.g., Hudson, 1987; Butler, 1992), though James Kahn, president and CEO of the museum, denies this (Leroux, 1993, p. 15). However, this doesn't mean that the exhibit does not serve Ameritech's (and by extension, the communication industry's) interests. Indeed, in the preliminary proposal for the exhibit, two of the explicit goals were to "create favorable attitudes regarding the information industry by providing an exciting view of the potential of the information age and depicting the benefits of technology to consumers (rather than just showing technology at work)" and to "reflect favorably on Ameritech and Illinois Bell" (Museum of Science and Industry [MSI], 1991, p. 1). Kenneth Hudson notes that the corporate-sponsored exhibits at the MSI not only are blatant advertisements for their sponsors but are not critical at all. He writes, "the voice that comes out of the Museum of Science and Industry is unmistakably that of the Establishment" (Hudson, 1987, p. 106; quoted in Butler, 1992, p. 53).

We should not be surprised at the level of commercialization and commodification prevalent at the museum. Though the museum is not a "private" venture (it receives both Chicago Park District and state funds [Danilov, 1982]), it still has to draw crowds (and donations) to justify and support its existence. Increasingly, museums in general have come into competition with commercial ventures, especially those associated with the tourist and leisure industries (i.e., theme parks, shopping malls) (Morton, 1988, pp. 137-138). These spaces have much in common as spaces of consumption.[4] Museums of science and industry not only have to deal with "a bewildering array of products, from television to shopping malls, but also . . . the consumers that go with them" (Morton, 1988, p. 129). This includes both consumers of industrial products and consumers of the exhibition itself. Public museums have to struggle against the tendency to become mere state-sponsored "trade shows," while at the same time competing with the visions of science and industry presented elsewhere (particularly Disney's EPCOT Center in Florida). They must present cultural capital as well as economic capital. Nevertheless, what these museums present are the reified products of an industrial society. As Walter Benjamin wrote concerning world fairs, museums are "places of pilgrimage to the fetish Commodity" (quoted in Bennett, 1988, p. 94). In fact, "the museum visit has itself become a commodity" (Morton, 1988, p. 137); MSI started charging for admission in 1991.

The difference between a museum and a mall is that the museum ostensibly has a pedagogical function; that and the fact that all of the objects displayed are not immediately for sale in the museum. Eilean Hooper-Greenhill (1992) writes of contemporary museums:

> Shops, restaurants, rest and orientation areas occupy space that in the past would have contained objects and displays. The percentage of space within the building allowed for the display of objects is reduced in favor of spaces to display people. . . . As shops take over gallery spaces, museum exhibits are returned to storage, and items for sale take their place. Objects for looking at are replaced by objects for purchase. Museum visitors as lookers and learners are repositioned as consumers. (p. 202)

The Museum of Science and Industry is no exception and provides three museum stores[5] at which visitors can purchase replicas of artifacts or other related items. Like the modern mall, the museum also has a "food court": six restaurants, including a Pizza Hut. It also houses a movie theater, a giant Omnimax/IMAX screen that shows documentaries such as *The Fires of Kuwait, Flight, Antarctica,* or *The Rolling Stones: At the Max.* This last screening represents the museum's intent to "draw new audiences to the Museum" (MSI, 1992, p. 10). The museum also attempts to reach out to "diverse" audiences (especially children) by direct appeals to popular culture in staging temporary exhibits like "Star Trek: Federation Science" and "Super-Heroes: A High-Tech Adventure," though the audiences responding to these exhibits in the end may not be that diverse. The museum provides a space that visitors traverse in such a way as to articulate themselves into the relations of power represented by that space and in that space.

My argument in this chapter is that the Museum of Science and Industry's Communications Exhibit presents a particular stratification of Technology and Language (in other words, a configuration of social space), and that this exhibit is responding to a similar stratification in the social formation. The argument will proceed in two stages: (1) How this stratification is achieved through the medium of the museum and the exhibit itself; and (2) how visitors to the museum are articulated into this stratification (i.e., how they are placed in relation to these technological systems and within the relation of technology and language).

The Exhibit

The Communications Exhibit (in its various forms) has been a part of the Museum of Science and Industry for decades; the chairman of Illinois Bell was on the board of trustees when the museum opened in 1933 and the chair of Ameritech currently serves there as well. The 8,000-square-foot exhibit space has a very prominent location: immediately to the right after entering the museum,[6] it is situated directly across from the main museum store. An estimated 80% of museum visitors pass through the exhibit (MSI, 1991, p. 1), which consists of four sections (see Figure 5.1): a foyer, the main gallery, a small theater (called "Worldspeak"), and the Whispering Gallery (two large parabolic lenses at either end of a short corridor that allow visitors at either end to whisper to each other).

The foyer has a series of television monitors on the left showing (simultaneously) an edited compilation of scenes (many humorous) from popular culture that have to do with the telephone. On the right are a series of pillars with short quotes from a variety of sources that serve as the epigraph(s) to the exhibit. Many of the quotes are from well-known science experts who would be expected to present (or have been known to express) either celebratory views of technology or positive notions of technological progress, such as Isaac Asimov, Arthur C. Clarke, chairs of computer or communication firms; or they are from technological determinists such as Ithiel de Sola Pool and Marshall McLuhan.

Those voices raised in dissent against the march of technology (mainly Henry David Thoreau, President Rutherford Hayes, and Josef Stalin) are placed as humorous in their ignorance (i.e., Hayes: "That's an amazing invention, but who would want to use them?" or Thoreau: "We are in haste to construct a telegraph from Maine to Texas, but Maine and Texas may have nothing to say to each other"). Placed in this context, Stalin's ideological critique of Western technology systems (he vetoes Trotsky's plan for a modern telephone system because it is counterrevolutionary) cannot be regarded or considered in any depth. Devoid of its own context, such statements come across as historically ignorant (like Hayes's), or curmudgeonly (like Thoreau's), or merely paranoid.

The main exhibit area consists of four "character areas." The first is "Dissolving Distances," which follows the development of the telephone; the second, "Making Connections," presents the "invisible" communication networks of cables, fiber optics, and airwaves (including

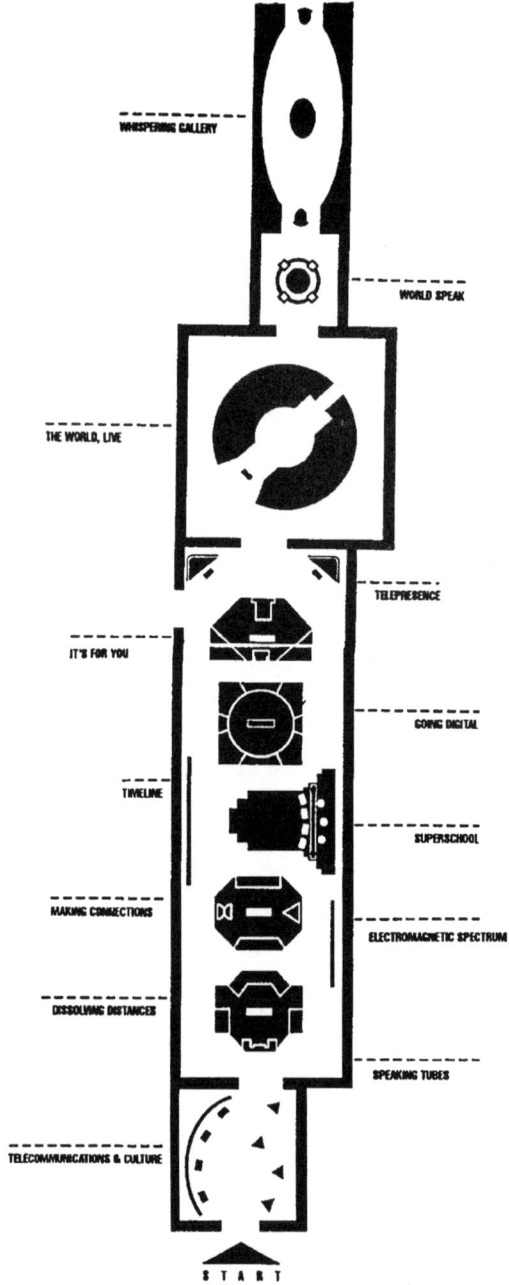

WHISPERING GALLERY

WORLD SPEAK

COMMUNICATIONS

THE WORLD, LIVE

TELEPRESENCE

IT'S FOR YOU

GOING DIGITAL

TIMELINE

SUPERSCHOOL

MAKING CONNECTIONS

ELECTROMAGNETIC SPECTRUM

DISSOLVING DISTANCES

SPEAKING TUBES

TELECOMMUNICATIONS & CULTURE

S T A R T

Figure 5.1.   The Exhibit Floorplan. (MSI, 1993, pp. 34-35)

cellular communication) as well as the development of signal switching techniques; the third, "Going Digital," explores "how digital technology provides a common language for all signals," and includes discussions of microelectronics and the convergence of communication and computer technologies; the fourth, "Staying in Touch," explores possibilities for connections with today's systems, not only the new technologies of the workplace but those of the home as well. This last area also presents a video of how new technologies are helping disabled persons, and two stages called "Telepresence" at which visitors can interact in a virtual reality–type environment.

In the middle of the main gallery is the "Superschool," which explains how telecommunications is transforming education. Along the left wall of the main area is a historical timeline indicating inventors and inventions. On the right wall is a station that explains the electromagnetic spectrum. Past the main gallery is a small theater that features a variety of live satellite feed programs from around the world as well as a prepared video program. Next to the theater is a globe that allows visitors to touch a country of their choice and hear a phrase from the language spoken there; it also indicates the density of telecommunications networks in that area. Finally, past the theater, is the Whispering Gallery.

Stratification

The theme of the exhibit is that "telecommunication enables a global society." And the global society that is presented by the exhibit is a society of voices, of languages, like the Worldspeak globe. Most of the exhibit deals with the history of U.S. communication systems, and it is only in two of the last stations that the U.S. formation is applied toward global ends (the Worldspeak station, and "The World, Live!" theater). The focus of the exhibit ends up being a global one, and in this the exhibit follows the globalization of capital and industry, especially the communications and information industries. Ameritech itself has shares in a New Zealand telecommunications firm and at least one other company in Eastern Europe, while also building cellular systems in Norway, Hungary, and Poland (Levinson, 1993, p. 45).

In a move that seems paradoxical, the exhibit makes technologies disappear, but it does so by foregrounding them. It makes visible and familiar the technological backdrop of everyday life, allowing the visitor to more readily accept and position themselves in relation to that technological system. One of the quotes from the foyer illustrates this point: Mark Weiser writes that "the most profound technologies are those that disappear. They weave themselves into the fabric of everyday life until they are indistinguishable from it."

It *seems* obvious, since this is communication technology, that the goal *is* to make the technology disappear. The outline for the exhibit by Aldrich/Pears Associates, the designers, defines telecommunication broadly as not just technologies "directly available via phone lines today but [those that] will almost certainly arrive that way in the future" (Aldrich, 1993, p. 6). However,

> playing counterpoint to this broad view is an underlying theme of the essence of telecommunication: conversations between people. Direct communication between people is not only the reason for telecommunication as a means of extending our reach, it is also a model for the development of better, more flexible, more efficient and user-friendly technologies and services. (p. 7)

This view is emphasized by the progression of the exhibit from speaking tubes, to telegraphs, to various models of telephones, and finally to fiber optics, digitalization, and "virtual presence." The focus is on an increase in *clarity* and a decrease in virtual distance; as a result, the instrument intrudes less and less. As a station toward the end of the main exhibit hall, entitled "Staying in Touch," states: "The telecommunications systems provides many options that improve communications and help us keep in touch anywhere and at any time. Anyone connected to a communications network has almost unlimited access to information and other people."

The end product of virtual presence is facilitated by two assumptions on the part of the exhibit. The first of these is the focus solely on the transmission view of communications (Carey, 1989). This allows the exhibit to bypass issues of content and politics. Second is the use of *speech* as the model of communication (rather than writing or asignifying practices). As Jacques Derrida (1976) has argued, speech has almost always effaced writing as a model of communication by having some understood link to *presence*. By being the more immediate form, speech is assumed to be primary to writing. For example, virtual presence does not seem to have been a concern of AT&T until the mid-1920s (almost a half-century after Bell was awarded his patent), when it began emphasizing the sociability and personal connections made possible by the telephone (Fischer, 1988). Since then it has become an explicit goal of the company as evidenced in its famous "Reach Out and Touch Someone" advertising campaign. The ideal of virtual presence is in no way endemic to telephone technology but is socially constructed.[7]

Paul Virilio argues that the new communication and information technologies, such as those presented in the exhibit, collapse not just space (distance to presence) but time itself into the immediacy of light-waves ("absolute speed"). This leads, he says, to a "real crisis of *immediate action,*" where

> an accident of a so-called real instant, is suddenly disconnected from its site of origin or inscription, from its here and now, for the sake of an electronic dazzle . . . where telecommanding, the so-called tact at a distance, would bring to completion the former technique of telesur-veillance of what is kept afar, or beyond our grasp. (Virilio, 1993, p. 7)

But he reminds us that though *exposure* replaces *succession* and *extension,* exposure is still "the space-time of a very real action facilitated by elec-tronic machines" (p. 7).

Though the focus of the MSI exhibit is on these electronic machines that bring us tele*presence,* what we end up with is the globe of the intensive moment, "The World, Live!" This station runs two programs: live satellite feeds from around the world and a recorded presentation.

> The multi-image theater presentation shows that a powerful telecom-munications network dissolves distance and barriers, linking us to the many diverse cultures of the world. Technologies that will be dem-onstrated in an upbeat, lively mood include simultaneous translation, telecollaboration, virtual reality, distance learning, and media bridging. (Aldrich, 1993, p. 29)

The technologies and technological systems presented in the exhibit are represented as advancing autonomously. This is confirmed by the focus on inventors and inventions throughout the historical sections of the exhibit and the timeline, and the provision of only minimal, if any, social context. The focus, like that of other science and technology museums, is on the products not the processes of technology (Bennett, 1988, p. 94). The history of communication technology becomes a pro-gressivist, evolutionary history where the telegraph begets the tele-phone, which begets the radio, which begets television, and so on, each stage an "improvement" on the others. The visitor is treated to an

endless, seemingly inevitable progression of technologies. But this historicization culminates in the elimination of history through the intensive *durée* of telepresence, of absolute speed (Virilio, 1993).

This seeming elimination of time and space does not eliminate the
interests of the state or of capital. The intensive dureé is still the product
of specific machines (Virilio, 1993, p. 7). The collapse of these categories
is still taking place within the specific space of the museum. By the end
of the 19th century, museums, especially museums of science and
technology, arranged their exhibits according to a nationalist ideology
(Morton, 1988, p. 132; see also Bennett, 1988, pp. 94-96). Not only this,

> [m]useums of science and technology, heirs to the rhetorics of progress
> developed in national and international exhibitions, completed the
> evolutionary picture in representing the history of industry and manu-
> facture as a series of progressive innovations leading up to the contem-
> porary triumphs of industrial capitalism. (Bennett, 1988, p. 90)

By 1990, national spaces seem to have been superseded by these new
communication and information technologies. Space, including national
space, collapses. Manuel Castells (1989) describes this as the move from
a space of places to a space of flows. However, this "teletopia" (Virilio's
term) is still a triumph of postindustrial capitalism, as Castells's analysis
points out. The space-time of the electronic machines is marked, coded,
territorialized by capital. And, despite appearances to the contrary, the
global space presented at the MSI is still a U.S. space—we are not
decentered on the network of communication and information technologies but centered at the endpoint of a national technological progress
toward teletopia.

Not only are these technologies represented as advancing autonomously toward a (nationalist and capitalist) future, but they are socially
deterministic as well. For example, the timeline begins with an introduc-
tory statement that reads: "Telecommunications has had a profound
effect on the modern world. Communications systems and the exchange
of information mold the cultural, political, social and economic fiber of
nations." At the end of the timeline, a panel reads: "Communication
technology has shaped society and helped create the information age. . . .
Advanced communications is bringing people of the world closer together, opening doors to information, enhancing knowledge and ena-
bling a better life for us all." "We," as a society, are then being molded
(and nudged and cajoled) into an information economy for our own

good. But, lest this conjure up Orwellian images, there are also assurances that technology won't leave "us" behind, that it waits for us to catch up. Though the technological systems themselves are seemingly developing autonomously, we are told that their *uses* are socially determined: That is, *we* decide how to implement these neutral tools that we have been given.

The particular stratification of social space that is presented in the Communications Exhibit consists of Language (taken broadly as the ability to intervene in reality and have effects) that is centered around presence and use, and Technology that is autonomous though user-friendly. Content is the telecommunications networks; expression is "use." Language here would seem to be expanding to global levels (especially the universal language of digitalization) through telepresence, while technology quietly shrinks. Such a situation would seem empowering for the human individual when viewed from a modernist perspective because of the modern articulation of language to presence and power that Derrida points out. Indeed, most arguments around the issue of the "public sphere" (and around democracy in general) are based on the presumption that language overpowers technology. An increase in technology, from such a viewpoint, would severely limit human agency (as we see in the arguments of technological determinism). And though the exhibit places the individual visitor within this scenario, the control that is supposedly available to the user (to decide the uses of these technologies or even to have effects on the system) is illusory. The stratification (and therefore the configuration and distribution of agency) is much different from what is superficially represented.

What we would seem to have here are two different shifts: One is in popular representations of technology such as AT&T's commercials and the rhetoric of the museum, both of which foreground the liberatory potentials of the new communication and information technologies; and the second is revealed by a more careful look at the new technologies themselves. It is this second that I see as being truer to the contemporary social formation, and its configuration is much different from that popularly represented.

Articulation

The institution of the museum acts as a disciplinary apparatus, providing a specific distribution of power through the arrangement of artifacts and visitors that is internalized by the visitors (see Bennett, 1988;

Foucault, 1977). The museum encourages a specific way of examining artifacts (and generally a way of seeing objects) that the visitors then apply to their own environment. The visitors are thus placed on the side of power. This placement allows the public to consent to the order of things, the arrangement of objects, the progression of ideas, that make up the dominant formation. Visitors gaze at themselves and at the city around them with the same disciplinary eye they turn on the artifacts on display. From the majestic steps of the front entrance to the building, one is allowed a view of not only Jackson Park but the Chicago skyline in the distance. This fact was not lost on Waldemar Kaempffert (1933), the first director of the museum:

> As the visitor emerges from the museum he [sic] will understand better the spectacle that greets his eyes— electric lights, the automobiles, the airplanes overhead, the towering hotels and apartment houses, the hard roads, Jackson Park itself. Chicago will seem a part of the museum —the last great exhibit in the technical progress of man. (p. 20)[8]

What the museum exhibit presents is a social space of communication and information technology.

Michel de Certeau (1984) makes a distinction between "space" and "place." Social space that is structured (i.e., a fairly stable network, a hegemonically overcoded space), he calls "place." Place is "the order (of whatever kind) in accord with which elements are distributed in relationships of coexistence" (de Certeau, 1984, p. 117). It is the location of power in that it is the preexisting condition (or set of conditions) in which we find ourselves and have to contend with. Place is stable; it preexists the individual. We can think of place as gridded: differentiated, coded, and territorialized.

"Space," on the other hand, is dynamic. "When one takes into consideration vectors of direction, velocities, and time variables," one has space (p. 117).

> It is in a sense actuated by the ensemble of movements deployed within it. Space occurs as the effect produced by the operations that orient it, situate it, temporalize it, and make it function in a polyvalent unity of conflictual programs or contractual proximities. (p. 117)

Space is a practiced place, a place with actors, with movement through/in/of places. Space is relatively deterritorialized. Place is relatively reterritorialized. Practice, the movement of actors and the flux of relations, tends to deterritorialize (in that possibilities not marked by codes and forms are actualized); but it also reterritorializes because these formations themselves are actualized. The movement through space does not actualize all the possibilities of that place. Indeed, what one has to work with is limited, structured. The museum exhibit presents a place (a cyberplace) that is then actualized by the visitor into a cyber*space*.

Place, de Certeau argues, is like a city in that there are walls that restrict one's movement, streets that allow certain types of movement (traffic) but only in determined directions, and so on. He writes that "a spatial order organizes an ensemble of possibilities (e.g., by a place in which one can move), and interdictions (e.g., by a wall that prevents one from going further)" (de Certeau, 1984, p. 98). Any single walk through a space (as the actualized place becomes) engages only some of the interdictions (you will encounter only a few walls, not all of them), while others remain unrealized. Likewise, only some of the possibilities for movement will be actualized. By walking through the city, the pedestrian "moves [interdictions and possibilities] about and . . . invents others, since the crossing, drifting away, or improvisation of walking privilege, transform or abandon spatial elements" (de Certeau, 1984, p. 98).

One's walk creates possibilities not accounted for by the city's struc-tures[9] and thus deterritorializes. But the walk reterritorializes because some of the structures remain, the rules are followed (we enter buildings through doors, or we use sidewalks).

One approaches technology *like* one would approach social space, and one approaches technology *when* one approaches social space. Tech-nology, like place, preexists human actors. It is a complex articulation of potentials, of para- and epistrata. A technology is composed of a multi-plicity of social actors, of determining forces: molecular aggregates (NaCl, $C_8H_{10}N_4O_2–H_2O$, etc.); social needs; economic possibilities; re-lated processes, systems, and technologies; and so forth. These potentials are actualized and social space is created through the movement of actors through the place of technology. In other words, place becomes space through the living of the double articulation of language and technology (note that this does not necessarily mean merely through the *introduction* of language but rather through their articulation). That moment, the living of the double articulation, creates human social space and actual-izes the potentials of technological form (and linguistic structures and distributions as well). One can never approach technology in isolation, except in the abstract. Likewise, social places of power can be mapped only through their effects in the dynamic social space (from these effects, we may try to create an abstract model of that place).

The visitor to the Communications Exhibit is stitched into the social place presented by the exhibit primarily in two ways: One is by taking an active part in the exhibit experience, and the second is through the specific use of language. Thus both aspects of the stratification of social space (technology/language) are addressed. The Communication exhibit was designed with three primary audiences in mind: (1) students and teachers, (2) adult visitors, and (3) business and public dignitaries receiving VIP tours (MSI, 1991, p. 1). All audiences, the initial proposal writes, "will be best served by a fully interactive exhibit consisting of a series of hands-on experiences to help visitors *sense* what the future holds" (p. 2).

One of the attractions of museums is their reliance on what Alan Morton (1988) calls "the romance of the real," or that actual objects are on display. Museums of Science and Industry since the Deutsches Museum was founded in Munich around the turn of the century have added to this by designing their exhibits to be used and manipulated by the visitors. This hands-on experience fosters a sense of control in the individual over the equipment, that one has somehow mastered the technology by making it work. The appeal of the hands-on approach is emphasized by the fearful rise of "autonomous" technologies in the 20th century—in the context of the museum, one literally brings these technologies under one's physical control (Winner, 1977, p. 25). But as communication and information technologies intrude further into domestic space, they become ever more a part of our everyday lives, and so the prospect of an exhibit of communication technology becomes less attractive (why go to a museum to see or use a telephone?). The romance of the real then becomes a revealing, or dissection, of common technologies (phones, TVs) to show them in a new and privileged way or to show the technologies *behind* the technologies (switching technologies, the wires themselves, etc.). The MSI here plays with the tension that Robert Bud (1988) describes as between myth and machine. On the one hand, museums are considered "sacred" or "mythic" spaces where artifacts reside within an "aura" of authenticity (Bud, 1988, pp. 135-136). On the other hand, it is now a profane space where the sacred object is dissected into its various components for educational purposes. But then these components (switching devices, fiber optic cables, etc.) themselves take on the aura.

A visitor gains a sense of control over technology by making it work or by seeing what is usually hidden. This feeling of control is mirrored in the layout of the exhibit itself. Rather than being led through a determined progression of stations, the visitor is free to wander about (window shopping, an activity with which it has deep resonance[10]) and therefore control his or her own experience of the exhibit as well. But this freedom is designed into the exhibit: "The design [of the Communications Exhibit] parallels the principles set out in the Museum's MSI 2000 plan, favoring *nonlinear, multi-layered experiences* appealing to visitors with a variety of learning styles," and the thematic structure follows "a *nonlinear* storyline [*sic*]" (Aldrich, 1993, p. 1). The exhibit is designed to allow visitors to traverse the exhibit in their own styles (according to their own interests and needs) and still get the message of the exhibit.[11] Michel de Certeau (1984), writing about the city, says that

> the walker actualizes some of these possibilities [of the place]. . . . But he [*sic*] also moves them about and he invents others, since the crossing, drifting away, or improvisation of walking privilege, transform or abandon spatial elements. (p. 98)

But the spatial order in the case of the exhibit tries to assume a certain amount of drifting in the first place. Remember that de Certeau distinguishes between "style" (a singular processing of the symbolic environment) and "use" (the normative code) (p. 100). The individual visitor will exhibit his or her own style of use, which the exhibit tries to presuppose via its "nonlinear storylines"; and this whole particular movement— that of the visitor as *flâneur*—is profoundly modern (and masculine; cf. Massey, 1994). Though the visitors have some freedom, the exhibit nevertheless has a determined structure (the progress of technology). For example, the main exhibit hall culminates in the telepresence stages, at which visitors can creatively exhibit their style but only within the context of the technological system, within "use." In the context of the MSI exhibit, the resistance and freedom de Certeau sees in "style" is severely constrained by the technological coding of "use" of the new communication and information networks.

Along with the practice of traversing the exhibit physically and handling it manually, the exhibit discursively articulates the visitor into a subject position within the stratification by the select use of "you" and "we" to help the visitor explicitly identify with the goals and progress of the U.S. communications industry. For example, at the end of the timeline is the following passage:

> *Our Challenge:* It is up to each of us to help plan and shape what the future will bring. How will we communicate in the future? How will we direct our technological capabilities? What new developments would you like to see?

By this strategy, visitors are placed in the position where they can supposedly control the direction and use of these technologies (which the exhibit also says are developing autonomously). This strategy is mirrored in the activity packet distributed to teachers and students (MSI, 1993), which ends with the students' developing their own communication technology. The global communications network, the exhibit says at one point, is the biggest machine in the world; and it is a machine that we can control from our phones (and, now, modems).

One of the factors drawing us to the exhibit is that not only are we seeing what we otherwise might not have seen, but we are touching what we are not allowed to touch elsewhere (try reconfiguring your cable TV connection or, God forbid, hooking it up yourself). We control these technologies in the MSI because we have little control outside the museum space. The exhibit fosters a sense of control that is false because from our phones, modems, and interactive televisions, we do not have any control over the system itself or most of its workings. The global language of digitalization is part of Technology, not Language. What Virilio (1993) calls "telecommanding" ("the so-called tact at a distance," p. 7), though achieving almost immediate effects at a distance, does it within the possibilities (the coding or norms) of the technological system. Here technology and language are not at odds but seem to be in synch in a technicist stratification: Technology expands globally, language shrinks to that of "use." The term *use* is conflated with *control*, so that individual use of these technologies is thought to have actual effects independent of the normative constraints of the system.[12] But this is not to push Deleuze's use of "language" into individualist, voluntarist notions of power. The focus on individual uses of technologies is merely part of this particular configuration of language. The reduction of language to "use" indicates the general inability to intervene in reality and achieve effects except through technological means, or means deeply resonant with technological configurations.

For Virilio, the abandonment of actual effects accompanies an abandonment of the body through telepresence. The "plugged-in" human being, complete with multiple prostheses and interfaces, becomes the virtual equivalent of a paraplegic. The shift toward this new stratification results in the creation of a *terminal citizen*.

> The shift is ultimately felt in the very body of every city dweller, as a *terminal citizen* who will soon be equipped with interactive prostheses whose pathological model is that of the "motorized handicapped," equipped so that he or she can control the domestic environment without undergoing any physical displacement. We have before us the catastrophic figure of an individual who has lost, along with his or her natural mobility, any immediate means of intervening in the environment. The fate of the individual is handed over, for better or for worse, to the capacities of receivers, sensors, and other long-range detectors that turn the person into a being subjected to the machines with which, they say, he or she is "in dialogue"! (Virilio, 1993, p. 11)

There seems to be a convergence, he writes, of the politics of disability ("I demand that a global politics for the handicapped become a strong axis of social Europe," says François Mitterand [quoted in Virilio, 1993, p. 11]) and the increasing teleactivity of the so-called "able" (or "valid"). However, the politics of disability argues for "the inalienable right that the handicapped person has to live as others do and therefore *with others*" (pp. 11-12), while "able" terminal citizens become increasingly isolated and inert. In the literature of cyberpunk it is therefore not surprising to have computer hackers refer to their nonvirtual selves as "meat" (see Hayles, 1993a). In this context, we have to see as ironic the positioning in the Communications Exhibit of the video presentation regarding the benefits of these new technologies for the disabled next to the telepresence stages (which flank the passageway that leads eventually to the "Imaging Technologies" exhibit beyond—an exhibit that ends with a demonstration of virtual reality).

If we shift Virilio's argument from one of body versus machine (which leaves us not only within the modern dialectic of Master/Slave, but in the problematic of identity) to one of the stratification of technology and language, and if we ignore possible arguments as to what constitutes the "natural mobility" of a human being, we see that the growing inertia of the terminal citizen is that of the reduction of language to "use" rather than merely (the possibly very real) passivity of the body per se.[13] It is the inability to achieve effects outside of the technological system, or rather, outside the normative coding that territorializes these technological systems. This is the passivity not just of the immobile body but of the ineffectual agent.

There is a consistent emphasis on the interiority of cyberspace—from Gibson's (1984) definition of it as a consensual hallucination to John Parry Barlow's definition as the place we are when we're on the phone (in Elmer-Dewitt, 1995). "By emphasizing its interiority rather than the geopolitical and cultural interfaces that form it, the ideology of cyberspace is enforced instead of being critically thought out" (Gabilondo, 1995, p. 429).

Let me be clear here as to what I am describing in this chapter. I am not attempting to describe a generalized, abstract social formation such as "postmodernism." Rather, this is a specific social formation within a specific national and economic location. Actually, I should say that what is being described (in AT&T's commercials and Ameritech's exhibit) is one possible corporate version of what the social formation should be. It is a version that I am attempting to unpack and critique. At the same time, I wish to show the ways that the social formation has been shifting in the 1980s and 90s, and how these visions of teletopia are on the one hand responding to and working out of that shift, and on the other feeding into and influencing that shift.

What, then, are we to make of the MSI Communications Exhibit? It is more than simply an advertisement for Ameritech and the rest of the U.S. telecommunication industry; and, likewise, to conclude that it is hege- monic and establishmentarian is facile. The exhibit, like any other exhibit, is a disciplinary apparatus, one that positions visitors within discourses of power and structures of knowledge. We have seen the way the exhibit articulates the visitor into its social formation. But what we have also seen are the characteristics of that social formation over and beyond what its self-described characteristics are.

I will name this formation *the problematic of the terminal citizen*, a formation within which technologies appear increasingly autonomous and deterministic despite much advertisement to the contrary. The problematic of the terminal citizen is a formation in which agency is predominantly technological. Viewed in more traditional terms, as I have just done above ("autonomous" and "deterministic"), the problematic seems dire (indeed, we fall back into the apocalyptic proclamations of Ellul and

Marcuse that seem to be echoed by Virilio). Rather, we need to explore this technological agency; what are the possibilities of movement, attachment, resistance, and power within this particular formation? It may be a form of agency that we are not used to, but we may have to learn to maneuver in different terms.

How can we describe the formation in terms of Henri Lefebvre's three concepts of social space? The spatial practice in this formation is primarily technological and explicitly fosters a sense of individual control. This sense is emphasized by the exhibit's hands-on approach as well as the very everydayness of many of the exhibit's objects: telephones. Practice is characterized by this assumption of personal agency but is actually overcoded by the needs of the dominant system. We are users of the system but have little effect on how it is run or where it goes. More generally, our limited agency is exemplified in the "idiot button" that appears in more "user-friendly" computer software interfaces such as the Macintosh and Windows (Ullmann, 1995, esp. pp. 141-142). This is the button that appears at the bottom of a warning box. The warning may read that your hard drive has imploded, your book manuscript has disappeared, or that viruses are rampant in your system. The only thing the computer will let you do (besides physically turning it off) is click on the button. The button says, "OK." You have to accept the system's decisions. You have no option and no choice. But it makes you perform the action nonetheless; you must click to be in control.

The conception of social space prevalent in the exhibit is that of the globe within reach, the collapse of distance. Conceptually, the social space of the new assemblage is marked by ideas of control and efficiency, in other words, of a technicist agency. And we have discussed the representations of space—social space as it is lived—in examining the articulation of visitors into the exhibit.

As I said in an earlier chapter, culture is the particular arrangement of relations among these three concepts in social space. The culture represented in the exhibit, then, consists of the circulation of communication technologies that we feel are under our control and that allow us virtually unlimited agency. It is a culture undergirded by a criterion of efficiency and progress. This is the culture of the terminal citizen.

In these terms, what is striking about the culture of the new technological assemblage is that it is an overwhelmingly corporate culture. From the covers of *Wired* magazine, to cybersalons, pages on the World

Wide Web, to ever more popular and sophisticated CD-ROM video-
games, the culture of cyberspace is that of communication and information corporations. This is especially marked in the corporate presence in
the MSI exhibit. The very concept of culture (in addition to its practice
and representations) is intimately articulated to the conception of a free
market economy.

Lefebvre (1978) argues that "each mode of production has its space;
but the characteristics of space do not amount to the general characteristics of the mode of production" (p. 292; quoted in Gregory, 1994,
p. 382). In other words, we cannot say that social space is ultimately
determined by the mode of production (in a more traditional Marxist
base/superstructure theory), of which technology is a part. In other
words, the social space traced out in the exhibit is not *necessarily* corporate, and the new communication and information assemblage is not
necessarily capitalistic. I do not mean to ignore or dispute the mode of
production's obvious role in the determination of either technology or
social space. Manuel Castells (1989) argues fairly persuasively that what
he terms the informational mode of development (i.e., the forces of
production driven by information) has a profound impact on social
space.[14]

But we must remember that

> We are confronted not by one social space but by many— indeed, by
> an unlimited multiplicity or uncountable set of social spaces that we
> refer to generically as "social space." No space disappears in the course
> of growth and development: the *worldwide does not abolish the local.*
> (Lefebvre, 1991, p. 86)

Social space is always multiple, interpenetrable, contradictory, and
durable. We talk of social spaces. Global space does not eradicate local
space. In fact, what is taken to be global space is often solely a dominant
conception of global space that is but a local space writ large (global
space, as well as local space, is then ideological; i.e., The World, Live! and
the Worldspeak Globe). Capitalism is not necessarily a global phenomena, though it presents itself as such and attempts to so structure global
conceptual space (through universalizing terms). Likewise, though the
social space of a nation may be dominated by, for example, U.S. mass-
mediated representations, this does not mean that any particular local
social space within, overlapping, or adjacent to that national space is
necessarily so dominated.

It is here that Latour's long networks become useful. But if a social space is an actor-network, it is much more than simply political alliances among animate and inanimate actors; the network would also consist of the practices that make it up, renew it and transform it, as well as concepts of the network itself,[15] and the representational experience of the network. The purpose of this chapter is to describe the ways the exhibit "translates" the visitor into the network. The space of the exhibit is part of a longer network. We as visitors are translated to fit the National Information Infrastructure. National spaces and global spaces, then, are simply longer networks than local ones. James Hay (1993, p. 45) reminds us, "the very concepts of 'local' and 'global' are always *constructed* through media and other cultural discourses and through emerging and residual ways of imagining social relations." However, real differences (differences that cannot be collapsed into convenient abstractions like local and global) arise between these networks, differences in power. These differences in power do not occur simply by the enlistment of different actors but by their stratification, differentiation, and territorialization. Networks may move to open borders, deterritorialize, and reterritorialize, but they are always already territorialized to begin with. If we reduce postindustrial capitalism to just another long network, we ignore much of its power and influence on all aspects of social space and on the stratification of that space itself.

Notes

1. I would like to thank Bill Berry at the University of Illinois at Urbana-Champaign for his encouragement and resourcefulness in directing me toward the materials and people that are the sources for part of this chapter. In addition, I would like to thank Joe Vessely at Ameritech and Marvin Pinkert at the Museum of Science and Industry, who were both very helpful and generous.

   An earlier version of this chapter was presented at the International Communications Association Annual Conference in Albuquerque, NM, May 1995.

   The MSI holds all rights to exhibit text and associated exhibit preparation documents. These are quoted here with permission. *The opinions in this chapter are those of its author; they do not reflect the views of the MSI, Ameritech, or their employees.*

2. Officially, the exhibit is copyrighted by Ameritech; at the entrance to the exhibit, a plaque lists additional sponsors.

3. Bernard Finn's assessment of science museums is somewhat dated, but his discussion of the role of the curator in a science museum is relevant here (Finn, 1965).

4. Cf. Walter Benjamin's work on arcades and world expositions. See Buck-Morss, 1989.

5. "Sales Activities" in general account for 28% of museum revenue (MSI, 1992).

6. In a talk at the University of Illinois, Willard ("Sandy") Boyd, president of the Field Museum of Natural History in Chicago, mentioned that in our culture, at least, people tend to turn right on entering a space. This, then, is an assumption of museum designers, which places the Communications exhibit very prominently within museum space. ("Museums as Centers of Public Learning About Environmental and Cultural Issues," Program for the Study of Cultural Values and Ethics, University of Illinois at Urbana-Champaign, March 23, 1994.)

7. Carolyn Marvin (1988) argues that anxieties over presence in the early days of the telephone mask anxieties over crumbling class divisions. Older methods of visually assessing a person's class or race were erased by "telephonic anonymity," and methods of maintaining social distance and propriety were problematized (esp. chap. 2).

8. When the museum opened, Chicago was, in fact, part of the exhibit. The museum building was originally constructed as the Palace of Fine Arts for the 1893 World's Columbian Exposition, and is the last remaining structure from that Exposition's "Great White City." It was extensively renovated, and the MSI opened in 1933 in conjunction with Chicago's "Century of Progress Exposition" (see Kaempffert, 1933; I am also relying here on background information provided by the MSI).

9. For an example of such an unexpected movement, see Italo Calvino's Baron, leaping from tree to tree, never to touch the earth again (Calvino, 1980).

10. Again, see Benjamin's work; Buck-Morss, 1989.

11. An illustrative parallel can be found in Chris Riding's (1995) account of the MicroGallery, a virtual version of the British National Gallery, located in a new wing of the museum, that visitors can browse before negotiating the museum itself: "the system enhances the museum-goer's walk" (p. 246). And later:

> The key to the seduction of the MicroGallery lies in navigating the information and not in the information itself: the latter is always subordinated to the former. The seduction is the lure of the labyrinth and the aura of technology; one moves through it in the manner of a rhizome rather than a linear sequence. (pp. 248-249)

But, in the end, no matter how one moves it seems, it is still a canonical space that is being negotiated. What is interesting as well about the Micro-Gallery is that it is available on CD-ROM, so that after your visit you can not only purchase artifacts and replicas, you can take the whole museum home with you!

12. Langdon Winner makes a similar distinction. What I am calling "use" here roughly corresponds to what he refers to as "utilization," which is passive. "Use," in his terminology ("the whole line or sequence of thought, action and fulfillment" [Winner, 1977, p. 229]), corresponds more with de Certeau's "style of use," though without the focus on individual practice.

13. In any case, similar arguments about the potential passivity of the individual were used against the wide dissemination of books in the 19th century and television in the 20th.

14. Castells (1991): "Modes of development evolve according to their own logic; they do not respond mechanically to the demands of the modes of production or of other instances of society" (p. 11). However, he also argues, though not in these terms, that technology is autonomous.

15. And here the actor-network methodology of describing a network from the perspective of its actors becomes useful.

6

Welcome to Your Assemblage

In Chapter 4, I traced a shift in popular notions of technology. The chapter examined how a positive, social constructivist view of technology was being articulated to AT&T's global network of communication and information technologies. Through these new technologies, we (as individuals and as humans) become empowered and are able to solve the dilemmas of the past (e.g., the cold war) and it is hoped, prevent future crises.

Chapter 5 described how visitors to a museum are presented with, and articulated into, a similar vision of an empowering global network of communication and information technologies. This vision has more recently become a U.S. government policy in the form of the National Information Infrastructure. The policy itself has captured popular imagination and has been named the Information Superhighway.

The purpose of this chapter is to begin to explore this vision as it has been taken up in popular discourse, and in doing so, I will continue the analysis from the last chapter of the double articulation that constitutes the social space of the new technological assemblage. In particular, I hope to show how the advent of a terminal citizenry can be read in the debates.

Visions have believers, and this vision is no exception. In particular, it has a patron saint (Marshall McLuhan) and assorted sects of communitarians, libertarians, and luddites. To take the pulse, assess the dimensions of this vision, let us take a brief look at these visions and roles: policy struggles over the National Information Infrastructure (NII); the popularization of the NII; debates over access, abuse, and viability; AT&T's corporate telecommunity; the political struggles within *Wired* magazine; and the figure of the Intelligent Agent.

NII Assemblage

The National Information Infrastructure (or National Data Superhighway, Electronic Superhighway, Information Superhighway, Infobahn, or Information Highway) officially began in the fall of 1992 as a plan by then President-elect Bill Clinton and VP-elect Al Gore, Jr., to improve the country's economic infrastructure. As a plan for economic restructuring, the NII solidified trends that placed the nation's economic future in the hands of information and communication industries. Though these technologies have been dominant since the late 1970s, the U.S. government's involvement with them mainly has been confined to either regulation (e.g., the 1984 AT&T divestiture) or defense (e.g., SDI). Compared to other Western industrialized nations, the U.S. government's general attitude toward domestic communication and information technology in the last 20 years has been remarkably laissez-faire, except for extensive military investment, of course (Webster & Robins, 1986). Such an attitude is surprising, given that information is key to neo-Fordist economic formations and also has been considered a mode of production in its own right (Castells, 1989).

The NII proposal can be seen as an attempt to directly stimulate the United States' stagnating post–cold war economy. Rather than simply encouraging the development and expansion of specific industries, Clinton-Gore proposed the construction of a high-speed network of fiber optic lines, switching stations, and file-server supercomputer sites that would expand and enhance the domestic circulation of data. The government had already been financing the development of new technologies that could handle the speed, volume, and sophistication needed if the NII was to work. In 1991, for example, then-Senator Al Gore sponsored legislation (The High Performance Computing Act) to finance a National Research and Education Network (NREN), which would develop these new technologies and ideally speed up current abilities to transfer data by a factor of six (Markoff, 1993, p. 4).

What makes it possible to bring together such a diverse series of networks, or even consider such a thing, is the increase in "translatability" between different media and networks (fiber optics, coaxial cable, phone lines, analog and digital signals, television, telephones, databases, etc.).[1] This is referred to in the buzzwords of the NII as "convergence," which (from the perspective of information technology) amounts to digitalization.[2] Digitalization was one of the central themes of the MSI exhibit in the last chapter. With common technologies in place, it is the configuration (rather than composition) of the system itself and the media that dominate it that will play the greatest role in what the NII actually means.

The primary debate in late 1992, early 1993 (soon after the announcement of the administration's proposal at an economic roundtable) was not *whether* such a network should be built (i.e., if it was necessary or even feasible) but *who* should build it. Misunderstanding the government's position as actually wanting to build the infrastructure itself (an assumption that would place the administration further to the political left than its more centrist position), it was pointed out by industry sources that models and networks already existed. These included not just the Internet (which is the name given to a loose collection of services available over a decentralized series of computer networks) but other commercial data networks (Prodigy, America Online, etc.), plus cable television systems (and not just interactive cable systems), and the fiber optic networks of the long-distance telephone companies (AT&T, MCI, Sprint, and so forth) and the Regional Bell Operating Companies (RBOCs): Ameritech, Bell Atlantic, BellSouth, Nynex, Pacific Telesis, Southwestern Bell, and US West. If Gore's intention was to spur a reluctant telecommunications industry into action, as some have suggested (see, e.g., Markoff, 1993), he seems to have succeeded. But it should be noted that private industries are getting more actively involved in the NII probably because the government has already financed or is financing the expensive new technologies necessary (Markoff, 1993, p. 4).

The debate in early 1993, then, was not between a government built and run system and a private system (or systems), but rather between different combinations of the two. Gore's main arguments for government involvement with the project are: (1) Without government the private industry would not do much on its own; and (2) private companies would build private networks, and the network should be open to all Americans (Markoff, 1993, p. 4). In opposition to Gore are the phone companies, which do not mind the government developing new technologies for them but do not want a government network competing with the phone system; they would rather use or transform the current system. The RBOCs and cable companies do not want that competition either, but would center the NII around their own current systems.

The administration's model for the NII seems to be the Internet. The Internet began in 1969 as a Department of Defense Project called ARPAnet to create a computer network that could survive a nuclear attack[3] (Krol, 1993, p. 12). It was spurred by the same cold war mentality that justified the building of the freeways in the 1940s and 50s.[4] By the late 1970s, ARPAnet had been joined by other networks, most prominently NSFnet run by the National Science Foundation. The system was structured so that any computer on a network could access any other (even if they were different types of computers). As the networks were deliberately designed around the same hardware and software capacities (or "protocols"), networks could "talk" to one another, so that a computer on any one network could access a computer on any other network (potentially). This combination of independent networks is referred to as the Internet. In January 1993, soon after the proposal was announced, it was estimated that over 10 million people used the Internet (Markoff, 1993, p. 6). Just over a year later, there were an estimated 20 million users and 150,000 new users each month (Reinhardt, 1994, p. 49). Current, 1996, estimates range from 30 to 40 million. For example, America Online, a private computer network that provides access to the Internet, doubled its subscriptions between summer, 1993, and early 1994, and had to scramble to update its equipment to keep up with the demand ("The Net," 1994, p. 49).

The Internet, as it now stands, is a decentered, nonhierarchical organization of computer networks (see Krol, 1993). Control of each network is left to that system's System Administrator (or SysAdmin). Governance for the entire Internet is loosely provided by an oligarchical committee of SysAdmins, though most of their decisions concern the establishment, maintenance, and upgrading of standard equipment (e.g., trunk phone lines) and protocols to keep the Internet running smoothly. Information (data, messages, etc.) that passes through the Internet is not distributed by a central service like the Post Office. Rather, each packet of information is "locally intelligent" and routes itself to its destination. The route it takes depends on the state of various switchers and servers that it encounters. For example, if I am carrying on a correspondence with a colleague in Texas and send that person five different e-mail messages, each message may take a completely different route to get there. Distance really is fairly irrelevant to this system. The geography of the Internet is radically different from either the physical geography of, say, the United States, or the political geography of any cartographic representation.

The vast bulk of the traffic on the Internet is the transfer of data for research purposes (its original intent). What gains the highest profile are its more entertaining options: e-mail, newsgroups, Internet Relay Chats (IRCs), interactive environments such as Multi-User Domains or Dungeons (MUDs), games, and so on. They loom larger in popular consciousness than the actual percentage of traffic would indicate. These services provide multiple opportunities for affective attachment; as a result, there are discussion groups about almost anything (breakfast cereal, *Star Trek*, boats, politics, etc.).

The advantages to the system are many (apart from being able to survive a war—if any server or line goes down, messages automatically reroute themselves on remaining lines). It is possible to distribute messages cheaply to a large number of people (or to a select group of people) simultaneously without relying on a more centralized distribution service (public, like the USPS, or private like UPS). Also, not being part of a hierarchical system means that fairly free discussions (depending on the SysAdmin) can take place on newsgroups or IRCs (where people "chat," in real time, on-line). The Internet provides alternative media to disseminate information effectively. Groups are able to present alternative versions of events to those depicted in traditional media such as television or newspapers, or report events that those media do not cover. Such reports have been issued from China, Croatia, Iraq, and the Mexican state of Chiapas. Despite these possibilities for resistance and for resistant uses, access to the Internet is still somewhat privileged (limited, for instance, by the costs of computers and connections), leaving the Internet open to charges of elitism.

NII → Information Superhighway: Policy to Social Movement

The NII, as the proposal stood in early 1993, concerned mainly a network for data transfer for business and research. Only brief mention is made (e.g., in John Markoff's *New York Times* article) of the possibilities for entertainment—video on demand or interactive entertainment. But the prospect of a nationwide fiber optic network renewed proposals dating back to the late 1970s for interactive television (i.e., Videotext), high-definition television, and so on.[5] Soon it was not just the phone companies, computer industry, and government involved in these debates but the entertainment industry as well, particularly cable television, which saw the information highway as direct competition.

By April 1993, when the NII hit the major news magazines as cover stories, entertainment and leisure were the primary selling points and the proposal had taken on the popular title, the "Information Highway." Articles in *Time* magazine (April 12), for example, focused on the "communicopia of entertainment, information and interactive services" (Elmer-Dewitt, 1993, p. 52) and the multiplication (and eventual obsolescence) of television channels (Zoglin, 1993); while *Newsweek* (May 31) focused more broadly on "interactivity." Most articles concerned the impact of these technologies on the home and on leisure. The government's role regarding the Information Highway was clarified as not actually building it but playing a supporting and guiding role. *Time's* Elmer-Dewitt characterized the Clinton administration as "scrambling to see how the government can join in the fun" amidst the competition of cable and the telecommunication companies (p. 51). Vice President Gore stated that "[p]rivate industry will take the lead role, of course, and government will play the role of facilitator and administrator" (Belsie, 1993, p. 4).

The Internet itself has become a space of increased popular affective attachment, as indicated by its tremendous growth over the past 2 years (1995-1997). For example, a cousin of mine recently remarked that she wanted to get an e-mail address not because she needed one nor that there were particular activities she wanted to pursue, but simply to *have* one. An e-mail address (especially a specific type of address, including a homepage on the World Wide Web) is somewhat hip. Both *Newsweek* and *Time* have begun weekly columns on "Cyberspace," keeping up with the latest developments (mainly cultural) on the Net; and *Newsweek* launched the quarterly *Virtual City: Your Guide to CyberCulture* in fall, 1995. A recent poll found that though 57% of those polled "didn't know what cyberspace meant . . . 85% were certain that information technology had made their lives better" (Elmer-Dewitt, 1995, p. 6).

But the Internet is not without its debates. In terms of agency, three of the main debates concern access, the use or abuse of the system, and the viability of the system. The most prominent debate over the NII, as an expansion of the Internet, is precisely the question of access. On the policy level, access refers to the perceived social need for the NII to be available to all citizens—this is part of Vice President Gore's NII campaign—and relies on the vision of the Infrastructure as a national/ natural resource. Beyond the physical connections to schools and public sites like libraries, most of these debates concern access to information. The problem with questions of access is that they reify whatever it is that we are to have access to as something central to our lives without which we would otherwise be destitute. They, therefore, redirect debate away from the technologies or services themselves. It may be that lack of access proves a hindrance to the more equitable distribution of power, but first we need to examine how that service is being territorialized and what is territorializing it. Moreover, universal access is hardly realistic (since even telephones have not accomplished this yet—at least 7 million U.S. homes do not have a telephone [Ratan, 1995, p. 26]).[6] The access debates often play out among sweeping rhetorical gestures to the increased separation between the wired haves and the tired have-nots.[7] How such an elitist, separatist system would be much different from the situation today is hard to tell. Indeed, it is the split between the information haves and have-nots that has driven the proposal for a New International Information and Communication Order (NIICO) since the late 1970s, a proposal that I will be looking at more closely toward the end of this book.

How will the system be used, will it be used, will it be misused? This is the second debate. "Use," or "interactivity," is often confused with control (as we saw in the last chapter). Some distinctions along these lines are noted by writers in the field. For example, Denise Caruso, editor of *Digital Media*, contrasts "false interactivity" (merely choosing which movie to watch on TV) to "true interactive" or "complete viewer control," by which she means something along the lines of telepresence: "A user might stand in front of a monitor/receiver and just talk or listen, communicating with whatever or whomever is Out There. Images and voices would be beamed back and forth" (quoted in Kantrowitz, 1993, p. 44).

Andy Reinhardt, in *Byte*'s March 1994 cover story on the "Data Highway," makes a similar contrast between information *consumption* (mere use) on the Internet and *communication* (which implies control). Which direction the Highway develops in, Reinhardt (1994) argues, depends in part on the machinery and wiring of the Highway itself (p. 48). Allocating bandwidth into and out of homes and other sites determines the extent that individuals can move data *out* of their terminals—presumably in communication with other users—rather than just being able to send the signal requesting *The Home Shopping Network* at 7:30 and *The Terminator* at 7:50. Both Reinhardt and Kantrowitz worry that the potential of the Highway will not be met and users will merely be channel-surfing consumers (with little agency). But though wider bandwidth and interactive services and software are necessary in the production of more extensive effects, they are not sufficient to guarantee it.

What is considered use or abuse depends in part on where one stands and where one wants to go. The NII does provide the possibility for a fairly active agency (e.g., to be more than simply consumers). However, the geography of cyberspace is increasingly territorialized by capitalism and is increasingly user-friendly, which limits the possibilities of radical agency. Machines become friendlier, easier to use, only when our options are restricted. When using a computer, for instance, we are responding to its structures and the range of possibilities it allows or limits. The development of Graphical User Interfaces (GUIs, especially the popular "desktop" look as well as the virtual rooms of Microsoft's "Bob" interface), moving from the Macintosh to Microsoft's popular "Windows" and "Windows 95" and beyond to more icon-driven systems, further limits our effectiveness (Kantrowitz, 1994, p. 49).[8] In terms of the Internet, we can see this shift in the development of new user-friendly interfaces (both in interactive services like AOL as well as the World Wide Web "browser wars" between Netscape, Microsoft, and others). Such interfaces remove the user from direct access to the Unix command structure of the Internet. However, at the same time, these new interfaces allow greater numbers of users to work on the Internet without having to struggle with the complexities of Unix, a system, like DOS, that tends toward the arcane. Indeed, user-friendly access to the Internet is one of the major selling points of private data networks.[9] When considering agency and new technologies, a balance needs to be struck between the populism of the user interface and the actual possibilities of achieving effects.

What constitutes the "use" of the Highway is usually defined negatively, in terms of the abuse, or potential abuse, of the system. "Abuse" usually concerns issues of consumer privacy, advertising intrusion, government spying, and corporate spying on labor (Kantrowitz, 1993, p. 44). Interestingly, all of these center around *institutional* abuses of the system rather than individual abuses. Perhaps this derives from the ideology of individualism that pervades cyberculture—teenage hackers and fictional "console cowboys" (Ross, 1991). Individual abuses, most often "flaming" (the posting of inflammatory *ad hominem* statements about other users), are taken care of by the virtual community—the abuser is publicly reprimanded by other users.[10] At times, a certain retaliation in kind is carried out as the community attempts to flood, jam, and shut down the abuser's e-mail box. This sort of "frontier justice" is representative of libertarianism, which itself has a marked presence in discourses about the Internet. This is evidenced by *Wired* magazine's (a central publication for this information culture) foregrounding and support of organizations such as the Electronic Frontier Foundation (which lobbies Washington for individual rights in cyberspace) and prominent articles on the so-called hacker underground.

However, one question that runs under these others is that of the viability of the NII: Can it work? Indeed, one can trace a backlash of sorts against the proposal:[11] Convergence probably won't happen like they are describing it; telephone and cable signals are incompatible; no computer system could handle the potential demand (e.g., if several people in the same area want to watch the same film at slightly different times); consumers won't want it or won't use it; and so forth. The problem with this line of argument is that it is irrelevant. It does not matter if the systems and pipe dreams (or fiber dreams) are never realized, those are not the point. Vincent Mosco (1989a, 1989b) once argued of Ronald Reagan's SDI plans that the ability of SDI to do what it was designed to do did not matter (it probably would not work after all), because SDI was *already working* by successfully reorienting U.S. industrial, economic, and defense policies (and ideologies of defense). The same applies to the NII: *It is already working.* As Vice President Gore has said:

> We have already begun to implement the changes that were outlined
> in that policy and we are already seeing a response in the private sector.
> We have had a long series of meetings with industry groups who are
> beginning to shift investment priorities in accord with the vision that

President Clinton and I outlined earlier this year. We are already seeing a reallocation of funding within the federal programs by the appointees that have been put in place by the administration. (Belsie, 1993, p. 4)[12]

What the NII proposal is doing is setting the economic and industrial policy directions of Internet geography—a move that will have a powerful impact on the structure of global communication and information networks. It is under the name of the NII that the 1996 Telecommunication Bill was passed, allowing direct competition between cable television companies and local and long-distance telephone providers.

To expand the Internet into a free public service essentially would be to establish a socialist information network, an outcome that is not, alas, to be. Indeed, to allow the Internet to continue expanding at its current phenomenal rate as a government-sponsored service is anathema to an administration that seems intent on continuing the New Right's agenda of deregulation (despite attempts at passing universal health care) (cf. the aforementioned telecommunications bill).

The future of the NII, like that of the Internet, is almost entirely in private hands. The free and anarchic space that characterized the earlier days of the Internet (though how free and anarchic it really was is subject to debate) is being reterritorialized into a commercial space, an extension of U.S. entertainment industries.

What the NII actually is (or will be) depends on who is describing it: the government, cable (CATV) companies, telecommunication companies, or those on the Internet (Reinhardt, 1994, pp. 48-49). Each of these presents a different conceptual space. The government views the NII as an economic resource, an industrial infrastructure, and the redirection of industrial policy. Internet users (to risk overgeneralization) view the NII differently. The Internet usually characterizes itself around a sense of community that develops between its users and the free access to almost unlimited data. Users are wary of the commercialization and privatization of the Internet. Cable companies envision the NII as structured around interactive television, where programs and information services appear like multiple channels. The telecommunication companies envision a similar system but structured around their own networks of fiber optics, as opposed to the coaxial cable of CATV.

Individual users concerned about government censorship and oppression, corporations concerned about competition and production and R&D secrets,[13] and the federal government concerned about national security and economic infrastructure: Each of these positions generally takes up a different metaphor for the NII; for users it can be an ocean, for the corporations a highway, or for the government a railroad. What metaphor one chooses affects how one conceptualizes the space one moves through. This conceptualization affects, in turn, the possibilities for movement one considers.

One of the dominant views of the Internet (and, by extension, of the Information Highway) found within cyberculture itself is that of the Internet as *ocean*, usually accompanied by surfing references (i.e., *Wired's* monthly column, "Net Surf," and *Mondo 2000's* mission to "Surf the New Edge"). What is conveyed is a certain *attitude* toward the Net, that of the cyberpunk, the hacker, the (white, male) individual living on the edge.[14] The Net (as it is called) is a three-dimensional space as well; the ocean net is cyber*space*—space where information is "longing to be free" (in the words of *Mondo 2000*, a cyberspace magazine). This vision of a deterritorialized space of free information[15] is articulated to equally powerful metaphors of the Net as frontier (complete with "console cowboys"). The frontier is much like the beach, however, where the active participants are men-on-the-(new)edge; women are passive objects of domesticity or desire; and legality is ad hoc ("netiquette"). And, as Richard Slotkin (1985) writes, the myth of the frontier in American society functions "as rationalizer of the processes of capitalist development in America" (p. 34). The Internet is still a *capitalist* space, though not completely *commercialized*, yet. The freedom represented in these metaphors ignores or radically reduces the agency of the technologies themselves. Proponents of this view seem to have forgotten Norbert Weiner (1954), who coined the term *cybernetics* from the Greek, *kubernētēs*, which means "steersman." Cyberspace is in actuality (and despite popular conceptions) a *highly* territorialized space; a guided, directed, and governed space (*governor* derives from *kubernētēs* as well), all the way down to its von Neumann architecture (Hayles, 1993b, p. 184).

Cheris Kramarae (1994) has argued that new technologies are inevitably masculinized in Western culture but, once common, become "feminized." Therefore, as we move from those riding the "New Edge" to those "Homesteading the Electronic Frontier" (Rheingold, 1993)—a shift from libertarianism to communitarianism—we may find a less *overtly* testosterone-laden view of the Internet. Indeed, the second metaphor, that of the Net as *highway* (associated with the NII), tends to refer mainly to civic and economic infrastructures rather than the frontier (though it is highly resonant with patriarchal, suburban social structures). The Information Highway is perceived as a public resource (which is different from a free space or a frontier). It becomes reified, a commodity, the "standing reserve" of the information age. Its structure becomes more rigid and particular, and less ubiquitous, than the ocean metaphor. One must build on-ramps to the fiber optic trunks. Like the highways, where the trunks go from and to, and how much and what type of traffic they can carry (e.g., nonmotorized vehicles are not allowed on the Interstate) is a matter of strict regulation.[16] The Information Highway is then rigid and guided, patrolled, and controlled.

The problem with the term Information Highway, especially with the high-profile federal involvement by Vice President Gore, is that it is often equated with the Interstate Highway System (usually called, significantly, the "freeways"). But, at this point at least, the government has no plans to build anything approaching a free, public system. A more apt metaphor would be that of a private tollway. John Browning (1994), a contributing editor to *Wired*, likens the current information networks to a railway system rather than a highway system. Railroads are private, closely regulated monopolies whose cargoes are carefully monitored. Public access is increasingly restricted and its geographies even more determined and rarefied than the highways.

The NII as metaphor is extended and elaborated in future projections of social life. There are two types of such futurologies: cyberpunk science fiction (by William Gibson, Neal Stephenson, Bruce Sterling, et al.) and informational televisual programs (numerous TV specials on the Internet from PBS and such cable channels as Discovery, plus promotional videos provided by AT&T). Much attention has been paid to cyberpunk writings elsewhere, so I will not spend time on them here. But I do wish to provide a short introduction to the video material available by focusing on one video from AT&T. These types of videos represent and dramatize the vision of the new technological assemblage, making literal the considerations of agency and movement in the new social space.

Life in the Telecommunity

Given the amount of money to be made with a further shift to an information economy along the lines of the NII, it is hardly surprising that most of the non–science fiction projections of future life and possibilities of the NII are corporate-sponsored and corporate-centered. One of the most interesting (and at the same time representative) examples of corporate futurology is found in a 1993 promotional video from AT&T entitled, "Connections," which describes life in 2014.

The plot of the video centers around a young woman's wedding. The new technological assemblage allows her to not only stay in close contact with her fiance, but also to shop for wedding dresses (virtually) with her mother. Her mother, a medical doctor who specializes in prosthetics, is also seen consulting with a patient in a distant city through interactive technologies. Her father grounds the second plotline, which involves plans to tear down an old community center for a new housing complex. He, as deputy city planner, has to struggle with some protesters (led by a school principal, which leads to an excuse to tour a computerized classroom) who feel that the community needs a community center more than new housing. The video's strength is in effectively demonstrating the great possibilities of the new technological assemblage by showing how these technologies would be a part of everyday life (videophones, virtual reality games, teleconferencing, Intelligent Agents, etc.).

Three aspects of the video are particularly striking:

1. There is a focus on internationalization. This entails not only the expected (given the sponsor) long-distance videophone calls, but also travel. But, as the global vision at the end of the MSI exhibit is a national vision writ large, the globalization here needs careful examination. Despite the connectivity and mobility of the characters, one language has not become globally dominant; indeed, real-time translation software is one of the technologies most emphasized in the video. Questioning who is traveling and where they are traveling to is revealing. The plot involves a young American scientist who falls in love with a Belgian doctor while in a rug shop in Nepal. The exoticization of the Third World is evident as "authentic" folkwares become a niche market for a Euro-American elite (each rug is handmade, and takes a year to complete). Business must be booming as the old Nepalese rug merchant, though still living in a hut in the Himalayas, has an AT&T videophone (and can afford the long-distance rates). But perhaps I am being overly critical. After all, on one level this video is simply a fantasy designed to attract a certain segment of the American market.

2. Despite the emphasis on electronic connectivity (cyberspace as the new social space), one plotline explicitly involves altering design plans for a new housing project to allow for a community center

to be built. The emphasis on community (both physical and electronic) has political ramifications that I will discuss later. Viewing the tape cynically, however, reveals two aspects of this return to physical community (which is a literal and physical reestablishment of a democratic town square): First, the constituents who are in need of the community center are poor and, in being so, are unwired. They get a community center but may be cut off from the center of the electronic (and economic) community: cyberspace. In the video, this problem is solved through the use of new technologies in the schools. Second, the only way that the wired elite can have the time to congregate physically (a mother and daughter shopping for wedding dresses, etc.) is through the extensive array of obviously expensive technology at their fingertips. In particular: the Intelligent Agent.

3. The agency of individuals in the future society has greatly expanded through their technology. The reason for this: the Intelligent Agent, a software program that appears as the animated figure of a person on the computer screen. This person—an electronic personal assistant—carries out complex tasks for its owner (ordering tickets, arranging meetings, screening calls, etc.) and even is authorized to "stand in" for their owners and make certain business decisions. The Agent is becoming quite the darling of the cyberset. Present in most discussions of the future of the Internet, the Intelligent (or sometimes "virtual") Agent is representative of the great power that the new technological assemblage may grant us. It is, in fact, the latest in a long, long line of labor-saving devices that promise us more leisure time. It is this power, the power of agency, that is so seductive about those scenarios and about these technologies.

Futurology, once upon a time, was the domain of the Left, back when the Left stood for progressive (i.e., future-directed), even revolutionary ideas. However, futurology has institutionally been the domain of the Right since before the start of the cold war (Ross, 1991). Once RAND, and other money-intensive think tanks, started spinning out their range of possible futures (focused around the use of nuclear technologies, usually), the task of imagining the future fell to the military-industrial complex. That corporations have almost entirely taken over that function after the cold war has also to do with a shift in the relations between transnational corporations and the nation-state. Mattelart, Delcourt, and Mattelart (1984) describe the situation as such:

> Previously, firms saw themselves as the standard-bearers of an apoliti-cism that delegated all social functions to the invisible hand of the market. Today, the privatization process is pushing firms into a totally different relation with society, transforming them into pressure groups with new social responsibilities and political concerns. (p. 32)

Socially and culturally, corporations are playing an increasingly central role, and this is especially true of the social space that the vision of a new technological assemblage presents us with.

The Wired World

With regard to the new technological assemblage, *Wired* magazine has become one of the central sites in the politicization and culturization of information and communication corporations. Something of a pub-lishing phenomenon, *Wired* presents the communication and informa-tion corporate industry as a *culture*, and a highly politicized culture at that. *Wired* acts as a mouthpiece for a corporate political agenda. The magazine is not just selling computer technology and consumer goods (Absolut vodka, etc.) to computer users, it is selling a lifestyle and a politics as well.

Wired was launched in 1993, almost concurrent with the NII pro-posal, and has been called "a Rolling Stone of the computer generation" (*Newsweek*, January 17, 1994, p. 38). Others have said that it could be "the first successful lifestyle magazine of the emerging technoculture" (*New York Times*, May 29, 1994). It was voted *Adweek's* start-up magazine of the year for 1993 and has won an American Society of Magazine Editors' award for general excellence.

One striking aspect of the magazine is its attitude, or rather Attitude. Though more empty posturing than substance at times, *Wired* tries to play to the schizophrenic nature of the dominant segment of U.S. society: the baby-boomers, rebellious youth from the 1960s who are now wealthy and working for corporations (profile of average reader: male, 33, and making $81,000/year [Markoff, 1994]). What the magazine advocates is an interesting blend of corporate individualism or capitalist libertarian-ism. It calls for the radical freedom of the Internet through its very vocal support of the Electronic Frontier Foundation (EFF) and its own columns labeled "Cyber-rights Now!" But, on the other hand, it plays the corporate darling—and advertiser's dream—by showcasing the CEOs of major communication and information firms (featured on *Wired's* covers have been cable TV giant TCI's head John Malone pictured as the Road Warrior, Bell Atlantic CEO Ray Smith as Conan the Barbarian, and Frank Biondi and Ed Horowitz of Viacom as Beavis and Butthead; Sonic the Hedgehog was their first Man of the Year). Corporate takeovers are now hip. To be revolutionary, one need only buy the right products. Luckily, these products are listed every month in the Fetish section of *Wired*. As Jesse Drew (1995) has argued,

> The continuing "debate" over the National Information Infrastructure, the so-called information superhighway, has so far been a staged event. Mass-circulation magazines like *Newsweek* and *Time* have run cover stories about the coming "revolution" that are little more than industry PR. Lifestyle magazines like *Wired* and *Mondo 2000* stimulate consumer demand for new gadgets and informed acquiescence to governmental and corporate policies—in the name of spurious "liberation" and "empowerment." (p. 75)

Whether staged or not, *Wired* figures prominently in the unfolding debate about cyberspace and its culture. Two political strains can be discerned in *Wired* (and in cyberculture generally), and these are the appeals to communitarianism and libertarianism (and I use these terms broadly). Though opposites in some ways (dedication to the group versus dedication to the individual), these positions are not mutually exclusive.

First, there is the general appeal to a sense of community on the Internet (though it is a community of those who consider themselves rugged individualists, the lone pioneers connected across the wire). Indeed, in many ways, this has become a dominant feature of the Internet: It allows geographically disparate individuals to come together around any number of interests, hobbies, ideas, politics, etc. on newsgroups, MUDs, MOOs (MUD Object Oriented), e-mail lists, and so on. And there has been a strong need to protect this community equally from the government and consumerism and the corporations. The possibilities for community-building around politics is very real and is evident in Howard Rheingold's 1993 book, *The Virtual Community*. In his book,

Rheingold tells stories of the personal support, the caring community, available on-line. These electronic groups become families that take care of each other.

I am explicitly articulating Rheingold's work to the communitarian movement, though he himself does not necessarily advocate communitarianism. The communitarian movement, as it currently is constituted, preaches a *balance* of individual rights and community responsibility. Such a balance would be very appealing to the baby-boom generation seeking to assuage the dissonance between notions of responsibility and human rights and a protection of their own wealth, jobs, and positions.

Communitarianism is traceable in some form back to Alexis de Tocqueville's observations of Americans in the 19th century. It also has roots in John F. Kennedy's Inaugural Address, the Peace Corps movement, and so on (Derber, 1994). Its recent appearance arose with the 1985 book *Habits of the Heart* by Bellah, Madsen, Sullivan, Swidler, and Tipton, which examines the ways rampant individualism is destroying the fabric of U.S. society and upsetting the balance of individual rights and community responsibility that has been central to U.S. character. Coming as it did in the midst of Reaganomics, this was a significant book. Since then, communitarianism has gained steam as an intellectual and political movement: Both Bill Clinton and Al Gore (and other prominent figures) have signed a communitarian platform. This platform has been evident in Clinton programs such as health care reform and even in Hillary Rodham Clinton's latest book, *It Takes a Village*, about the importance of children to a society. Al Gore's frequent pleadings that the NII be open to community access through schools and libraries likewise shows communitarian tendencies.

But despite advertising itself as a broad-based movement, communitarianism belies a significant class interest (as do Rheingold's on-line communities). Sociologist Charles Derber (1994) refers to this as Professional Middle Class (PMC) communitarianism (p. 112). At the heart of communitarianism is a return to a moral standard and center for society. Though in some ways open and flexible, that moral center is also resoundingly culturally specific in its assumptions of such things as proper family structure. The movement also seems to go incredibly light on the corporate world (which could be what makes the movement so appealing to the PMC). As Derber argues, the movement ignores not only the rule of elites in social and cultural matters but also fundamental factors such as the restructuring of the U.S. industrial workforce into temporary, flexible, just-in-time labor. Taking a slightly more aggressive tone, Sivanandan (1996) argued that communitarianism "is a middle-class project for middle-class people to safeguard themselves from the excesses of the marginalized" (p. 9).

The careful balance between rights and responsibilities advocated by the movement betrays a particular class-based self-interest. Likewise, on the Internet, when push comes to shove, consumerism wins out over the community. This is evident in an example from *Wired* magazine. In 1994-1995, *Wired* started up its website, HotWired, an electronic twin to the print magazine. But these are fraternal twins, in that though they issue from the same source, each is unique as each strives to utilize the limits of its medium (the cyberzine has interactive chats, on-line art, and other happenings, while the paper 'zine experiments with information de- livery, fonts, and visually striking layouts). Rheingold was named as HotWired's executive editor. However, after a difference of opinion, Rheingold left (or was ousted) (Keegan, 1995). As Rheingold has said, "a glib and probably unfair way to state our differences is that [founder] Louis [Rossetto] wanted to create something cool for the sponsors and I wanted to create something cool for the people on the Web" (quoted in White, 1995). Consumerism won out over community. HotWired be-came one of the splashiest sites in cyberspace for corporate advertising. In that only a year or two earlier advertising was forbidden on the Inter-net, and also strongly opposed by the on-line community as it was at the time, the success of HotWired represents a shift in the central character of cyberspace to a more commercial arrangement.

However, it did not take as much to shift the character of the Internet as one might suspect. Community based on special interests (hobbies) is already on its way toward a consumerist-centered organization (rather than community based on community interests), where the dominant communities (e.g., newsgroups) are communities centered around lei-sure activities (e.g., *Star Trek*). This does not mean that communities centered around politics and community concerns do not exist, indeed thrive, on the Internet, but that they are increasingly less central.

As Sivanandan (1996) has put it in an issue of *Race and Class*:

> The community of the Internet is a community of interests, not of people. . . . [I]t is another example . . . of technological escapism substi-tuting virtual reality for reality. . . . And that plays straight into the hands of capital, for once these virtual communities are established—

and this is from a Wall Street report—there should be an opportunity for what they call "transaction related and advertising related revenue schemes" to be introduced. As Nat Wice has said, "For Wall Street, community is the new commodity." (p. 9)

The second political strain, then, evident in *Wired* (and in cyberspace generally)—and by now its dominant one—is the libertarian as corporate apologist. In this guise, *Wired* borrows all of the trappings of 1960s revolutionary jargon (including a logo of an upraised fist clenched around lightning bolts). It is an antigovernment, deregulatory stance that advocates not only the personal rights based on life, liberty, and the pursuit of happiness, but corporate rights based on the laws of the free market.[17] The standard bearer for this position seems to be the Electronic Frontier Foundation, a lobby group founded in the early 1990s to protect civil rights in cyberspace. The group's prominent battles have included the Clipper Chip and the Digital Telephony Bill. More recently, however, an article in *Wired* accused the group of selling out on the latter bill and becoming Washington insiders (being tarnished by working with government) (van Bakel, 1996). But at the same time, *Wired* out-deregulates the deregulators, profiling the exploits of computer hackers, crackers, and phone phreaks who seek to enter, take advantage of, and at times destroy both corporate and government/military computer systems.

The libertarian position takes technology to be the extension of rational individuals. It is little surprising that the figure of Marshall McLuhan has enjoyed such a renaissance. His brand of hip bon mot and technological determinism fits the new technological assemblage and can be found throughout *Wired*. McLuhan's work reminds us of the struggles in the 1950s and 1960s against the Organization Man and the One-Dimensional Man. *Wired* has named McLuhan its patron saint and includes his picture every month in the list of editorial staff along with an appropriately decontextualized quote.

The notion that technology is the extension of self arises in two ways in the literature on cyberspace. One is the cyberpunk literature. The second is the intriguing notion that we will *become digital*. So say the fervent believers of this vision of cyberspace, and followers of McLuhan. Nicholas Negroponte—whose significant infusion of early cash guaranteed that there would *be* a *Wired* magazine and earned him the status of having the prophetic last word in every issue—and fellow MIT professor William Mitchell lead the way in abandoning the physical world of atoms to play in the *City of Bits* (1995). Negroponte (1995) explains, for example, how much easier life will be once we stop shipping around atoms and start sending bits (once we "become digital"). Mitchell, whose 1995 book was also simultaneously published on-line as well as in more traditional paper form, explores the ways currently solid institutional and architectural spaces may be greatly transformed (or even vanish into thin air).

Abandoning the material realm to an electronic one helps one avoid discussing the very real problems that these electronic technologies are causing industrially and globally (i.e., in the realm of atoms). Such onto-logical legerdemain ignores displaced, underemployed, temporary workforces that are exploited (and expanded) by the new information economy with its flexible, just-in-time management.

> The wish to leave body, time, and place behind in search of electronic emulation of community does not accidentally intensify at a time when the space and time of everyday life have become so uncertain, unpleas-ant, and dangerous for so many. . . . [T]he flight into cyberspace is motivated by some of the same fears and longings as the flight to the suburbs: it is another "white flight." (Brook & Boal, 1995, p. ix)

Leaving "body, time, and place" behind is a way of extending one's reach, one's agency, one's ability to achieve effects. This decorporealization is also, as was discussed in Chapter 3, profoundly modern. In this pre-sumption that the new technology will extend one's individual agency, the figure of the Intelligent Agent (yes, that pesky servant who made an appearance in AT&T's video at the start of this section) is increasingly central. The Intelligent Agent makes appearances not only in the AT&T video (and other corporate videos) but also in Negroponte's and Mitchell's books. It also is referred to in the critical volume *Resisting the Virtual Life* (Brook & Boal, 1995). But no matter where it appears, the figure of the Intelligent Agent seems to be a wholly expected, welcomed, and unquestioned part of our future wired world.

The Intelligent Agent can be viewed as a labor-saving device. As such, it necessarily displaces labor by performing the expertise and skills of labor (Noble, 1986). But also, like most of such devices, it causes more labor by increasing normative expectations. More *can* be accomplished with its help, so more *must* be accomplished.[18] Within today's new technological assemblage, we are busier than ever and personally responsible for more information than at any other time in history.

In addition to adding to our information stores, the Agent also functions by limiting and selecting our information input. One of the figures in this scenario is the electronic newspaper, which knows the owner's interests and reports only on those that meet them. It is programmed to feed us only according to our special interests (the same interests that form the heart of the cyber-communities).

> Imagine a future in which your interface agent can read every newswire and newspaper and catch every TV and radio broadcast on the planet, and then construct a personalized summary. This kind of newspaper is printed in an edition of one. (Negroponte, 1995, p. 153)[19]

With this development runs the danger of the further balkanization of the cyberclass. For example, in describing the future house, Mitchell (1995) writes: "as networks and information appliances deliver expanding ranges of services, there will be fewer occasions to go out" (p. 100).

The Agent is an intriguing figure, however, in that it literally stands in for a popular conception of what great advances will be possible in individual agency in the new technological world. It is an essential part of terminal citizenry. McLuhan and libertarianism come together: The individual is now in complete control of its extended self. But in control of what? Control of consumption? A quote from Pattie Maes, a professor at MIT currently developing Intelligent Agent programs, is revealing: "We think it's important to keep the users in control, or at least always give them the impression they are in control" (quoted in Berkun, 1995, p. 117).

The terminal citizen is well represented in these discourses around cyberspace. It is the new *Dasein* (in Heidegger's term), the new Being: Being Digital. Characterized by having both the time and the resources to devote to a life on-line, the terminal citizen creates communities without commitment, and argues for freedoms that are illusory (given the configuration of the technological assemblage and the technicist stratification of this social space). The decorporealization of social space effectively ignores the structures of the technological assemblage (assuming them part and parcel of a linguistic assemblage of digitalization). The terminal citizen, being digital, is swept up in the maelstrom of the corporate territorialization of cyberspace.

Notes

1. I borrow the concept of translation from Bruno Latour (1988).

2. On digitalization and convergence, see Kantrowitz, 1993, p. 44, and Reinhardt, 1994, pp. 47-48.

3. This fact—that the Internet was created by the military to survive a nuclear attack—is often cited in the literature (e.g., Krol, 1993; and elsewhere), but not much is ever made of it (does it make the Internet somehow *dangerous?*). Manuel de Landa (1991) puts the ARPAnet in a broader context.

4. An interesting parallel here, which has not been lost on speech writers or reporters, is that Al Gore, Sr., championed the Interstate Freeway system, and Al Gore Jr. is following in his father's footsteps, in a way.

5. On Videotext, see Fedida and Malik (1979), Martin (1982), or Mayne (1982). Saffady (1990) provides an extensive, though now dated, bibliography on HDTV.

6. See also Robert Fortner's (1995) discussion of access and "impedient excommunication," esp. pp. 141-142.

7. See, e.g., Kantrowitz, 1993, p. 44, and Reinhardt, 1994, p. 74. "Tired/Wired" is a column in *Wired* magazine listing what *was* hip, and what is hip *now*.

8. On some of the problems, assumptions, and alternatives to standard GUIs, see Raskin (1993).

9. Furthering this trend toward the user-friendly, Microsoft released an operating system based on a rudimentary Intelligent Agent (named "Bob") who will explain the workings of the system for you and carry out tasks for you. Advanced versions of this concept can be found in AT&T's promotional video, "Connections," as well.

10. What has not been dealt with in the recent literature on the Information Highway is the potential for possibly the most harmful effects an individual might have on the system: the creation of computer viruses that pose even greater dangers the more technologies converge and the more "wired" we get.

11. Cf. Browning, 1994: "Get on Track: There Will Be No Info Highway"; Stahlman, 1994: "Backlash: The Infobahn Is a Big, Fat Joke"; Lewis, 1994: "Solve Real Problems: Avoid the Superhighway"; Grossberger, 1994: "Coming in Lashed."

12. Reprinted by permission from *The Christian Science Monitor*. © 1993, The Christian Science Publishing Society. All rights reserved.

13. For example, an individual hacker apparently posted software onto the Internet that could decode a company's proprietary source code, leaving it vulnerable to competitors. No official action was taken, though the individual was reprimanded by peers on the Internet (Steinberg, 1994, p. 130).

14. Andrew Ross (1991) refers to cyberpunk as part of "the remasculinized landscape of anarcho-libertarian youth culture in the 1980s" (p. 146).

15. The vision of a deterritorialized space of free information might be fruitfully compared to Jean-François Lyotard's (1984) proposal of free public access to all data banks (p. 67).

16. The decision of where to place highways, railroads, and fiber optic trunks is obviously highly political. We should remember the consequences for hundreds, if not thousands, of small towns that were missed by the interstates, and therefore vanished, cut off from a major source of income.

17. For a highly cynical look at *Wired*, see Keith White's 1995 article, "The Killer App: WIRED Magazine, Voice of the Corporate Revolution," *The Baffler, 6.* It can also be found at http://www.voyagerco.com/misc/killerapp/ killerapp.html

18. "The technology of humanity turns these social products of our acts into conditions of survival, thus putting us under obligation. We are the masters of the Earth, and we are constructing a world that is almost universally miserable and that is becoming the objective, founding *given* of our future" (Serres, 1995, p. 177).

    When the question of labor-saving devices is raised, we must always ask whose labor is saved, and whose is increased? See Cowan, 1983.

19. Material excerpted from *Being Digital* (1995) by Nicholas Negroponte is used by permission of Alfred A. Knopf, Inc.

7

It's a Small World After all: Rethinking the NIICO and the GII

The GII

Not content with the plan of simply wiring the United States, in March 1994 Vice President Gore proposed the creation of a Global Information Infrastructure (GII) at the meeting of the International Telecommunications Union (ITU) in Buenos Aires. This chapter is about global communication and information networks.

The imposition of the new technological assemblage on a global scale (with its accompanying politics, culture, and problematic) will have particular consequences on the lesser developed countries (LDCs), which are, to a great extent, "unwired." Such consequences may include the reinforcement of relationships of dependency and unequal exchange and the resurgence of an informational neocolonialism. Discourses that label LDCs as "unwired," however, establish relations of negativity (they are not us, they are not wired, they are not developed) that reintroduce orientalism and neocolonialism. That information infrastructure can be crucial to the betterment of life in a country cannot be denied. But proposals of how to develop these countries always have a specific method in mind, a particular model of "infrastructure," for example, and a specific notion of what is "better." Alternative schemes that might be more appropriate for a culture or nation are swept aside (or completely ignored) in the desire to be the most technically developed. We see here the same progressivist notion of technology that we saw in the museum, that color televisions are "better" than black and white, which are "better" than radio, and so forth. (This desire is ingrained in the nations themselves in that urban elites often want the color televisions and satellite dishes; the West is not completely to "blame," then.) These proposals also tend to attribute a certain passivity to LDCs (they have to be wired, they have to be developed), in that aid is always coming from the outside and ignores their own great cultural, political, and economic histories. That these nations may not boast central high-speed infrastructures as the United States does (or proposes) does not mean that computer networks do not exist on a more grassroots level within and among these LDCs. It was from grassroots bulletin board systems that much of what is now the Internet grew, not through a centralized, trunk- like system like the NII. The rhizomatics of information infrastructure.

I want to take as a starting point for this chapter an image that accompanied a *New York Times* article of April 26, 1994. The article, "AT&T Proposes Sea Cable That Would Encircle Africa," concerned a proposal by AT&T to establish a ring of fiber optic cable around Africa to connect not only the African continent with the rest of the world but the various African nations with themselves. The system would be owned and managed by Africans (which may mean additional international debt). On the whole, the project may have merit, but what I want to focus on is the accompanying graphic. What is striking about this map is the image of Africa encircled by a dark black line that plugs into the coast at several points. It is, it seems, a sort of CybAfrica, a Frankenstein monster animated by the life-giving electrodes inserted in its flesh. The cyborg imagery resonates with colonialist aspirations to "penetrate" the "dark continent" to a disturbing effect. The image of an encircled and plugged continent disturbs, and it is this feeling that I want to explore in this chapter. But at the same time, the positive political possibilities inherent in a minoritarian deterritorializing machine (as the cyborg has become in this book) and in grassroots computer networks are not to be denied. The question, then, is how to approach international communication as cyborg politics?

Gore's proposal to the meeting of the ITU of a "planetary information network" mentions, as primary advantages, education, the exchange of ideas, and contacts with families and friends (this last one is resonant with the public relations efforts of U.S. long distance companies).[1] But the central concern of the GII, according to Gore, is economics: the creation of a "global information marketplace." The GII is seen as a spur to global economic growth. At his most technologically determinist, Gore stated that "a primitive telecommunications system causes poor economic development," and that an advanced information network is "an essential prerequisite to sustainable development."

Thus, the GII is "key to economic growth for national and international economies." Gore argues this point through a double analogy: First, that the GII is analogous to the United States' NII (implying the intended imposition of U.S. capitalist structures globally). Second, that the positive economic impact foreseen for the NII is analogous to the positive economic impact that the development of the United States' transportation infrastructure had in the mid-20th century. That the economic boom of the 1950s might have been the result of World War II itself and the Korean War rather than simply the creation of more highways is not mentioned. Gore, however, sees participation in the GII as crucial to the well-being of every nation. He says, "I fervently hope this conference will take full advantage of this potential for economic growth, and not deny any country or community its right to participate in this growth." But should not the ITU also not deny any country or community its right *not* to participate in the GII (or how to participate)? The right not to connect, incidentally, *is* mentioned by the AT&T proposal to wire Africa.

To describe what would be the founding principles of the GII, Gore turns to the five principles he had stated for the construction of the United States' NII: Encourage private investment; promote competition; create a flexible regulatory framework; provide open access to the network for all information providers; and ensure universal service. All but the last of these outline a very specific form of capitalism (and were discussed in the last chapter). The last, "universal service," is rapidly becoming axiomatic in its own right (cf. debates over "universal" health care). This axiom, paradoxically, functions properly (i.e., achieves the needs of capital) only when it works unevenly or not at all. Under the sign of this principle, the inequalities that drive capitalism are entrenched as status quo. More than simply a rhetorical trope in recent political debate, the term is becoming, I would argue, an organizational principle.

However, Gore stresses the democracy of the GII: It will be built (privately) in a democratic effort, and "the distributed intelligence of the GII will spread participatory democracy" and "will in fact promote the functioning of democracy." Indeed, "the GII will be a metaphor for democracy itself." The democracy that the GII would describe is that of a decentralized system in which each citizen would be considered "the human equivalent of the self-contained processor" (in Gore's terms; this is the *terminal citizen*, in my terms). The result would be "a new Athenian Age of democracy," which is an odd metaphor from a man who just promised "universal service," which the Athenian Age most assuredly did not provide.

Insofar as the GII does allow the possibility of access to vast amounts of decentralized information and the possibilities for organizations to develop regardless of the structures of nation-states (i.e., because of the same possibilities that the Internet now offers), a GII may be a very positive move. In other words, to the extent that the GII would be decentralized, following Gore's proposal, it presents us with multiple political possibilities. But here we would need to heed the lessons of the rapidly centralizing Internet. To the extent that the technology is provided by a particular nation, group of nations, or even a particular cartel of corporations, and places minor nations in a position of economic and technological dependency, I would be very cautious (see Hamelink, 1983; Pacey, 1983). Likewise, to the extent that the purpose of a particular structuration of a GII is simply to increase the potential market for Western commodities (and here Gore writes that "information is a treasure that must be shared to be valuable"; in other words the larger the potential market the greater the respective valuations of U.S. information), I am against such a proposal (but against such a particular structuring rather than against the idea of a GII generally). Also, following from the last chapters, the consequences of the globalization of terminal citizenry need to be very carefully examined.

I do hope to tread here between the negativities of the informatics of domination (Haraway [1991a] warns of the "final imposition of a grid of control on the planet" [p. 154])—found in this chapter under the guise of media imperialism—and the positivities (utopias) of some of the U.S. government's information policy proposals. But just because the GII (if it appears) is not necessarily either the doom or the savior of the world does not mean that it is neutral. Likewise, if the GII is constructed under the sign of capitalism, that does not mean that all its functions will be capitalist; however, it still will function, generally, within the capitalist axiomatic.

I want to talk briefly here about the axiomatic functioning of capitalism (and capitalism's axioms) because an understanding of this functioning of capitalism is important to any analysis of global relations. Not only this, the primary capitalist axioms that we will be dealing with in this chapter are decidedly modernist, and to address these axioms, we need to recognize them as such and present an alternative that is not based within the modern episteme.

Axioms are seemingly self-evident statements regarding the production of goods, relations to the state, or other matters. They are "the operative statements that constitute the semiological form of capital" (Deleuze & Guattari, 1987, p. 461); they are the principles by which capital works. Capital adds or eliminates axioms depending on its needs. As examples of axioms appearing since World War II, Deleuze and Guattari (p. 462) cite the Marshall Plan, new forms of assistance and lending, and transformations within the monetary system (e.g., the Bretton Woods Agreement).[2]

Whereas capital tends toward the universal, axioms arise in response to specific, local situations. Axioms vary from place to place, though some axioms are common to global capital as a whole. "Every capitalist formation constructs or, more accurately, is constituted and enabled by its specific axiomatics" (Grossberg, 1992, p. 349). "The *immanent axiomatic* finds in the domains it moves through so many models, termed *models of realization*" (Deleuze & Guattari, 1987, p. 454). If an axiom is a principle by which capital operates, then a model is a law, policy, or structure. Specific models of realization of axioms are taken up by states. States combine and arrange these models "according to [their] resources, population, wealth, industrial capacity, etc." (p. 454). Each axiom may have many varied models of realization depending on local circumstances; but these models are isomorphic in that they arise from the same axioms.

All states, then, are isomorphic as they depend on or encounter capitalism and its axiomatics.[3] In other words, though particular configurations vary, they all have similar general forms (i.e., the nation-state) because they are either built on capitalist axiomatics or are attempting to reject them. In particular, the states of the center are isomorphic because they share common relations of production (the axiomatic as a whole). Variations occur depending on differences in modes of production (the particular combination of axioms taken up by each state) (p. 464). For example, relations between North and South (center and periphery, First and Third Worlds) reveal polymorphy in that, though the relations of production are capitalist, the modes of production are not necessarily capitalist (p. 465). What is important in this relation is the fact that "the polymorphy of the Third World States is partially organized by the center, as an axiom providing a substitute for colonization" (p. 465).

Though "the axioms of the periphery differ from those of the center" (p. 465), the overall axiomatic is consistent. The relations between center and periphery are partially determined by the center. What has been happening in the last 20 or 30 years is a seemingly mutual determination or exchange of determinations between center and periphery (p. 468). The periphery becomes the site of heavy industrial production, while the center becomes a peripheral site of "post-industrial activities" centered around information and automation (p. 469). This creates "peripheral zones of under-development inside the center, internal Third Worlds, internal Souths" (p. 469).

The shifting core-periphery relation is made possible by new information and communication technologies (the new technological assemblage); the very technologies that the center now proliferates and relies on, having abandoned heavy production to the periphery.[4] Indeed, in part through these technologies the core is no longer geographically bound. These technologies are central to what is referred to as the post-industrial society, neo-Fordism, and other variations. Castells argues that capitalism has shifted to what he calls a new mode of development, that of information.

Within this new mode of development are two axioms of capital that are crucial to our overall discussion: *the axiom of information*, which states that information is a commodity (Castells, 1989; Schiller, 1983);[5] and *the axiom of neutral technology*, which states that a technology's origins do not matter and its uses are socially determined. This second axiom is clearly based within the modern episteme, as is, we shall see, the response to it (which is that both the origins and uses of technology are socially determined). Both axioms are global but have varied models of realization.

Shifting Space

It is in the communications industry's best interests to present the current technological assemblage as one that will increase our individual power and will bring happiness to all. Thus, we have the assorted visions of AT&T's telecommunity, cyberspace, and The World, Live! My own, Deleuzian, reading of the situation looks at the stratification of social space and sees an increase in technology and a resulting shrinkage of language. I see the possibilities of terminal citizenry.

But my reading is not meant to echo the warnings of countless previous prophets about the deindividualizing, dehumanizing influence of modern autonomous technology, or the enslavement of humanity by its machines, because I am not arguing in terms of the human/technology split. Rather what is *human* is changing—or, in other words, what it is to be an *agent* in our society is changing. Human agency always consists of both technological and linguistic agency, the particular configuration of each and the relations between the two depend on the overall stratification of social space. That change is taking place, and that this particular change is taking place, is neither good nor bad in and of itself. What is important is that it is changing without a conceptual apparatus to help us negotiate within the changing conditions. What we are consistently presented with are modernist visions of individual freedom that do not ring true in the end. What I have tried to do here is to theorize a basis from which we can begin to address (or address better) the changing configurations of our social space.

What I would like to do now is to summarize the differences between the three epistemes outlined in Chapters 1 through 3 by showing how the problematic of the GII has been addressed from each perspective. In this way, I hope to tie together the various threads of this analysis and point to some ways in which we may want to begin to rethink global communication policy.

I would like to insert a brief word here about my objects of analysis in this chapter. The focus of most of the critique is on policy *proposals* rather than concrete networks, current regulatory frameworks, corporate restructuring, and so on, and this is for several reasons. First, I am dealing with the proposals of the New International Information and Communication Order (NIICO) because it is an as-yet-unrealized alternative to the dominant trends in current communication and information structures *generally*. Here, I am deliberately painting the current global situation with very broad strokes to move quickly on to my central concerns. Secondly, the information landscape is transforming so rapidly that it seems expedient to step out of the flow somewhat and indicate the range of possibilities being considered. And that is what these proposals are, for the most part: possibilities. When considering social space (and the specific articulations of Technology and Language that constitute it), I am not interested just in space as practiced but also space as conceptualized and represented. Working on the level that I have chosen allows me to consider more fully the abstract configurations guiding the structures of social space and the ways it is lived.

NIICO: Fighting Modernism With Modernism

The New International Information and Communication Order (NIICO) represents one of the most broad-based and extended movements resisting the domination of lesser developed countries by Western industrialized nations (such as the United States). It focuses on the problem of unequal flows of information and still represents a valid caution regarding such projects as Gore's GII.

The call for a NIICO originated in the Non-Aligned Movement,[6] which was itself a product of the decolonization movement of the 1950s, 60s, and 70s. The Non-Aligned Movement (representing a group of nations primarily from the Third World), while not aligning themselves *a priori* with either the capitalist or the socialist states, did not profess neutrality on international issues (and historically have sided more with the nondeveloped socialist states), but rather wanted to have the option to provide an independent voice (Vilanilam, 1989, pp. 23-24). If Deleuze and Guattari (1987) are correct and the relations between the First and Third Worlds are not only dominated by the center but organized by it (p. 468), then the Non-Aligned Movement can be seen as an attempt to cut through the overcodings of individual states to try to address directly the workings of capitalism that were transforming not only global relations but relations within and among Third World states as well.[7]

The Non-Aligned Movement had two primary proposals: a New International Economic Order (NIEO) and a New International Information and Communication Order (NIICO). The NIEO directly addresses the capitalist axiom of unequal exchange, especially with regard to the unequal flows of capital, resources, and so on. The NIICO, which this section of the chapter will focus on, addresses the unequal flows of information and communication (which, it was argued, were central to the construction and maintenance of social space as well as the individual's relations to the social [e.g., Traber, 1980]). It was one of the tasks of the Non-Aligned Movement, and later supporters of the NIICO in UNESCO, to attempt to link the NIEO and NIICO. If it is *explicitly* agreed that information is a commodity, then this is easily done. However, representatives from the capitalist West worked hard to dissociate the two terms (the information axiom is *assumed*, but *unspoken*) by shifting the terms of the debate onto ostensibly neutral grounds: hardware and news (journalism). Such a move assumes that technology is neutral (the axiom of neutral technology) and that questions on the flows of information can be reduced to questions about news coverage (ignoring the fact that the bulk of information transferred across borders is about banking, corporate trade, entertainment, etc.). To the extent that the NIICO *was* reduced to discussions about the news, the West succeeded.[8]

The NIICO was influenced by two paradigms of media research: *development communication* and *media imperialism*. Development communication was based on the research of such figures as Daniel Lerner (1958) and Wilbur Schramm (1964) (see also Lerner & Schramm, 1967). Development communication supported the implementation and growth of

> technology-based communication networks which, regardless of message and content, tended to create, by reason of its inherent characteristics, a climate suited to development. It was supposed to generate the psychic ambience within which economic and productive activity occurred. (Jayaweera, 1987, p. xviii)

But the countries that were subject to this paradigm ended up "getting effectively sucked into a particular mode of development, a development that is dominated and controlled by the global capitalist system" (p. xvi). Needless to say, the early development communication paradigm assumed that technology was neutral at worst and modernizing (used in a neutral, yet positive, way) at best.[9] My difficulty with the use of the term *development* in general (i.e., in Gore's speech or the ITU proposal) is that the term carries with it an assumed telos that needs to be investigated in each case.

Opposed to development communication (to a certain extent) was the second paradigm of media research, media imperialism, which influenced the call for a NIICO. Central to the NIICO is the assumption that the domination of information and communication resources leads to the domination of culture and therefore the social. This was the (problematic, yet influential) thesis of cultural imperialism, which stated that imperialism was not just political or economic but cultural as well, and so was carried through the media. As the majority of films, television programs, and other media material circulating throughout the world were (and still are, but to a lesser extent [see Roach, 1990, p. 294]) of U.S. origin, the United States became the primary target of these attacks.

Colleen Roach (1990) points out that the work of the central researchers in the cultural (or media) imperialism paradigm (if we may call it that)—for example, Herbert I. Schiller and Armand Mattelart—focused primarily on the structural aspects of global communication flows (p. 293).[10] These researchers argued that not only were the transnational corporations (TNCs) (which at the time were rapidly expanding) and media industries mutually supportive, but some media companies *were* important TNCs in and of themselves. Also, the TNCs and media industries were supported by, and supported, Western military expansion, creating "a relatively new military-industrial-communications complex" (Roach, 1990, p. 293). Schiller (1983), for example, argues that most information technologies were invented and developed in and for military organizations; the technologies were rapidly picked up by American corporations; and all along, the technologies were supported, protected, and put into use by the capitalist state (p. 18).[11] The view of technology in this paradigm is that, though it *presents* itself as neutral, technology "is produced according to the specifications of a particular system" and its use is dominated by that system as well (Schiller, 1980, p. 22). Though this view counters the axiom of neutral technology, it still remains within the modern episteme.

The Non-Aligned Movement called for the establishment of a "new international order in information" at their 1976 meeting in Tunisia. This proposal was fueled by media research and theories of cultural imperialism (such as Nordenstreng and Varis's 1974 study of communication flows for UNESCO, as well as the theories of Schiller and Mattelart). The Non-Aligned Movement was faced, on the one hand, with the West (especially the United States) whose preferred aid to the Third World came in forms consistent with the model of development communication (which only furthered the fears of the media imperialists) and, on the other with the prospects of ever more intrusive communication technologies such as Direct Broadcast Satellites and the establishment of the ISDN.[12] The NIICO was meant to be a means of "democratizing and decolonizing the system of international relations in the information field" (Kleinwachter, 1986, p. 63).

What are now acknowledged to be the principles of the NIICO were set out in a 1980 meeting of the Intergovernmental Council of the Non-Aligned Movement in Baghdad (Capriles, 1980; Gonzalez Manet, 1986). The NIICO was to be based on the following:

(a) The fundamental principles of international law, notably self-determination, sovereignty and non-interference;
(b) The right of people and individuals to an objective picture of reality by means of accurate and comprehensive information;
(c) The right of every nation to develop its own independent information system, in particular by regulating the activities of transnational corporations;
(d) The right of every nation to make known worldwide its interests, aspirations, and its political, moral, and cultural values;
(e) The right of every nation to resist, within constitutional limits, the distribution of false or distorted information;
(f) The right of every nation to participate at governmental and non-governmental level in the international exchange of information under favorable conditions. (cited in Gonzalez Manet, 1986, p. 48)

After several years of discussion, the call for a NIICO moved to UNESCO in the mid-1970s. At its 1978 General Conference in Paris, UNESCO passed the "Declaration on Fundamental Principles Concerning the Contribution of the Mass Media to Strengthening Peace and International Understanding, to the Promotion of Human Rights and to Countering Racialism, Apartheid and Incitement to War"; the title explains its intent. The "Mass Media Declaration" (as it was referred to) called for "a free flow and a wider and better balanced dissemination of information" (cited in Nordenstreng, Gonzalez Manet, & Kleinwachter, 1986, p. 227).

In response to the Mass Media Declaration, the western industrialized countries (led by the United States) shifted tactics from flat out opposition to that of cooperation so that they would have more influence in the decision-making process. A "Marshall Plan" for international telecommunications was proposed in which the West would gladly help developing countries establish their own communication and information infrastructures (Nordenstreng, 1986, p. 17; Schiller, 1989, pp. 299-303).[13] This plan had several advantages (most of which derive from the development communication paradigm): it made the United States look like a benefactor to the poor; it allowed the West to further establish *its* technology in these countries (making them dependent on the West for expert knowledge, service, spare parts, etc.);[14] and (most important) it attempted to shift the terms of the debate onto purely technological grounds—to define the issue as technological imbalance (technology seen, of course, as neutral) rather than imperialism. This plan, as Kaarle Nordenstreng points out (1986, p. 13), was obviously meant to derail the Mass Media Declaration, then still being deliberated. The attempt failed, however, and the declaration passed.[15]

To help solve some of the arguments that were ongoing about the Mass Media Declaration, UNESCO established the International Commission for the Study of Communication Problems chaired by Sean MacBride (and subsequently referred to as the "MacBride Commission"). These arguments included disagreements over the meaning of "freedom of the press," the "free flow" of information, development, and so on. The MacBride Commission's mandate was "to study the totality of communication problems in modern societies" (MacBride, 1980, p. xvii). The commission was comprised of representatives from a broad spectrum of political and economic circumstances. That a report was produced at all is evidence of the continued state of cooperation and compromise (especially on the part of the United States).

The MacBride Report was often praised for its scope and the fact that it attempted to bring together a great variety of communications problems to be discussed in a global context. It is often criticized, however, for failing in its details, for not going into enough depth on certain subjects.[16] It has also been criticized for not providing an overarching theoretical framework (e.g., Opubor, 1980) or even an adequate definition of a NIICO (e.g., Capriles, 1980). As this was essentially a compromise document, it is doubtful that such a unifying framework could have been agreed on without taking up either of the opposed ideological positions on the subject. For example, an acknowledgment of unlimited "free flow" of information would have been perceived as a declaration of the Western perspective (i.e., the West, with its extensive media resources, could flood the rest of the world with its information and ideology). Likewise, the call for the "wider and more balanced dissemination of information" from the Mass Media Declaration (a phrase that troubled the Western states) would have been perceived as a threat to the dominance of the U.S. media empire. The latter phrase (the "wider and more balanced dissemination of information") was toned down in the report by emphasizing that the NIICO was a *process* (and therefore was not an immediate threat). That there were dissenting opinions, printed both with the MacBride Commission's report and in other forums, is hardly surprising. But the fact remains that the Commission's report was approved by all member states of UNESCO, including the United States.

Despite the unanimous passage of the report, those representing the West were growing increasingly dissatisfied with developments around the NIICO and proceeded to attack the proposal as totalitarian, stating that the NIICO favored government control of information and the licensing of journalists (both of which were untrue).[17] The election of Ronald Reagan ensured the further distancing of the United States from the NIICO. In 1984, the United States threatened to resign from UNESCO if the NIICO was not abandoned; it also cited apparent mismanagement of the organization and the supposed politicization of UNESCO. In January 1985, it followed through on its threat and withdrew from UNESCO, followed by Britain and Singapore.

Since then, UNESCO has made moves to "reform" itself. Amadou Mahtar M'Bow of Senegal, the director general of UNESCO who fully supported the NIICO movement, was replaced by Federico Mayor of Spain in 1987. Mayor quickly endorsed the United States' "free flow" position and actively tried to distance himself and UNESCO from the NIICO (see Roach, 1990). In recent years, not only has UNESCO stopped printing the English language edition of the MacBride Report, but also actively opposed the publication of Preston, Herman, and Schiller's (1989) book on U.S.-UNESCO relations (Roach, 1990). Though the NIICO no longer has an open forum for international policy debate in UNESCO, the debate still continues in other forums. The Non-Aligned Movement sponsors regular MacBride Roundtables in Communication to discuss recent developments. Nongovernmental organizations such as the World Association for Christian Communication (WACC) also support the movement, advocating a more grassroots approach to the issues (see Traber & Nordenstreng, 1992). In other words, they propose that issues such as appropriate technologies, the right to communicate, and the establishment of democratic communication systems be decided not on an international level (not right away, in any case), but on the local level, through the support of churches, educational institutions, and other ecumenical nonprofit groups.[18]

Strategic (De)Linking

An extended attempt to address the drawbacks of the NIICO's response to the Western domination of global information flows can be found in what is referred to in different cases (and with different emphases) as theories of national sovereignty, cultural autonomy, or delinking. In this section, I will focus on Cees Hamelink's 1983 book, *Cultural Autonomy in Global Communications: Planning National Information Policy*, which I take to be fairly representative of this position. Hamelink cuts through the Western, capitalist arguments about neutral technology and the free flow of information and states that "the real issues are at the level of the distribution of social power" (p. 72).

Hamelink argues that there is a new, subtler, more pervasive, mode of cultural imperialism. He terms this "cultural synchronization," in which a great diversity of traditions and cultures are being destroyed by the imposition of a world or global culture. Unlike "classic" cultural imperialism, this synchronization is carried out not by direct domination, ownership, or control but through a system of dependencies established between Third and First World cultures. The cultures of the Third World are brought into resonance with that of the "global culture," which is actually the global capitalist market.[19] The daily rhythms of individual nations are made to match those of the global flows of capital.

Diversity, then, is being destroyed. But Hamelink (1983) argues that this is not simply the result of cultures clashing or meeting; it is through a *one-way* flow of ideas, the lack of *exchange* between cultures (p. 4). So when Hamelink advocates "cultural dissociation" as the only solution to the problem, he does not mean cultural isolationism.[20] Rather, he advocates the dissociation of the South from the North and the establishment, instead, of *regional* links (South-South, so to speak): "Delinking or dissociation, although central, is but one side of the coin in national information policy and planning. It must be complemented by building a new pattern of regional, horizontal linkages among developing countries" (p. 122). What is crucial for Hamelink is the cultural autonomy of a people, meaning by this "a society's capacity to decide on the allocation of its own resources for adequate adaptation to its environment" (p. 6). Autonomy and an organization of *interindependence* should be the basis of a new world order. Most of the arguments on both sides of the NIICO debate not only tended to reduce "information" to "news" but also focused simply on the reform of the current system and an interdependence among states (p. 83). Such an integrationist model, Hamelink argues, "might bring minor marginal improvements, but it will integrate the Third World countries in an international system that operates against their very interests, impedes their emancipation, consolidates existing dependency relations and both creates and legitimizes cultural synchronization" (p. 98). This process only would be accelerated with the establishment of a GII as it is now proposed: Countries would become circuits in the overall network; the flow of information would follow the overarching logics of capital rather than being the result of interactions among agents (states, groups, individuals).

One of the (many) critiques of the cultural (or media) imperialist view is that it fetishizes a certain form of the nation-state. When arguing against the dilution or outright destruction of a nation's culture, the question is seldom asked, "Whose culture is being destroyed?" By reifying a nation's culture, by taking one form of it to be the "true" culture, one ends up supporting not the nation as a whole but the dominant, often urban, group (or a rural nostalgia). Other cultures, other peoples, who are subordinate in the power structure of the nation, marginalized and impoverished, are ignored, their needs not met. The center/periphery(ies) imbalance that the NIICO seeks to address is not only an international problem but one that lies *within* every nation (see Ekwelie, 1985). The problem with the international policy arena (and this includes UNESCO, the Non-Aligned Movement, etc.) is that those representing each nation usually represent only the dominant group within those nations. Colleen Roach (1990) writes:

> While it was not uncommon to find [NIICO] literature referring to national elites as part of the problem the movement was trying to combat, one did not find writers referring to the problem posed by the national elites *within* the ranks of the [NIICO]. (p. 297)

Cees Hamelink (1983) *does* realize the dangers posed by national elites and argues that each nation should develop a National Information Policy "not at the cost of monopoly by certain social classes but through balanced participation of all social sectors" (p. 105). He writes that

> the national elite provides the nationalist legitimation of the dependency system, the local marketing knowledge, and the "native" capital,

which represents in many dependent countries an increasing share of industrial investment. (p. 7)

He acknowledges here that the social groups initially drawn into modernization or development schemes are the urban elites. And, though he notes that the Western media primarily affect the urban elites more than the rural minorities, "if the ruling elite accept imported social models . . . their action will certainly be decisive for the economic and cultural environment of the rest of the population" (p. 7).

Colleen Roach (1990), making a case for delinkage, draws together Hamelink's work with that of Samir Amin (1989) to argue for the necessity of cultural dissociation and national self-reliance. She writes that

> Hamelink's analysis, like that of Samir Amin, connects delinkage to the problem of national elites. Amin has consistently stressed in his writings that delinkage from world capitalism is only one part of the self-reliance process; the other is necessarily that of developing a national development policy that is a truly "popular force." In short, self-reliance is necessarily that of the people. (1990, p. 301)

She concludes by writing, "it therefore seems evident that a dissociation model implies delinkage not only from capitalism but from national elites" (p. 302). Roach asserts that the way out of the false dichotomy between transnationals or national elites is by the recognition of "the people" as a political actor in the realm of economic, cultural, and communication policy making. By "people power," Roach means "the new reality of grassroots groups struggling for change" (p. 303). Roach's approach emphasizes certain aspects of the recent changes of direction of the NIICO, those being the focus on local and grassroots organizations rather than governmental or intergovernmental organizations. She stresses that such a project "must advance a project for democratic socialism" (p. 303). To this end, she recognizes a recent shift in terminology from "international" to "world" communication order, de-emphasizing the role of states.

The delinking thesis has some resonance with the amodern episteme of technology, that based on agency. It shifts the terms of the debate onto the problem of (to use Latour's terms) the translation of Third World cultures into that of the global flow of capital, and the recognition of how technologies act as delegates for human action. This position does not demonize technology (that would be to remain within the modern episteme) but, rather, advocates the necessity for shorter actor-networks that better respond to specific conditions. This perspective realizes that the problem is one of agency rather than simply a problem of imbalances of one type of social element (like the inadequacy of technology). Following this perspective, then, the GII would more appropriately be based on grassroots computer networks rather than (or in addition to) more centralized, trunklike systems.

Flows

The delinking thesis has its merits and is an important step toward addressing the inequality of global information flows, but there are also several issues that it leaves unaddressed. For example, it seems to assume a universal distribution of agency, and to assume that agency always works in the same ways; it also assumes that if it were not for certain structures of domination (from the industrialized West as well as urban elites, and we should add socialist authoritarianism), universal agency could be realized. To a lesser extent, Hamelink's book also seems to assume a universal distribution of resources; finally, it assumes that all nations could be self-sufficient if not for Western imperialism.[21] It is because there is an unequal distribution of resources that I believe that some degree of regional interdependence is still necessary.

One possible cause of these problems is that Hamelink's book leaves unquestioned the notion of the nation-state as a continuing actor in these processes (despite a focus on relations within the nation-states themselves). Hamelink (1983) does note that the political boundaries of many of the Third World nation-states are the result of colonialism and are therefore problematic (p. 27); but the question of the nation-state form itself (which Deleuze and Guattari argue is axiomatic) is not addressed. Hamelink tends to conflate the terms *nation* (a term that I take to refer to a particular form of territorialization: the affectual articulation to a particular geography that is not necessarily physical, i.e., spiritual or ideological) with *nation-state* (a political term concerned more with differentiating than territorializing). International does not necessarily mean the same thing as intergovernmental (or interstate). Hamelink does correctly caution us that the general use of the term *national culture* is misleading because what is often taken for a national culture is often a combination (by colonizing powers) of disparate traditions (often reflecting the needs of an urban elite), or simply because there is no single national culture (pp. 27-28).

But Hamelink (1983) also assumes a certain environmental determinism: "Every type of human society is characterized by the neces- sity to adapt to its environment" (p. 1). Multiple environments would then produce diverse societies. Such a construction does not consider diasporic nations that are not tied to any one environment and often belong to several at once; it also assumes that nations do not move. This omission throws into question Hamelink's notion of cultural auton- omy, which he defines as "a society's capacity to decide on the allocation of its own resources for adequate adaptation to its environment" (p. 6). The notion of cultural autonomy is important, but any notion of "adequacy" will need to be very specifically defined within each social group in question and delinked from particular notions of Nature and the environment.

I applaud the focus of this approach on local issues and the attempt to avoid hierarchical organizations implicitly or explicitly modeled after Western ones, but we cannot focus *only* on the local—that would be to fall into a global relativism. Also, as Michel Serres (1995) has argued, "a philosophy of the fragmentary is conservative" (p. 120). His example is a vase: The larger it is the more fragile it is; fragments are heartier, more resistant, harder to break. "Consequently, when you create a fragment, you seek refuge in places, in localities, which are more resistant than a global construction" (p. 120). Fragments and localities are not to be avoided, however. We must grasp the global as well, though this is riskier and requires courage: the local *and* the global, the local *in* the global, and the global *in* the local. On the policy level, this means that the NIICO has to balance global flows of information (usually among states or other similar large-scale public organizations) with one of UNESCO's other proposals, the Universal Human Right to Communicate.[22] The problem in asserting the Right to Communicate is that it brings the discussion back under the shadow of modernism, with its specific notion of the individual. Such notions pose problems for cultures in which the social group is accorded more weight than the individual (Servaes, 1988).

The above comments are not meant as a rejection of the delinking thesis but, rather, as a corrective. My questions above arise out of a different approach to technology, the machinic (or Deleuzian) episteme. Thus, my questions concern axioms, flows, and the distribution and territorialization of social space. Such a perspective will give us a better understanding of many of the elements in a social system (and a realization that all the elements will never be accounted for in any one scheme), especially the multiple articulations of humans to machines, and the resonance that any technological assemblage has with other assemblages on other planes (such as planes of logic, religion, chemistry, etc.) that cut through that social space. It will also allow a better understanding of the particular possibilities for agency within any particular space (and the stratifications that produce them). I wish to indicate here some of the general directions such an analysis might take, and present some of the questions that it would ask.

A Deleuzian perspective calls for a minoritarian approach to the GII. Axioms are majoritarian (and the power of the majority *is* an axiom, its dominance is immanent to its social situation), and in this, they can manipulate only the functions recognized by the majority[23]—those that fit in its system. We can refer to these functions as denumerable since they are recognizable and "countable" by the majority, even if their number is infinite. As the First/Third World split continues (and the split between the "wired" and "nonwired" on the Information Superhighway), more and more functions escape the axioms; this is a situation similar to Latour's modernity: As purification progresses, more and more hybrids fall through the cracks (Latour, 1993). As more control is taken over the Internet—as its diverse sites synchronize with commercial logic—more users will turn back to alternative, grassroots uses of the same technology (BBSs, for example). It is only in the proliferation of local freenets (community-based, nonprofit Internet access providers) that we can find competing definitions of culture (practice, concept, and representation) to that of the wired world described in the last few chapters. Those that escape the axiom are referred to as minoritarian. A minority is not constituted by number (indeed, many of today's so-called minorities outnumber the majorities, e.g., blacks in South Africa). Rather, a minority is constituted by "the relations internal to the number," "by the gap that separates them from this or that axiom constituting a redundant majority" (Deleuze & Guattari, 1987, p. 469). Minorities are nondenumerable and thus escape the axiomatic. Minorities can (and do) constitute nations, but not nation-states (which are axiomatic). Deleuze and Guattari (1997) write,

> It matters little that the minorities are incapable of constituting viable
> States from the point of view of the axiomatic and the market, since in

> the long run they promote compositions that do not pass by way of the capitalist economy any more than they do the State-form. The response of the States, or of the axiomatic, may obviously be to accord the minorities regional or federal or statutory autonomy, in short, to add axioms. (p. 470)

In other words, a minoritarian approach would question the nation-state as a default organizational model and bypass the state system, creating trans-state networks that promote, for example, the distribution of goods apart from state-regulated trade.[24] This would work as well for the distribution of information. The Internet currently allows networks of distributed intelligence to be established that routinely cross state borders, the content and traffic of which cannot realistically be regulated by the state (short of severing all phone lines). For example, there is the case of the United States' failed attempts to keep encryption software within its political borders. As I've noted earlier, the geography of the Internet is not that of traditional political geography. The establishment of such radical networks occurs not just within the United States and Western Europe, but within South America as well, where not only are South-South links being constructed but particular transcontinental feminist groups are flourishing (Reeve, 1994). If the GII is to be a private network, a joining of private networks, or even a joining of state networks, it promises simply to draw these minor nations further into the axiomatic, imposing additional axioms concerning the commodification of information, the centralization of networks, and so forth. But as a minoritarian network, a GII has radical possibilities.

Deleuze and Guattari (1987) point out that there are four particular flows that "torment the representatives of the world economy or of the axiomatic" (p. 468). These are flows of matter-energy, population, food, and the urban flow. The flows are problems that are created by the axiomatic itself, but that its axioms will not solve (by equally distributing food, or supplying appropriate and adequate sources of power, etc.). These flows return from the periphery (even the peripheries within the center) to the center as decoded flows.[25] "The more the decoded flows enter into a central axiomatic, the more they tend to escape to the periphery, to present problems that the axiomatic is incapable of resolving or controlling (even by adding special axioms for the periphery)" (p. 468). The axiomatic creates for itself problems that it will not solve, which leads to problems it cannot solve, which leads to the growth of minorities and multiplicities that elude the axiomatic. These four flows, then, are key sites for any international policy geared to counteract capitalism and its unequal flows of information.

Mahatma Gandhi once wrote:

> I do not want my house to be walled in on all sides and my windows stuffed. I want the cultures of all lands to be blown about my house as freely as possible. But I refuse to be blown off my feet by any. (quoted in Chifwambwa, 1985, p. 28; and Hamelink, 1983, p. 26)

Cees Hamelink (1983) takes this to mean that "acquisition of an independent identity is thus of primary importance" (p. 31). However, following Grossberg (1993), I feel that it is a recognition of the need to construct a place from which to stand and act within the global flows of space. This place may be in flux, changing through articulations and deterritorializations concerning other places and spaces. These places from which to act are necessarily the result of territorializing machines (which organize sites of attachment and possibilities for movement). Thus, the solution is not to posit a politics of identity that consists in the acquisition of some quickly reified "independent identity," or posit any necessary (physical, archeological, anthropological, or historical) connections to any particular space (or environment), or that may lapse back into Enlightenment notions of the individual, but rather a politics of space.

It is important that we understand these flows (of matter-energy, population, food, and the urban flow) *as flows*, as vectors, rather than understanding them by the points that they connect. To understand information as a flow necessarily assumes a consideration of the technologies with which the flows are wrapped up, and the codings and resonances of their energy stream (be they flashes of light in a fiber optic cable on the Information Highway or the resonances of soundwaves in air as verbal messages are passed). Meaghan Morris (1988a), writing about Michel de Certeau, makes a statement about travel stories that I believe is applicable to this approach to global information flows:

> The travel story, therefore, does not consist of process contained and directed by origin and destination, nor does it oscillate between "perspectives" on reality. It is itself a movement organized (like any spatial story) between both prospective and retrospective mappings of place *and* the practices that transform them. (p. 38)

From this episteme, a machinic episteme, there is no *a priori* reason that some flows (such as banking information or American satellite broadcasts) should take precedence over others (farm reports, gossip, travelers' tales, stories) in any particular situation (analysis or policy). It is not that we can and should treat all flows equally—but we *must* examine the ways flows are consistently *weighted* socially (and economically, affectually, etc.), in other words, the ways they are territorialized. From this, the rest of the analysis will follow, and we may be better able to change to a more equitable and balanced flow.

Bringing these conclusions and recommendations regarding global flows back to the NII and the U.S. social space that has been the focus of this book, I have two things to say. First, if indeed agency is increasingly technological, then we must find ways of analyzing and responding to that stratification. This new social space (cyberspace, if you will) is not inherently authoritarian, totalitarian, or capitalist, but it is a space where corporations and capitalist interests have had little difficulty making inroads, structuring and territorializing that space. In that within a more technologically dominant social space we move differently, then any critical intervention into that space requires at the very least a new *attitude* (in all its senses) toward space, the social, and technology.

Second, we must find alternative narrative structures (apart from modernist, linear ones such as the frontier/ homesteader myth being invoked by discourses around the Internet) to understand events in cyberspace and social space; narratives that do not isolate technology from the human or isolate cyberevents from the institutionalized structures of poverty, racism, and sexism that lie outside the wired world. In doing this we must construct a more equitable social space for all.

> Politics is active experimentation, since we do not know in advance which way a line is going to turn. Draw the line, says the accountant: but one can in fact draw it anywhere. (Deleuze & Parnet, 1987, p. 137)

Notes

1. The text of Gore's speech that I am working from was posted to an Internet list, IAMCRNET, by Howard Frederick, to whom I am grateful. All of Gore's quotes in this next section come from this source.

2. Larry Grossberg cites as a further example "the Fordist response to labor unions constituted everyday life as an axiomatic that incorporated the free

time of labor into the accumulation of capital through the dispersal of consumption. Similarly, the Fordist response to the relation of labor and machine involved an axiomatic of the regulation of space and time within the factory" (Grossberg, 1992, p. 349).

3. Deleuze and Guattari (1987) point out that "even the so-called socialist States are isomorphic, to the extent that there is *only one world market*, the capitalist one" (p. 455).

4. Deleuze and Guattari (1987) argue that the war machine now dominates the axiomatic; that since the automatization of the war machine after World War II, the war machine has become something else. "It is politics that becomes the continuation of war; *it is peace that technologically frees the unlimited material process of total war.* . . . More than that, the States no longer appropriated the war machine; they reconstituted a war machine of which they themselves were only the parts" (p. 467).

   Behind the invention and development of new communication and information technologies is the war machine. That this task was taken up by the state military apparatus is purely secondary in that the technology *exceeds* that apparatus and is exterior to the state itself. In places, the state still appropriates and dominates the war machine, but global communication and information technologies exceed the state, enfold the state. The war machine opposes the state appropriations of communication and information technology. Within communication and information networks, then (within global information space), there is both the striated, regularized, gridded space of the state, and the smooth, deterritorialized space of the war machine. In any communication or information system, there is always some element(s) that exceed it, that escape it *from within.*

5. A development in this regard would be a proposal that was put before Congress in April 1993 that would allow the Library of Congress to charge for access to data. Donald Curran, the associate librarian for the Library of Congress, states, "There is quite a lot of entrepreneurial interest in rendering library services in the future." Opponents to the bill worry that the fees fly in the face of the Library's democratic tradition of equal access. The Library claims, however, that it will still provide "basic, core library services" free; though what exactly those are is unstated (Richards, 1993).

6. The Non-Aligned Movement (NAM) sought to be an international policy-making body. However, the views voiced by (and in) the NAM did not necessarily represent the concerns of all those nations' citizens. Rather, the views presented were usually those of national elites, ruling blocs, or cosmopolitan intellectuals.

7. In this discussion, I do not mean to idealize the NAM or ignore the very real political struggles that compromised it. Armand Mattelart (1994) writes of supporters of the NAM and NIICO: "Indeed, examples were not lacking of

governments that, while taking the lead in demanding a new communication order and creating agency pools in the name of cultural identity, did not shrink from muzzling the press *in domo*, imprisoning journalists and banning from the large or small screen their filmmakers, who were obliged to go into exile" (p. 183).

8. See Hamelink, 1980, 1983, for a discussion of some of the consequences of the reduction of "information" to "news."

9. On recent developments in the development communication paradigm that move it away from this position, see, e.g., Jayaweera and Amunugama, 1987.

10. Some of political economy approaches to the mass media are based on assumptions similar to the media imperialists; cf. Guback, 1982.

11. For more on the military's hand in the invention and development of high technologies, see Castells, 1989, esp. chap. 5; Levidow and Robins, 1989; Mosco, 1989a; Noble, 1986; Smith, 1985; and Tirman, 1984. The now classic study of corporate involvement in research is Noble, 1977.

12. DBS, or Direct Broadcast Satellites, bypass any national controls over information by being able to transmit directly to home and local antennas. Also, during the 1970s, the West strove to establish the Integrated Services Digital Network (ISDN), which would dominate global communications and force Third World nations to conform to its technologies, standards, and so on. It promised to do wonders for global communication and technological compatibility but effectively created the only game in town, so to speak. Both of these technologies promise to play a central role in any GII.

13. Remember here that Deleuze and Guattari (1987) cite a Marshall Plan approach as an axiom (p. 462).

14. As you may recall from the theorizing of technology earlier in the book, any technology is necessarily a part of a system—a system both of other technologies, and also reaching into other planes: the social, the chemical, the biological, the linguistic. It is impossible to break all the articulations that make each technology possible, though it is less difficult, superficially, to rearticulate that technology into a new social situation (i.e., a "developing" culture), yet it will still retain many of its articulations to its original system.

15. As a result of this move by the West, and a similar call for technical assistance by several Third World countries, UNESCO set up the International Programme for the Development of Communication (IPDC).

16. For example, issues of women and communication are mentioned, but only briefly; Gallagher, 1984, 1985; Roach, 1990.

17. For detailed accounts of the United States' and U.S. press's attack on the MacBride Report, the NIICO, and UNESCO, see Coate, 1988; Giffard, 1989; Preston, Herman, and Schiller, 1989; and Roach, 1987.

18. See Traber and Nordenstreng, 1992; plus special issues of *Media Development* (the journal of the World Association for Christian Communication) throughout the 1980s; and a special issue of *Media, Culture and Society*, edited by Colin Sparks and Colleen Roach, 1990.

19. See Jameson's (1984) notion of postmodernism as a global "cultural dominant" that masks the working of capitalism.

20. The dissociation or delinking thesis is often subjected to a *reductio ad absurdum* by opponents of this position. For example, Colin Sparks writes, in opposition to his co-editor Colleen Roach's advocacy of "delinkage" as the way forward:

    if there is one central political lesson to be drawn from the 1980s it is of the failure of autarchic development, either in single countries or in blocs such as Comecon. The failure of the strategy even in its Soviet stronghold has demonstrated that it is in the long run impossible to withdraw from the world and world market. If "socialism in one country" is now demonstrably an impossibility, then *a fortiori*, communication in one country is impossible. (Sparks & Roach, 1990, p. 279)

    He goes on to describe the various economic horrors that result if one delinks oneself from the global market.

21. For example, Andrew Ross (1994) argues against the prevalent myth that Pacific Islanders lived in a paradise, in balance and harmony with nature, until the coming of the Europeans.

22. On the "Right to Communicate," see the special issue of *Media Development*, 1988, issue 4; also Splichal and Wasko (eds.), 1993.

23. The terms *majority/minority* do not refer to number, but rather to relations to the dominant power structure. The majority is an axiom in that, for example, regardless of actual numbers, white males still remain the "understood" majority, and therefore remain in positions of power.

24. "The question has always been organizational, not at all ideological: is an organization possible that is not modeled on the apparatus of the State, even to prefigure the State to come?" (Deleuze & Parnet, 1987, p. 145).

25. It is significant that these flows come from the periphery, from the South. Deleuze and Parnet (1987) write (with remarkable faith):

    [I]magine that between *the West and the East* a certain segmentarity is introduced, opposed in a binary machine, arranged in the State apparatuses, overcoded by an abstract machine as the sketch of a World Order. It is then from *North to South* that the destabilization takes place, as Giscard d'Estaing said gloomily, and a stream erodes a path, even if it is a shallow stream, which brings everything into play and diverts the plane of organization. A Corsican here, elsewhere a Palestinian, a plane hijacker, a tribal upsurge, a feminist movement, a Green ecologist, a Russian dissident—there will always be someone to rise up to the south. . . . The great ruptures, the great oppositions, are always negotiable; but not the little crack, the imperceptible ruptures that come from the south. We say "south" without attaching any importance to this. We talk of south to mark a direction that is different from that of the line of segments. But everyone has his [*sic*] south—it doesn't matter where it is—that is, his line of slope or flight. Nations, classes, sexes have their south. (pp. 131-132, emphasis in original)

Conclusion: Technology Is License to Forget

> There is a sense in which all technical activity contains an inherent tendency toward forgetfulness. Is it not the point of all invention, technique, apparatus, and organization to have something and *have it over with?* . . . Technology, then, allows us to ignore our own works. It is *license to forget.*
>
> Langdon Winner, *Autonomous Technology*

In his book *Autonomous Technology,* Langdon Winner (1977) argues that our reliance on technologies allows us to ignore the political effects of their function. We delegate tasks to our lieutenants, as Latour would put it, so we do not have to worry about them any more. The responsibility for that function is then diffused. We don't have to worry about pollution, global warming, unemployment, the atomic bomb, or repetitive strain injury. They remain external to us, for the most part, and little is done as a society to alleviate them. Winner would argue that one of the reasons for this laissez-faire attitude is the rise of autonomous technology—the common notion that technologies are value-neutral and self-developing. I argue in this book that autonomous technology is part and parcel with the modern (as a social and cultural formation) and results in part from the logic and horizons of the modern episteme, which separates our tools from ourselves. To "remember" technology, we have to put ourselves back on the same playing field as technologies. This book has been one attempt to do this, by arguing in terms of agency.

I place "remember" in quotes above because technology is never actually forgotten. It is always, every day, present in our lives. And, like the return of the repressed, eventually makes its presence felt, proliferating despite attempts to ignore it. This is especially true of communication technologies: They become such a part of our functioning that they disappear from active view, from critical consideration, they disappear into their content and into our communicative habits.

At the intersection of technology and social space is habit. Habit is a memory, a bodily memory. Technologies are not forgotten, rather they move from conscious memory to bodily memory. They come out in our hands, eyes, backs, shoulders, and in the repetition of our thoughts. They make their presence felt in our interfaces, interactions, in our ways of moving, in our ways of thinking, in our feel for the game, in our habitus. But it is not just habit that we are concerned with here, habits being the accretions of our movement through space, because the space we move through (and our subsequent memory of it, the effects etched on our brain and body) is always already stratified. Human social space is the stratification of technology and language. The shifting of this stratification alters who we are (because it *is* who we are) and what we can do (because it is a stratification of agencies and effects).

Therefore, the promise of a new stratification—a new technological assemblage and discursive assemblage—needs to be carefully examined. Call the new social space that incorporates this assemblage, cyberspace. But that term strikes me as more utopian, and much more geographically, culturally, and economically specific, every day. To examine this new space requires new tools, new methods, a shift in our perceptions. Specifically, it is a threefold project, or method, that I propose:

One, to examine critically the changing nature of technology and its concrete and prescriptive effects: What is being encultured in new technologies, and what do new technologies enculture? What social structures and operating criteria are reimposed by continued use of older (call them residual) technologies? In other words, this is a critical examination of the technological stratum, the effects of bodies on bodies, specifically the effects of technological bodies on other bodies and vice versa.

Two, examine the linguistic, discursive, and conceptual dimensions associated with technology. These are the discourses that play out on our television screens, in our films, in our policies, and in our daily lives. This is the critical examination of the linguistic stratum.

Three, examine the living of these two strata; the relationship between them embodied in everyday life, in habit, in culture, in practice, and in representations. How does one live one's life within a social space that offers a heavily overdetermined technological agency, while claiming to offer the unlimited freedom to accomplish anything through a new linguistic agency (as is promised about cyberspace)? For example, how is it that we enter the Museum of Science and Industry as students and tourists and exit as terminal citizens?

I have often been critiqued for seeming overly technophobic, or at least curmudgeonly, in my critical stance toward new technologies (and old technologies, for that matter). But it doesn't mean that technologies are bad or evil just because we've posed difficult or negative questions about them. In posing questions, I am not posing their answers as well. Indeed, we cannot know the answers in advance of the questions being asked (if we do, they are not the right questions), and we cannot know the answers that will be given for each specific iteration of a question from a particular moment and position. I believe that it is our duty to ask such questions, and then carefully consider for ourselves (as individuals or social groups) the consequences of the answers. But the questions must be posed. To be a technological curmudgeon (or, let's say it, a luddite) is not to reject technology *a priori* and *in toto*, but to reject the acceptance of technology *a priori* and *in toto* (without asking questions). And we also must realize that there are never technology questions that only can be answered by technology answers. In that technologies have resonance with other planes, other strata, technology questions can have discursive answers, moral answers, cultural answers, and so forth.

There are far too many pronouncements about the future of the new technologies being made these days for me to state any final, grand conclusion about the Internet or cyberspace here. And I would never presume to speak for all aspects of its varied terrain. Besides, such pronouncements either reiterate the same things said of the printing press, telegraph, telephone, radio, television, computer, and so on, or are quickly outdated (and thus would not be useful by the time this book sees print). Making such a survey or statement was never the purpose of this book. Rather, what I hope I have done here is to reveal some of the epistemological underpinnings of our commonsense approaches to the role of technology in our lives and our societies and cultures, to examine why arguments about technology do seem so repetitive and circular, and to present a different perspective that gets us out of the rut of the modern and better explains some of the ways technology and social space intertwine, interact, and are mutually constitutive.

References

Adcock, C. (1983, October). Dada cyborgs and the imagery of science fiction. *Arts Magazine*, pp. 66-71.

Aldrich/Pears Associates. (1993, February 12). *Exhibit content outline: Communications: Your link to a better life.* Vancouver, BC, Canada: Author.

Alperovitz, G. (1995). *The decision to use the atomic bomb and the architecture of an American myth.* New York: Knopf.

Amin, S. (1989). *Eurocentrism.* New York: Monthly Review Press.

Anderson, B. (1983). *Imagined communities: Reflections on the origin and spread of nationalism.* New York: Verso.

AT&T. (1993). *Connections: AT&T's vision of the future* [Video].

Balbus, I. (1982). *Marxism and domination: A neo-Hegelian, feminist, psychoanalytic theory of sexual, political and technological liberation.* Princeton, NJ: Princeton University Press.

Baudrillard, J. (1983). *Simulations* (P. Foss, P. Patton, & P. Beitchmann, Trans.). New York: Semiotext(e).

Baudrillard, J. (1988). *The ecstasy of communication* (B. Schutze & C. Schutze, Trans.). New York: Semiotext(e).

Bellah, R. N., Madsen, R., Sullivan, W. M., Swidler, A., & Tipton, S. M. (1985). *Habits of the heart: Individualism and commitment in American life.* New York: Perennial.

Belsie, L. (1993, May 11). Al Gore seeks government as technology "facilitator." *Christian Science Monitor*, pp. 1, 4.

Beniger, J. R. (1986). *The control revolution: Technological and economic origins of the information society.* Cambridge, MA: Harvard University Press.

Bennett, T. (1986). The politics of "the popular" and popular culture. In T. Bennett, C. Mercer, & J. Woollacott (Eds.), *Popular culture and social relations*. Philadelphia: Open University Press.

Bennett, T. (1988, Spring). The exhibitionary complex. *New Formations*, 73-103.

Bennett, T. (1990). *Outside literature*. New York: Routledge.

Berkun, S. (1995). Agent of change. *Wired, 3*(4), 116-117.

Berman, M. (1988). *All that is solid melts into air: The experience of modernity*. New York: Penguin.

Bijker, W. E., Hughes, T. P., & Pinch, T. (Eds.). (1987). *The social construction of technology systems: New directions in the sociology and history of technology*. Cambridge, MA: MIT Press.

Bogue, R. (1989). *Deleuze and Guattari*. New York: Routledge.

Bommes, M., & Wright, P. (1982). "Charms of residence": The public and the past. In R. Johnson et al. (Eds.), *Making histories: Studies in history writing and politics*. London: Hutchinson.

Borgmann, A. (1984). *Technology and the character of contemporary life: A philosophical inquiry*. Chicago: University of Chicago Press.

Bourdieu, P. (1990). Social space and symbolic power. In *In other words: Essays toward a reflective society* (pp. 123-139). Stanford, CA: Stanford University Press.

Boyer, P. (1985). *By the bomb's early light: American thought and culture at the dawn of the atomic age*. New York: Pantheon.

Brook, J., & Boal, I. A. (Eds.). (1995). Preface. In *Resisting the virtual life: The culture and politics of information* (pp. vii-xv). San Francisco: City Lights.

Brooks, J. (1976). *Telephone: The first hundred years*. New York: Harper & Row.

Browning, J. (1994, February). Get on track: There will be no info highway. *Wired*, pp. 65-66.

Bruno, G. (1990). Ramble city: Postmodernism and *Blade Runner*. In A. Kuhn (Ed.), *Alien zone: Cultural theory and contemporary science fiction* (pp. 183-195). New York: Verso.

Buck-Morss, S. (1989). *The dialectics of seeing: Walter Benjamin and the Arcades Project*. Cambridge, MA: MIT Press.

Bud, R. (1988). The myth and the machine: Seeing science through museum eyes. In G. Fyfe & J. Law (Eds.), *Picturing power: Visual depiction and social relations* (pp. 134-159). New York: Routledge.

Butler, S. V. (1992). *Science and technology museums*. New York: Leicester University Press.

Callon, M. (1987). Society in the making: The study of technology as a tool for sociological analysis. In W. Bijker, T. P. Hughes, & T. Pinch (Eds.), *The social construction of technology systems: New directions in the sociology and history of technology* (pp. 83-103). Cambridge, MA: MIT Press.

Callon, M. (1993, May 7). Social ordering [Lecture]. University of Illinois, Urbana-Champaign.

Callon, M., & Latour, B. (1981). Unscrewing the big Leviathan: How actors macro-structure reality and how sociologists help them do so. In K. Knorr-Cetina & A. Cicourel (Eds.), *Advances in social theory and methodology: Toward an integration of micro- and macro-sociologies* (pp. 277-303). Boston, London, and Henley: Routledge & Kegan Paul.

Calvino, I. (1980). Baron in the trees (A. Colquhoun, Trans.). In *Our ancestors* (pp. 72-284). London: Picador.

Cameron, J. (Director). (1984). *Terminator* [Film].

Cameron, J. (Director). (1991). *Terminator 2: Judgment day* [Film].

Čapek, K. (1923). *R.U.R. (Rossum's Universal Robots): A fantastic melodrama* (P. Selver, Trans.). Garden City, NY: Doubleday.

Capriles, O. (1980). Some remarks on the new international information order. In C. Hamelink (Ed.), *Communication in the eighties: A reader on the McBride* [sic] *Report* (pp. 30-32). Rome: IDOC International.

Carey, J. W. (1989). *Communication as culture: Essays on media and society.* Boston: Unwin Hyman.

Castells, M. (1989). *The informational city: Information technology, economic restructuring and the urban-regional process.* Cambridge, MA: Blackwell.

Chifwambwa, G. S. (1985). Communication technology and tradition must be compatible. *Media Development,* (4), 28-30.

Christians, C. (1989). A theory of normative technology. In E. Byrne & J. Pitt (Eds.), *Technological transformation: Contextual and conceptual implications* (pp. 123-139). Boston: Kluwer.

Coate, R. A. (1988). *Unilateralism, ideology, and U.S. foreign policy: The United States in and out of UNESCO.* Boulder, CO and London: Lynne Rienner.

Cohn, C. (1989). Sex and death in the rational world of defense intellectuals. In M. R. Malson, J. F. O'Barr, S. Westphal-Wihl, & M. Wyer (Eds.), *Feminist theory in practice and process* (pp. 107-138). Chicago: University of Chicago Press.

Colombat, A. P. (1991). A thousand trails to work with Deleuze. *SubStance, 20*(3), 10-23.

Connerton, P. (1989). *How societies remember.* New York: Cambridge University Press.

Copleston, F. (1985). *A history of philosophy* (Vol. 6). New York: Image.

Cowan, R. S. (1983). *More work for mother: The ironies of household technology from the open hearth to the microwave.* New York: Basic Books.

Danilov, V. J. (1982). *Science and technology centers.* Cambridge, MA: MIT Press.

de Certeau, M. (1984). *The practice of everyday life* (S. Rendall, Trans.). Berkeley: University of California Press.

De Landa, M. (1991). *War in the age of intelligent machines.* New York: Zone.

Deleuze, G. (1984). *Kant's critical philosophy* (H. Tomlinson & B. Habberjam, Trans.). Minneapolis: University of Minnesota Press.

Deleuze, G. (1989). *Cinema 2* (H. Tomlinson & R. Galatea, Trans.). Minneapolis: University of Minnesota Press.

Deleuze, G. (1993). *The Fold* (T. Conley, Trans.). Minneapolis: University of Minnesota Press.

Deleuze, G. (1994). *Difference and repetition.* (P. Patton, Trans.). New York: Columbia University Press.

Deleuze, G., & Guattari, F. (1983). *Anti-Oedipus: Capitalism and schizophrenia* (R. Hurley, M. Seem, & H. R. Lane, Trans.). Minneapolis: University of Minnesota Press.

Deleuze, G., & Guattari, F. (1987). *A thousand plateaus: Capitalism and schizophrenia* (B. Massumi, Trans.). Minneapolis: University of Minnesota Press.

Deleuze, G., & Guattari, F. (1994). *What is philosophy?* (H. Tomlinson & G. Burchell, Trans.). New York: Columbia University Press.

Deleuze, G., & Parnet, C. (1987). *Dialogues* (H. Tomlinson & B. Habberjam, Trans.). New York: Columbia University Press.

Derber, C. (1994, November/December). Individualism runs amok in the marketplace. *Utne Reader,* pp. 111-117. Reprinted from *Tikkun, 8*(4).

Derrida, J. (1976). *Of grammatology* (G. C. Spivak, Trans.). Baltimore: Johns Hopkins University Press.

Dick, P. K. (1982). *Do androids dream of electric sheep?* New York: Ballantine (original work published 1968).

Doctorow, E. L. (1995, August 14-21). Mythologizing the bomb. *The Nation,* pp. 149, 170-173.

Doll, S., & Faller, G. (1986). "Blade Runner" and genre: Film noir and science fiction. *Literature and Film Quarterly, 14*(2), 89-100.

Drew, J. (1995). Media activism and radical democracy. In J. Brook & I. A. Boal (Eds.), *Resisting the virtual life: The culture and politics of information* (pp. 71-83). San Francisco: City Lights.

Ekwelie, S. A. (1985). African nations must redirect information flow. *Media Development,* (1), 27-29.

Ellul, J. (1964). *The technological society* (J. Wilkinson, Trans.). New York: Vintage.

Elmer-Dewitt, P. (1993, April 12). Take a trip to the future on the electronic superhighway. *Time,* pp. 56-58.

Elmer-DeWitt, P. (1995, Spring). Welcome to cyberspace. *Time* (Special Issue), pp. 4-11.

Fedida, S., & Malik, R. (1979). *Viewdata revolution.* New York: Wiley.

Feenberg, A. (1991). *Critical theory of technology.* New York: Oxford University Press.

Ferguson, E. S. (1965, Winter). Technical museums and international exhibitions. *Technology and Culture,* pp. 30-46.

Fermi, R., & Samra, E. (1995). *Picturing the bomb: Photographs from the secret world of the Manhattan Project.* New York: Abrams.

Finn, B. S. (1965, Winter). The science museum today. *Technology and Culture,* pp. 74-82.

Fischer, C. S. (1988, January). "Touch someone": The telephone industry discovers sociability. *Technology and Culture,* pp. 32-61.

Fortner, R. (1995). Excommunication in the information society. *Critical Studies in Mass Communication,* 12(2), 133-154.

Foucault, M. (1977). *Discipline and punish: The birth of the prison* (A. Sheridan, Trans.). Harmondsworth, UK: Penguin.

Francavilla, J. (1991). The android as Dopplegänger. In J. B. Kerman (Ed.), *Retrofitting "Blade runner": Issues in Ridley Scott's "Blade runner" and Philip K. Dick's "Do androids dream of electric sheep?"* (pp. 4-15). Bowling Green, OH: Bowling Green State University Popular Press.

Furman, N. S. (1990). *Sandia National Laboratories: The postwar decade.* Albuquerque: University of New Mexico Press.

Gabilondo, J. (1995). Postcolonial cyborgs: Subjectivity in the age of cybernetic reproduction. In C. H. Gray (Ed.), *The cyborg handbook* (pp. 423-432). New York: Routledge.

Gallagher, M. (1984). Parallels and paradoxes of women and the NWICO. *Media Development,* (2), 2-6.

Gallagher, M. (1985). Women and the NWICO. In P. Lee (Ed.), *Communication for all: New World Information and Communication Order* (pp. 33-56). Maryknoll, NY: Orbis.

The genius behind the bomb [Television program]. (1992, September 29). (*Nova,* no. 1911). PBS.

Germain, G. (1993). *A discourse on disenchantment: Reflections on politics and technology.* Albany: SUNY Press.

Gibbins, D. (Director). (1991). *Eve of destruction* [Film].

Gibson, W. (1984). *Neuromancer.* New York: Ace.

Giffard, C. A. (1989). *UNESCO and the media.* New York and London: Longman.

Gledhill, C. (1980). "Klute" 1: A contemporary film noir and feminist criticism. In E. A. Kaplan (Ed.), *Women in film noir* (pp. 6-21). London: BFI.

Gonzalez Manet, E. (1986). Issues and developments. In K. Nordenstreng, E. Gonzalez Manet, & W. Kleinwachter (Eds.), *New International Information and Communication Order: Sourcebook* (pp. 43-60). Prague: International Organization of Journalists.

Gray, C. H. (1989). The cyborg soldier: The U.S. military and the post-modern warrior. In L. Levidow & K. Robins (Eds.), *Cyborg worlds: The military information society* (pp. 43-71). London: Free Association.

Gray, C. H. (Ed.). (1995). (With H. J. Figueroa-Sarriera & S. Mentor). *The cyborg handbook.* New York: Routledge.

Gray, C. H., Mentor, S., & Figueroa-Sarriera, H. J. (1995). Introduction: Constructing the knowledge of cybernetic organisms. In C. H. Gray (Ed.), *The cyborg handbook* (pp. 1-16). New York: Routledge.

Gray, C. H., & Mentor, S. (1995). The cyborg body politic and the new world order. In G. Brahm, Jr., & M. Driscoll (Eds.), *Prosthetic territories: Politics and hypertechnologies* (pp. 219-247). Boulder, CO: Westview.

Gregory, D. (1994). *Geographical imaginations.* Cambridge, MA: Blackwell.

Grossberg, L. (1992). *We gotta get out of this place: Popular conservatism and postmodern culture.* New York: Routledge.

Grossberg, L. (1993). Cultural studies and/in new worlds. *Critical Studies in Mass Communication, 10*(1), 1-22.

Grossberg, L. (1995). The space of culture, the power of space: Cultural studies and globalization. In I. Chambers & L. Curti (Eds.), *Common skies/Divided horizons: The postcolonial question* (pp. 169-188). London: Routledge.

Grossberger, L. (1994, January 10). Coming in lashed. *Mediaweek.*

Guback, T. (1982). *Transnational communication and cultural industries.* Paris: UNESCO.

Hamelink, C. (1980). The NIIO: The recognition of many different worlds. *Media Development,* (4), 3-6.

Hamelink, C. (1983). *Cultural autonomy in global communications: Planning national information policy.* New York: Longman.

Haraway, D. (1991a). A cyborg manifesto: Science, technology, and socialist-feminism in the late twentieth century. In *Simians, cyborgs, and women: The reinvention of nature* (pp. 149-181). New York: Routledge.

Haraway, D. (1991b). The promise of monsters: A regenerative politics for inappropriate/d others. In L. Grossberg, C. Nelson, P. Treichler, with L. Baughman & J. M. Wise (Eds.), *Cultural studies* (pp. 295-337). New York: Routledge.

Haraway, D. (1991c). Situated knowledges: The science question in feminism and the privilege of partial perspective. In *Simians, cyborgs, and women: The reinvention of nature* (pp. 183-201). New York: Routledge.

Hay, J. (1989). *Updating the family album: Historical narrative and the production of popular memory in a television culture.* Paper presented at the Seventh International Conference on Culture and Communication, Philadelphia.

Hay, J. (1993, Summer). Invisible cities/visible geographies: Toward a cultural geography of Italian television in the 90s. *Quarterly Review of Film and Video,* 35-48.

Hayles, N. K. (1993a). The materiality of informatics. *Configurations, 1*(1), 147-170.

Hayles, N. K. (1993b). The seduction of cyberspace. In V. A. Conley (Ed.), *Rethinking technologies* (pp. 173-190). Minneapolis: University of Minnesota Press.

Hayward, P., & Wollen, T. (Eds.). (1993). *Future visions: New technologies of the screen.* London: BFI.

Heidegger, M. (1977). *The question concerning technology and other essays* (W. Lovitt, Trans.). New York: Harper Torchbooks.

Hersey, J. (1946). *Hiroshima.* New York: Bantam.

Hoddeson, L., Henriksen, P. W., Meade, R. A., & Westfall, C. (1993). *Critical assembly: A technical history of Los Alamos during the Oppenheimer years, 1943-1945.* New York: Cambridge University Press.

Hooper-Greenhill, E. (1992). *Museums and the shaping of knowledge.* New York: Routledge.

Hudson, K. (1987). *Museums of influence.* New York: Cambridge University Press.

Hunter, S. (1989, October 22). 1945-1989: Facing the bomb on film [review of *Fatman and Little Boy*]. *Baltimore Sun.*

Illich, I. (1973). *Tools for conviviality.* New York: Harper & Row.

Jameson, F. (1984). Postmodernism, or the cultural logic of late capitalism. *New Left Review, 146,* 53-92.

Jarvis, J. (1989, March 6). [Review of "Day One"]. *People,* pp. 11-12.

Jayaweera, N. (1987). Introduction. In N. Jayaweera & S. Amunugama (Eds.), *Rethinking development communication.* Singapore: AMIC.

Jayaweera, N., & Amunugama, S. (Eds.). (1987). *Rethinking development communication.* Singapore: AMIC.

Jeffords, S. (1993). The big switch: Hollywood masculinity in the nineties. In J. Collins, H. Radner, & A. P. Collins (Eds.), *Film theory goes to the movies* (pp. 196-208). New York: Routledge.

Jonas, H. (1984). *The imperative of responsibility: In search of an ethics for the technological age.* Chicago: University of Chicago Press.

Kaempffert, W. (1933). *From cave-man to engineer: The Museum of Science and Industry founded by Julius Rosenwald: An institution to reveal the technical ascent of man.* Chicago: Lakeside.

Kantrowitz, B. (1993, May 31). An interactive life. *Newsweek,* pp. 42-44.

Kantrowitz, B. (1994, February 14). The metaphor is the message: Technology: A software icon is worth 1,000 words. *Newsweek,* p. 49.

Keegan, P. (1995, May 21). The digiterati! *New York Times Magazine,* pp. 38-45, 86-88.

Kershner, I. (Director). (1980). *Empire strikes back* [Film].

Kershner, I. (Director). (1990). *Robocop 2* [Film].

Kleinwachter, W. (1986). Aims and principles. In K. Nordenstreng, E. Gonzalez Manet, & W. Kleinwachter (Eds.), *New International Information and Communication Order: Sourcebook* (pp. 61-93). Prague: International Organization of Journalists.

Kojève, A. (1969). *Introduction to the reading of Hegel* [Assembled by Raymond Queneau] (A. Bloom, Ed.; J. H. Nichols Jr., Trans.). New York: Basic Books.

Kolb, W. M. (1991). Script to screen: "Blade Runner" in perspective. In J. B. Kerman (Ed.), *Retrofitting "Blade Runner": Issues in Ridley Scott's "Blade Runner" and Philip K. Dick's "Do Androids Dream of Electric Sheep?"* (pp. 132-153). Bowling Green, OH: Bowling Green State University Popular Press.

Kramarae, C. (1994, March 23). *The language of cyberspace: Searching for social messages* [Jubilee Lecture]. University of Illinois at Urbana-Champaign.

Krol, E. (1993). *The whole Internet user's guide and catalog.* Sebastapol, CA: O'Reilly & Associates.

Krupnick, J. (1989, March 5). "Day One" for the bomb [Review]. *Newark Star-Leader.*

Latour, B. (1988). Mixing humans and nonhumans together: The sociology of a door closer. *Social Problems, 35,* 298-310.

Latour, B. (1993). *We have never been modern* (C. Porter, Trans.). Cambridge, MA: Harvard University Press.

Latour, B. (1994, October 11). *Will modernization continue? Reflections on science and democracy* [Lecture]. University of Illinois at Urbana-Champaign.

Latour, B. (1995). The "Pédofil" of Boa Vista: A photo-philosophical montage (B. Simon & K. Verresen, Trans.). *Common Knowledge, 4*(1), 144-187.

Law, J. (1987). Technology and heterogeneous engineering: The case of Portuguese expansion. In W. E. Bijker, T. P. Hughes, & T. Pinch (Eds.), *The social construction of technology systems: New directions in the sociology and history of technology* (pp. 111-134). Cambridge, MA: MIT Press.

Lefebvre, H. (1978). *De l'état: Vol. 4. Les contradictions de l'état moderne* [The state: Vol. 4. The contradictions of the modern state]. Paris: UGE.

Lefebvre, H. (1981). *De la modernité au modernisme (Pour une métaphilosophe du quotidien)* [From modernity to modernism (for a metaphilosophy of the quotidian)]. Paris: L'Arche Editeur.

Lefebvre, H. (1991). *The production of space* (D. Nicholson-Smith, Trans.). Cambridge, MA: Blackwell.

Lenin, V. (1969). *Collected works: Vol. 42. Supplementary material: October 1917–March 1923.* London: Lawrence and Wishart.

Lentz, K. M. (1993). The popular pleasures of female revenge (or, rage bursting in a blaze of gunfire). *Cultural Studies, 7*(3), 374-405.

Leonard, J. (1989, March 6). Masters of the universe [Review of "Day One"]. *New York,* p. 97.

Lerner, D. (1958). *The passing of traditional society: Modernizing the Middle East.* New York: Free Press.

Lerner, D., & Schramm, W. (Eds.). (1967). *Communication and change in developing countries.* Honolulu: East-West Press.

Leroux, C. (1993, February 28). Back to the present. *Chicago Tribune Magazine,* pp. 10-15.

Levidow, L., & Robins, K. (Eds.). (1989). *Cyborg worlds: The military information society.* London: Free Association.

Levinson, M. (1993, October 25). Dial U for uncertainty. *Newsweek,* pp. 44-45.

Lewis, J. (1994, February 7). Solve real problems: Avoid the superhighway. *PC Week.*

Lifton, R. J., & Mitchell, G. (1995). *Hiroshima in America: A half-century of denial.* New York: Avon.

Lipsitz, G. (1990). *Time passages: Collective memory and American popular culture.* Minneapolis: University of Minnesota Press.

Lofficier, R., & Lofficier, J. (1987, July). The primordial "Star Wars." *Starlog,* pp. 17-20.

Lucas, G. (Director). (1977). *Star wars* [Film].

Lukács, G. (1971). *History and class consciousness: Studies in Marxist dialectics* (R. Livingstone, Trans.). Cambridge, MA: MIT Press.

Lyotard, J.-F. (1984). *The postmodern condition: A report on knowledge* (G. Bennington & B. Massumi, Trans.). Minneapolis: University of Minnesota Press.

MacBride, S. (Ed.). (1980). *Many voices, one world: Communication and society, today and tomorrow.* New York: Unipub.

Marcuse, H. (1964). *One-dimensional man.* Boston: Beacon Press.

Markoff, J. (1993, January 24). Building the electronic superhighway. *New York Times,* section 3, pp. 1, 6.

Markoff, J. (1994, May 29). Conversations/Louis Rossetto: The view from cyberspace: The revolution will be digitized. *New York Times,* p. O31.

Marquand, R. (Director). (1983). *Return of the Jedi* [Film].

Martin, J. (1982). *Viewdata and the information society.* Englewood Cliffs, NJ: Prentice Hall.

Marvin, C. (1988). *When old technologies were new: Thinking about electric communication in the late nineteenth century.* New York: Oxford University Press.

Marx, K. (1973). *Grundrisse.* Harmondsworth, UK: Penguin.

Marx, K., & Engels, F. (1982). *Collected works* (Vol. 38). London: Lawrence and Wishart.

Massey, D. (1994). *Space, place, and gender.* Minneapolis: University of Minnesota Press.

Massumi, B. (1992). *A user's guide to capitalism and schizophrenia: Deviations from Deleuze and Guattari.* Cambridge, MA: MIT Press.

Mattelart, A. (1994). *Mapping world communication: War, progress, culture* (S. Emanuel & J. A. Cohen, Trans.). Minneapolis: University of Minnesota Press.

Mattelart, A., Delacourt, X., & Mattelart, M. (1984). International image markets. In C. Schneider & B. Wallis (Eds.), *Global Television.* (pp. 13-33). Cambridge, MA: MIT Press.

Mayne, A. (1982). *The videotex revolution.* Fareham: October Press.

McLuhan, M. (1964). *Understanding media: The extensions of man.* New York: Signet.

McLuhan, M., & Fiore, Q. (1967). *The medium is the message.* New York: Bantam.

Melehy, H. (1995). Images without: Deleuzian becoming, science fiction cinema in the eighties. *Postmodern Culture, 5*(2).

Michaels, E. (1994). *Bad Aboriginal art: Tradition, media, and technological horizons.* Minneapolis: University of Minnesota Press.

Mitchell, W. J. (1995). *City of bits: Space, place, and the infobahn.* Cambridge, MA: MIT Press.

Morris, M. (1988a). At Henry Parkes Motel. *Cultural Studies, 2*(1), 1-47.

Morris, M. (1988b). Politics now: Anxieties of a petit-bourgeois intellectual. In *The pirate's fiancee* (pp. 173-186). New York: Verso.

Morton, A. (1988). Tomorrow's yesterdays: Science museums and the future. In R. Lumley (Ed.), *The museum time-machine* (pp. 128-143). New York: Routledge.

Mosco, V. (1989a). *The pay-per society: Computers and communication in the information age.* Norwood, NJ: Ablex.

Mosco, V. (1989b). Strategic offence: Star Wars as military hegemony. In L. Levidow & K. Robins (Eds.), *Cyborg worlds: The military information society* (pp. 87-112). London: Free Association.

Mumford, L. (1963). *Technics and civilization.* New York: Harcourt Brace Jovanovich.

Mumford, L. (1967). *Technics and human development.* New York: Harcourt Brace Jovanovich .

Museum of Science and Industry. (1991, July 3). Exhibit proposal. Chicago: Author.

Museum of Science and Industry. (1992). *Annual Report.* Chicago: Author.

Museum of Science and Industry. (1993). *Teacher's guide & student activity tour to accompany the communications exhibit.* Chicago: Author.

Negroponte, N. (1995). *Being digital.* New York: Knopf.

The net: An apology from America offline. (1994, February 14). *Newsweek,* p. 49.

Noble, D. F. (1977). *America by design: Science, technology and the rise of corporate capitalism.* New York: Oxford University Press.

Noble, D. F. (1986). *Forces of production: A social history of industrial automation.* New York: Oxford University Press.

Nordenstreng, K. (1986). The rise and life of the concept. In K. Nordenstreng, E. Gonzalez Manet, & W. Kleinwachter (Eds.), *New International Information and Communication Order: Sourcebook* (pp. 9-42). Prague: International Organization of Journalists.

Nordenstreng, K., Gonzalez Manet, E., & Kleinwachter, W. (Eds.). (1986). *New International Information and Communication Order: Sourcebook.* Prague: International Organization of Journalists.

Nordenstreng, K., & Varis, T. (1974). *Television traffic: A one-way street?* Paris: UNESCO.

O'Sullivan, T. (1991). Television memories and cultures of viewing, 1950-65. In J. Corner (Ed.), *Popular television in Britain: Studies in cultural history* (pp. 159-181). London: BFI.

Opubor, A. E. (1980). Groping towards elusive concepts. In C. Hamelink (Ed.), *Communication in the eighties: A reader on the McBride [sic] report* (pp. 4-7). Rome: IDOC International.

Pacey, A. (1983). *The culture of technology.* Cambridge, MA: MIT Press.

Penley, C. (1990). Time travel, primal scene and the critical dystopia. In A. Kuhn (Ed.), *Alien zone: Cultural theory and contemporary science fiction cinema* (pp. 116-127). New York: Verso.

Preston, W. J., Herman, E. S., & Schiller, H. I. (Eds.). (1989). *Hope and folly: The United States and UNESCO 1945-1985.* Minneapolis: University of Minnesota Press.

Pyun, A. (Director). (1989). *Cyborg* [Film].

Pyun, A. (Director). (1993). *Nemesis* [Film].

Raskin, J. (1993, December). Down with GUI's. *Wired,* pp. 122-123.

Ratan, S. (1995, Spring). A new divide between haves and have-nots? *Time* (Special issue), pp. 25-26.

Reeve, C. (1994, July 10). Latinas lead the world in networking. *Chicago Tribune,* p. 1.

Reinhardt, A. (1994, March). Building the data highway. *Byte,* pp. 46-74.

Rheingold, H. (1993). *The virtual community: Homesteading on the electronic frontier.* Reading, MA: Addison-Wesley.

Rhodes, R. (1986). *The making of the atomic bomb.* New York: Simon & Schuster.

Richards, M. (1993, April 8). Library of Congress sets off debate with its plan to sell computer data. *The Christian Science Monitor.*

Richardson, J. H. (1994, August). Iron Jim. *Premiere,* pp. 44-55, 97.

Ricoeur, P. (1980, Autumn). Narrative time. *Critical Inquiry,* pp. 169-190.

Riding, C. (1995). Drowning by Microgallery. In J. Brook & I. A. Boal (Eds.), *Resisting the virtual life: The culture and politics of information* (pp. 243-251). San Francisco: City Lights.

Roach, C. (1987). The position of the Reagan administration on the NWICO. *Media Development,* (4), 32-37.

Roach, C. (1990). The movement for a New World Information and Communication Order: A second wave? *Media, Culture and Society, 12,* 283-307.

Ross, A. (1991). *Strange weather: Culture, science and technology in the age of limits.* New York: Verso.

Ross, A. (1994). *The Chicago gangster theory of life: Nature's debt to society.* New York: Verso.

Saffady, W. (1990). *High definition television: A bibliography.* Westport, CT: Meckler.

Sargent, J. (Director). (1970). *Colossus: The Forbin project* [Film].

Sargent, J. (Director). (1989, March 5). *AT&T presents: Day one* [Television program]. Script by David W. Rintels. New York: CBS.

Schatz, T. (1993). The new Hollywood. In J. Collins, H. Radner, & A. P. Collins (Eds.), *Film theory goes to the movies* (pp. 8-36). New York: Routledge.

Schiller, H. I. (1980). Will advanced communication technology create a new order? *Media Development,* (4), 22-24.

Schiller, H. I. (1983). The communication revolution: Who benefits? *Media Development,* (4), 18-20.

Schiller, H. I. (1989). Is there a United States information policy? In W. J. Preston, E. S. Herman, & H. I. Schiller (Eds.), *Hope and folly: The United States and UNESCO, 1945-1985* (pp. 285-312). Minneapolis: University of Minnesota Press.

Schivelbusch, W. (1986). *The railway journey: The industrialization of time and space in the 19th century*. Berkeley: University of California Press.

Schramm, W. (1964). *Mass media and national development*. Stanford, CA: Stanford University Press.

Schumacher, E. F. (1973). *Small is beautiful: Economics as if people mattered*. New York: Harper & Row.

Schumacher, E. F. (1977). *A guide for the perplexed*. New York: Harper Colophon.

Scott, R. (Director). (1982). *Blade runner* [Film].

Serres, M., with Latour, B. (1995). *Conversations on science, culture, and time* (R. Lapidus, Trans.). Ann Arbor: University of Michigan Press.

Servaes, J. (1988). The right to communicate is a basic human right. *Media Development*, (4), 15-17.

Shannon, C., & Weaver, W. (1949). *The mathematical theory of communication*. Urbana: University of Illinois Press.

Simpson, L. (1995). *Technology, time, and the conversations of modernity*. New York: Routledge.

Sivanandan, A. (1996). Heresies and prophecies: The social and political fall-out of the technological revolution: An interview. *Race & Class, 37*(4), 1-11.

Slack, J. D. (1984). *Communication technologies and society: Conceptions of causality and the politics of technological innovation*. Norwood, NJ: Ablex.

Slotkin, R. (1985). *The fatal environment: The myth of the frontier in the age of industrialization, 1800-1890*. New York: Atheneum.

Smith, M. C. (1986). *Stallion gate*. New York: Random House.

Smith, M. R. (Ed.). (1985). *Military enterprise and technological change: Perspectives on the American experience*. Cambridge, MA: MIT Press.

Sparks, C., & Roach, C. (1990). [Editorial.] *Media, Culture and Society, 12*, 275-281.

Splichal, S., & Wasko, J. (Eds.). (1993). *Communication and democracy*. Norwood, NJ: Ablex.

Springer, C. (1991). The pleasure of the interface. *Screen, 32*(3), 303-323.

Stahlman, M. (1994, March). Backlash: The infobahn is a big, fat joke. *Wired*, p. 73.

Stanley, M. (1978). *The technological conscience: Survival and dignity in an age of expertise*. Chicago: University of Chicago Press.

Star, S. L. (1991). Power, technology, and the phenomenology of conventions: On being allergic to onions. In J. Law (Ed.), *A sociology of monsters? Power, technology, and the modern world* (pp. 27-57). Oxford: Blackwell.

Steinberg, S. (1994, January). Hypelist: Cryptography. *Wired*, p. 130.

Street, J. (1992). *Politics and technology*. New York: Guilford.

Taylor, B. C. (1992). The politics of the nuclear text: Reading Robert Oppenheimer's *Letters and Recollections. Quarterly Journal of Speech, 78*(4), 429-449.

Taylor, B. C. (1993a). "Fat Man and Little Boy": The cinematic representations of interests in the nuclear weapons organization. *Critical Studies in Mass Communication, 10,* 367-394.

Taylor, B. C. (1993b). Register of the repressed: Women's voice and body in the nuclear weapons organization. *Quarterly Journal of Speech, 79*(4), 267-285.

Tirman, J. (Ed.). (1984). *The militarization of high technology.* Cambridge, MA: Ballinger.

Traber, M. (1980). Editorial: Towards a New International Information Order (NIIO). *Media Development,* (4), 1-2.

Traber, M., & Nordenstreng, K. (Eds.). (1992). *Few voices, many worlds: Towards a media reform movement.* London: World Association for Christian Communication.

Turner, G. (1993). *Film as social practice* (2nd ed.). New York: Routledge.

Ullmann, E. (1995). Out of time: Reflections on the programming life. In J. Brook & I. A. Boal (Eds.), *Resisting the virtual life: The culture and politics of information* (pp. 131-143). San Francisco: City Lights.

Van Bakel, R. (1996). How good people helped make a bad law. *Wired, 4*(2), 133-135, 181-186.

Verhoeven, P. (Director). (1987). *Robocop* [Film].

Vilanilam, J. (1989). *Reporting a revolution: The Iranian revolution and the NIICO debate.* London: Sage.

Virilio, P. (1993). The third interval: A critical transition. In V. A. Conley (Ed.), *Rethinking technologies* (pp. 3-12). Minneapolis: University of Minnesota Press.

Virilio, P. (1995). *The art of the motor* (J. Rose, Trans.). Minneapolis: University of Minnesota Press.

von Auw, A. (1983). *Heritage and destiny: Reflections on the Bell system in transition.* New York: Praeger.

Vonnegut, K. J. (1969). *Slaughterhouse five, or the Children's Crusade, a duty-dance with death.* New York: Dell.

Warner, W. (1992). Spectacular action: Rambo and the popular pleasures of pain. In L. Grossberg, C. Nelson, P. Treichler, L. Baughman, & J. M. Wise (Eds.), *Cultural studies* (pp. 672-688). New York: Routledge.

Weart, S. R. (1988). *Nuclear fear: A history of images.* Cambridge, MA: Harvard University Press.

Webster, F., & Robins, K. (1986). *Information technology: A luddite analysis.* Norwood, NJ: Ablex.

Weiner, N. (1954). *The human uses of human beings: Cybernetics and society.* New York: Da Capo.

White, H. (1987). *The content of the form: Narrative discourse and historical representation.* Baltimore, MD: Johns Hopkins University Press.

White, K. (1995). The killer app. *The Baffler, 6.*

White, M. (1989). Television: A narrative—a history. *Cultural Studies, 3*(3), 282-300.

Williams, R. (1974). *Television: Technology and cultural form.* New York: Schocken.

Williams, R. (1989). Culture is ordinary. *Resources of Hope* (Robin Gamble, Ed.). New York: Verso.

Winner, L. (1977). *Autonomous technology: Technics-out-of-control as a theme in political thought.* Cambridge, MA: MIT Press.

Winner, L. (1993). Social constructivism: Opening the black box and finding it empty. *Science as Culture, 3*(3), 427-452.

Wyden, P. (1984). *Day one: Before Hiroshima and after.* New York: Simon & Schuster.

Zoglin, R. (1993, April 12). When the revolution comes what will happen to . . . *Time,* pp. 50-55.

Index

About the Author

J. Macgregor Wise is Assistant Professor of Media Studies at Clemson University. A former Assistant Editor of the journal *Cultural Studies*, he received his Ph.D. in Speech Communication from the University of Illinois at Urbana-Champaign. Greg grew up in Southeast Asia and the Middle East and currently resides in Atlanta with his wife, Elise, and their two dogs.